BRITISH WARSHIPS OF THE SECOND WORLD WAR

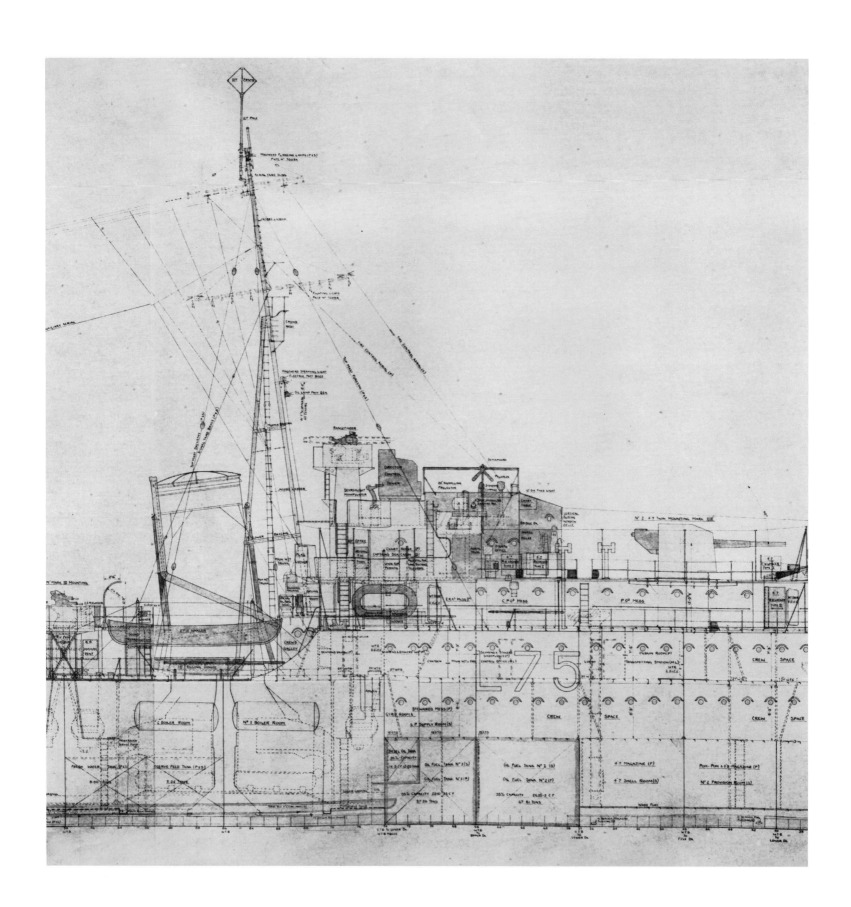

BRITISH WARSHIPS OF THE SECOND WORLD WAR

JOHN ROBERTS

The Blueprint Series is published
in association with the National Maritime Museum

CHATHAM PUBLISHING

LONDON

Frontispiece. Detail of HMS *Eskimo,* Profile (as fitted) Vickers
Armstrongs, Newcastle, 9 March 1939.
(Neg No 622301)

First published in Great Britain in 2000 by Chatham Publishing,
61 Frith Street, London W1V 5TA

Chatham Publishing is an imprint of Gerald Duckworth & Co Ltd

British Library Cataloguing in Publication Data
A catalogue record for this book is available from the
British Library

ISBN 1 86176 131 7

Designed and typeset by Martin Richards

Printed and bound in Great Britain by Bookcraft (Bath) Ltd

CONTENTS

INTRODUCTION

The National Maritime Museum holds one of the largest archives of technical drawings of ships in existence. Although this collection includes vessels of all types, the larger part relates to warship design and within this group the vast majority are official Admiralty draughts of Royal Navy ships and craft. These latter drawings represent an important source of historical information as they provide a detailed record of the appearance and particulars of the majority of the Royal Navy's fighting ships over the past three centuries. This book provides an insight into part of this collection – the Admiralty drawings for the period from 1920 to 1945. It includes both ships designed and built during that time and the older vessels of the fleet that were subjected to the type of major reconstruction that warranted the production of substantially new drawings.

Given the number and types of vessels that served with the Navy during this period, it would be impractical to cover even major warships on a class by class basis. As far as possible the vessels chosen have been included to give a broad coverage of ship development during the period, with particular bias towards fighting ships (as opposed to auxiliary vessels), ships designed after 1920 and the major units of the fleet (*ie* escort vessels and larger). At the same time account has had to be taken of the quality of the original drawings with respect to both suitability for reproduction, amount of detail and interest of content. In several instances, whilst searching out the originals, an intended inclusion, which was viewed as of particular interest or an ideal example of the type, was abandoned or replaced because drawings were either missing or unsuitable. These problems were most severe with the small and auxiliary war vessels constructed, or adapted to naval use, during 1939-45 where both the quality and number of drawings available is much lower than that with warships of what might be described as the main fleet. Good drawings of the vast amphibious invasion fleet constructed during the war are few and difficult to locate, and almost non-existent where landing craft are concerned, hence the limited coverage of these important vessels.[1] A similar situation applies to other small craft and auxiliary fighting vessels. Presumably the majority of these drawings were not retained post-war because they were regarded as 'hostilities only' material rather than part of the mainstream of warship development. Some exception is found with coastal forces where, although the overall coverage is again limited, there is a very good collection for Vosper craft, which includes examples of most of the types they constructed.

The primary groups of drawings in the Admiralty collection are the general arrangement plans for ships as designed and the 'as fitted' drawings of the ships as built, the former representing the ships at the end of the Admiralty design process and prior to construction and the latter providing a record of the ships as actually completed. Many of these drawings, particularly the earlier ones, could be seen as works of art, being drawn with considerable care in various coloured inks, but this is incidental to their purpose and it is worth remembering that they are engineering drawings intended to fulfil a practical purpose. Practically all the drawings in this book are of the 'as fitted' type, these being chosen precisely because they show ships as they actually were. A considerable number of other types of drawings from the Admiralty Collection are held by the Maritime Museum, mostly general layouts and details but these are not as complete in their coverage as the design and 'as fitted' general arrangement drawings. In some cases there are so few samples of particular drawings that they serve simply as examples of the type and it seems reasonable to conclude that the principal general arrangement drawings were retained for record purposes whilst much else was discarded. On a ship-to-ship basis this gives a considerable variation in available detail with some classes having substantial additional drawings surviving while others have little more than the main general arrangement sets.

The design process

To understand the purpose and place of the Admiralty drawings it is necessary to follow the design process that generated them. In the period covered by this book this process was initiated from a set of 'Staff Requirements' which were prepared at the direction of the First Sea Lord, who was also the Chief of Naval Staff (CNS). The officers of the Admiralty's Staff Divisions[2] carried out this work with reference, when necessary, to other Admiralty departments to produce a specification for armament, machinery, speed, endurance, protection, dimensional limitations, etc. Once an initial set of requirements was established, they were updated to meet altered circumstances (technical, tactical, strategic and international) as and when considered necessary. Thus, the requirements for fleet destroyers were updated regularly but in comparatively minor ways during the nine years from the 1927 Programme ('A' class) to the 1935 Programme ('I' class). Following this, however, the introduction of a major change in destroyer design, in the shape of the large 'Tribal' class destroyers of the 1935 Programme necessitated a substantial rewrite of the 'Staff Requirements' albeit based on previous practice. By way of contrast, battleship 'Staff Requirements' were produced in 1928 in an unfulfilled anticipation of the renewal of capital ship construction in 1931. These requirements were not reconsidered again until five years later when preparations began for the Second London Naval Limitation conference, which was due to take place in 1935-6.

In the formal process, the 'Staff Requirements', having been approved by the Board (of Admiralty), were passed via the

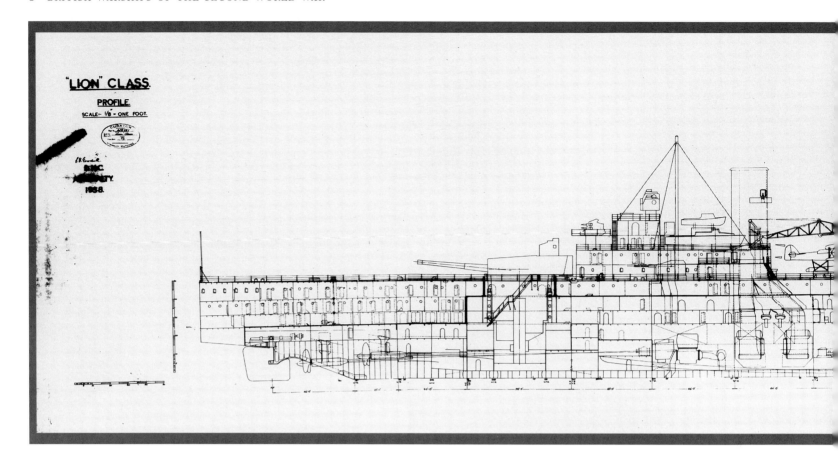

Lion Class, Profile, DNC, Admiralty, 1938. This design profile is one of the general arrangement set for the Lion *class battleships whose construction was first suspended and then cancelled during the Second World War. It serves as a good comparison with the 'as fitted' drawings that appear later in this book – particularly those of the* King George V *which belong to the same design group. As can be seen the lack of small detail (mostly items which would be worked out by the builders) gives the drawing greater overall clarity and the primary fittings, compartmentation, machinery and armour can therefore be viewed a little more clearly. Note that the drawing is signed by the DNC, S V Goodall (just above the 'DNC' printed at top left on the drawing).*
(Admiralty No 615251)

Controller (Third Sea Lord) – the senior Sea Lord responsible for material – to the Director of Naval Construction (DNC) for the preparation of initial design studies. These 'outline designs' were worked out comparatively quickly using information from previous designs, model experiments and estimation but were nevertheless still accurate enough to give a close match to the final dimensions and particulars of any design. In practice this process was not quite so neat, particularly with large ships. In preparing the requirements the Staff might well have called for design studies at an earlier stage. This was done to provide a basis on which to formulate the requirements, some assurance that the specification could be met in practice or to gain some idea of the size of vessel necessary to provide the features they had in mind. Thus by the time the Board had approved the requirements, the DNC might well have already prepared a number of design studies. In addition the investigation of a design by the Construction, or other technical departments, might well result in modification of the 'Staff Requirements' either during preparation or at a later date. Whatever the route, the initial output from the design department was used by the Controller and/or DNC to decide on which arrangement should be carried forward to the 'Sketch Design' stage.

The sketch designs were worked out in much greater detail and involved consultation with the other principle technical departments of the Admiralty – those of the Director of Naval Ordnance (DNO), the Director of Torpedoes and Mining (DTM) and the Engineer-in-Chief (E-in-C). The DNO and DTM providing esti-

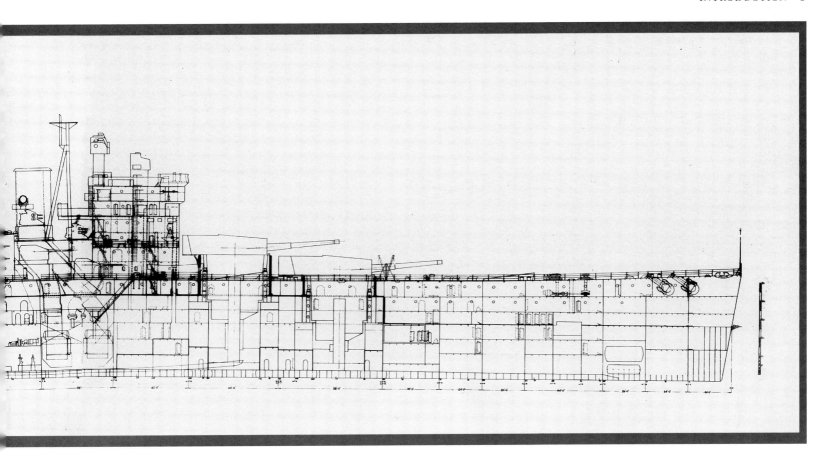

mates of the space and weight required for the armament and the E-in-C similar information for the machinery (the latter based on the DNC's estimate of the power required to achieve the desired speed on a ship of the proposed form and dimensions). The output from this process was one or more sketch designs in the form of small-scale general arrangement drawings, a legend of particulars giving the general details of the ship, a weight distribution, a provisional scheme of complement and the estimated cost. These would be examined at a meeting of the Controller and the senior members of the Naval Staff[5] who would decide on a design (or a choice of designs) for submission for full Board approval. At both these stages it was possible for modification of the design to be requested but once it had full Board approval the DNC's department was clear to proceed with the design in detail. This process involved:

1) Calculating in detail the weights, stability, trim, buoyancy, structural strength and the likely effects of damage to the ship's structure from enemy attack.

2) Preparation of specifications describing all aspects of the ship and its structure, fittings, machinery, armament, etc, the type and quality of materials to be used, methods of construction, standards of workmanship and so on.

3) Preparation of large scale drawings, including:
   a) Detailed general arrangement of the ship – profile, plans of all decks and a set of transverse sections.
   b) Sheer drawing (often referred to as a 'lines' plan) showing form of ship's hull and consisting of a sheer plan (simple longi-

tudinal elevation of hull showing position of principal decks, bulkheads, etc and giving the location of the water lines and frame lines shown in the other views), half-breadth plan (plan view of port side only – hence 'half' breadth – showing water 'lines') and body plan (end-view of hull showing frame 'lines' – fore end to right and aft end to left of a common middle-line) all on one sheet. A separate table of offsets, which specified the hull form in terms of dimensional co-ordinates, was also drawn-up.
   c) Sketch of rig showing, in plan and profile, detail of the masts, yards, booms, rigging, and wireless aerials (in some cases a separate wireless rig was produced) etc.
   d) Armour diagram (if required) showing positions, type and thicknesses of protection.
   e) Constructional transverse sections (usually one amidships, one forward and one aft) to show general arrangement of scantlings.
   f) Arrangement of boilers, uptakes and funnels, auxiliary machinery, pipes, propeller shafting, etc.

Once again this work was carried out in consultation with other technical departments, now expanded to include the more junior departments, such as electrical engineering, signals and naval equipment. In the cases of ordnance, machinery and various other items of equipment, design and its associate drawing work was carried out by outside contractors. Of these the most important was Vickers-Armstrongs Ltd which, apart from being a major warship shipbuilder and manufacturer of naval machinery, was the principal supplier of naval guns and mountings to the Admiralty. The development of machinery, weapons and armour was, moreover, an ongoing process not necessarily directly linked to any particular warship's design.

With the design process complete, the Technical and Naval Staff departments of the Admiralty examined the completed documents and signified their agreement in a book provided for the purpose. Following this, the DNC would formally sign off the completed design prior to it being submitted first to the Controller and Assistant Chief of Naval Staff (ACNS) and then to the Board for final approval. At this point, having received the Board Stamp, the design could not be further altered without the agreement of the Board. Some allowance was provided for alterations and additions to the design by the provision of a 'Board Margin' – an addition to the design weights, over and above those actually required, to provide for contingencies – but Board approval was still required before this allowance, or part of it, could be used. The final design could now be passed to one of the Royal Dockyards in order for construction work to commence and/or sent out for tender from a private shipbuilder. Separate contracts were placed for:

1) Hull, hull fittings and electrical equipment.
2) Main and auxiliary machinery.
3) Armour (if applicable).
4) Armament.
5) Miscellaneous machinery and equipment (aircraft catapults, anchor machinery, cranes, etc).

It was common for shipbuilders to take the contracts for both hull and machinery, as most of the principal shipbuilders also manufactured machinery. During the war, when the organisation of war construction demanded much greater central control over manufacturing resources, the tendering process was largely superseded by the direct placement of contracts. Even before the war, with the heavy demands resulting from the rearmament programme of the late 1930s, the Admiralty directly selected the contractors for the *King George V* class battleships. In addition, it was common for contracts for heavy gun mountings and armour to be placed in advance of that for the ship itself and before the design process was complete. This was done to ensure that these items, which were subject to long production periods, were available for fitting in the ship at the required point in the building process. It should be noted that it was not advisable to leave these items to be fitted at a late stage in construction. The gun mountings for a battleship, for example, had to be fitted before the main propelling machinery and propeller shafts could be correctly aligned.

Although the above was the generally accepted procedure, there were major exceptions, particularly during the war, when much of the design work was carried out by the contractors. This often involved taking over the design process at some intermediate stage,

probably to relieve the Constructor's Department of its heavy workload. The most extreme example of this is the responsibility for the design of the *Colossus* class aircraft carriers, which was taken over by Vickers in 1941, immediately after the initial requirements had been set. This was, however, more usual with smaller vessels such as destroyers and escorts where there was a greater commonalty of design from one class to another. An outline general arrangement drawing and an intimate knowledge of Admiralty specifications were all that were required by such specialist warship builders as Thornycroft and Yarrow. Designs directly submitted by shipbuilders, either to promote their own ideas or to meet some specific Admiralty requirement, were the other major exception. In the case of 'shipbuilder' design, perhaps the best known is that for the 'Flower' class corvettes which, unusually, was the product of a merchant shipbuilder. This originated with a sketch design from Smiths Dock for a coastal escort based on the whale-catcher *Southern Pride* and was subsequently worked out in detail by that firm with only minor assistance from the Admiralty.

Construction

Using the Admiralty design as a basis, the builders, both the private yards and the Royal Dockyards, were responsible for the preparation of detailed construction drawings, the production of which would begin before a ship was laid down and continue throughout its construction. When more than one ship was to be built to a given design, the usual case with warships, one builder was chosen as the 'lead shipbuilder' and prepared the more important constructional drawings which were then passed on to the other builders. Each yard produced its own copies of these drawings and added their own detailed drawings as required – modifying these as necessary to suit their own practices. Such work was substantial and involved the generation of thousands of drawings; the more important of which would be submitted to the Admiralty for approval by the DNC.

Sister-ships were seldom identical because the builders had a relatively free hand when it came to the detailed fitting-out of ships with such items as cable and pipe runs, the sighting of minor equipment and electrical fittings and the detail of accommodation arrangements. They also had some minor leeway in the structural arrangements to accommodate their own methods and equipment. However, they were not totally free to do as they pleased as the construction of all Royal Navy ships was monitored by Admiralty Overseers. These were a mixture of constructors, naval officers and technical officers, with a senior constructor serving as the 'Principal Ship Overseer' or 'Warship Production Superintendent'. Apart from ensuring that the ship, and the materials with which it was being built, were to specification, they served in an advisory capacity to the builders in clarifying the design intent and in resolving points of detail. They also ensured that the builders took care with the arrangement of fittings and equipment and that these were correctly and conveniently arranged for their intended purpose. Any points of dispute or major queries were referred back to the DNC's department for resolution or clarification.

'As fitted'

The final group of draughts produced was the 'as fitted' drawings that served to record the details of the ship as she actually was on entering service and provided a permanent reference for use by the Dockyards and the Admiralty. The general arrangement drawings in this group, and the ones primarily used for this book, were similar to those produced at the design stage – profile, plans of decks, transverse sections and rig – but included more detail and, of course, any changes in the design adopted during construction. Whilst the ship itself was fairly well-represented in these general arrangements, some fittings were seldom drawn in full detail. The ship's boats, for example, were normally shown only by a broken outline to indicate their position, while the illustration of gun mountings could vary from a reasonable outline to little more than an indication of its principal centre-lines. The ship's machinery also received little more than outline representation but details of this, and the other items mentioned, were of course available from other drawings.

Production of the 'as fitted' drawings was, again, the responsibility of the contractor and, although following similar conventions of style, these varied in small ways and in degree of detail from builder to builder and from draughtsman to draughtsman. There was also a variation with time; the general arrangement drawings had become progressively less involved from 1900 onward and by the time of the Second World War the pressure on limited resources had reduced many to comparative simplicity. However, there are always some that show more detail than others – again the result of different standards from different builders. For big ships the 'as fitted' drawings were generally produced to a scale of $1^{1}/_{8}$in = 1ft (1:96) and for destroyers and smaller vessels at $^{1}/_{4}$in = 1ft (1:48). Exceptions included the rig drawings, which were normally half the scale of the main drawings, and small craft, such as coastal forces vessels, which were usually $^{1}/_{2}$in = 1ft (1:24). More than one set of 'as fitted' drawings were produced, one of these serving as the 'master set' while the others were regarded as copies.[4]

Apart from the principal general arrangement drawings mentioned above, there were large numbers of separate 'as fitted' drawings for such items as the distribution of hull plating, ship's services (pumping arrangements, ventilation, water, steam, electrical distribution, hydraulic power, etc), bridge layout, compartment layouts and equipment and fittings arrangements. In addition there were general arrangement and detail drawings for the ship's machinery and armament (produced by their manufacturers), together with printed manuals detailing the features and operation of all these major items.

Refits and modernisations

This was not always the end of the process for the 'as fitted' drawings. Occasionally when ships were brought in for major refit, the general arrangement drawings were updated by the dockyard drawing office. Originally this involved indicating deletions by placing cross marks on the removed fitting or structure and drawing new items directly on the original in a particular colour of ink, indicated by a note below the drawing's title such as 'modified in green at Portsmouth March 1929'. This process did not have a strict structure, the modification of drawings was fairly intermittent and was normally only applied to one set of the drawings. Most 'as fitted' drawings remained unmodified throughout their life, despite alterations to the ship, while a few were updated so often that the clarity of the original was seriously compromised. For major changes this system was largely superseded in the 1930s by the production of 'fly sheets' to the original drawings. These detailed the modifications made on a separate sheet – showing either part or all of the area covered by the original. This, when used in conjunction with the original, provided full details of the new arrangement with considerably less risk of confusion. Unfortunately, relatively few of these additional drawings appear to have been preserved.

In the case of the major reconstructions of capital ships and cruisers which took place during 1933-41 the changes were so comprehensive that completely new sets of 'as fitted' drawings were produced. Examples of both the 'fly sheet' and the new 'as fitted' drawings can be found in these pages. These together with the original drawings represent the work of men whose skill has been all but lost. In the years since the Second World War the use of bow pens, coloured ink and heavy linen drawing media have gradually given way to more advanced but less demanding techniques, initially to simpler, and more cost-effective, drawings and improved drawing instruments and, more recently, to the introduction of computer-aided design.

Acknowledgments

The author wishes to thank the Staff of the Brass Foundry at Woolwich for their assistance, particularly Meridith Sampson who generously contributed both time and effort to locating suitable plans from the Admiralty Collection. My thanks are also due to D K Brown, RCNC for his help in clarifying certain points in the Admiralty's design process and drawing production system.

WARSHIP DESIGN IN PEACE AND WAR

At the close of the First World War Britain possessed the largest navy in the world. It had, moreover, a high proportion of new ships and was well advanced in all areas of naval science and design as a result of the accelerated development generated by the war. Substantial advances had been made in naval aviation, anti-aircraft equipment, the development of ordnance, fire control systems and equipment, submarine and anti-submarine warfare, night fighting techniques and communications. Alongside these a great deal had been learnt about warship design – particularly in relation to capital ships and their protection – and the efficient management and conduct of a naval war. The technical developments were generally summarised under the heading of 'the lessons of the war' but in many cases these only represented the initial stages of the development process. It is not therefore surprising to find that the majority of inter-war advances in naval technology had been initiated in the latter years of the First World War and the period immediately following. However, the greatly accelerated pace of wartime development slowed to a dangerous extent during the period 1919 to 1936, primarily because of the extreme financial restrictions imposed on defence spending.

This decline began in 1919 with the government imposition of the 'Ten Year Rule' which required the armed services to plan their expenditure on the basis that no major war would take place for 10 years. The ruling was made self-perpetuating in 1927 but was eventually rescinded in 1932 when it was realised that the relatively stable state of international affairs that existed in the 1920s no longer applied. For the Navy a further limit was added in 1920 with the adoption of the 'one-power' standard to replace the pre-war 'two-power' standard. This set the size of the future British Navy as at least equal to that of the next largest navy in existence – in other words that of the United States of America. These restrictions, together with the need to revitalise peacetime industry and trade, combined with the general anti-war feeling of the time, led to a major reduction in the Naval Estimates in the post war period. This low level was maintained into the mid-1930s partly due to the lack of any real threat of a major naval war and, more importantly, to the deterioration in the world economy which culminated in the 'Wall Street Crash' of 1929. It must be added, however, that until the early 1930s Britain was still spending more money on her fleet than any other country (when she was pushed into second place by the USA). The Royal Navy was, moreover, to remain the world's largest, in terms of numbers of ships, throughout the period between the wars. During this time Britain also built more warships than any other country – in large part due to the limited construction programmes of other navies, particularly that of the United States. In fact the drive to keep up British strength in terms of ship numbers, together with the high cost of running and maintaining the fleet, contributed to a shortage of funds for other purposes – particularly experimental work and the development of new weapon systems and improved machinery.

Supply and demand

Britain did not possess the industrial capacity that she had once enjoyed and despite the apparent appearance of being ahead of the game – at least until the mid-1930s – the restrictions on naval spending seriously curtailed Britain's ability for rapid expansion in time of war. The relatively low level of warship construction and the slow progress of development programmes for naval equipment produced a run-down in the industries and skills that supplied them and made a rapid recovery in time of crisis a near-impossibility. This was particularly the case in those areas requiring specialist plant and machinery such as the manufacture of armour plate, heavy guns and their mountings and fire control equipment. Even more serious was the reduction of personnel, which extended over the full range of skills from naval architects to shipyard labour. Recovery began in the mid-1930s but the training of such personnel takes years and, with the additional wartime demands on men for the armed services, the British naval construction and armament industries continued to suffer shortages throughout the Second World War. The effects manifested themselves most clearly in the work overload suffered by the Admiralty's Construction department, the difficulties in gun mounting supply and the wartime reduction of the battleship construction programme – particularly during the 1937-42 period. The latter years of the war proved less troublesome but this was in part due to the supply of equipment from, and access to the repair and refit facilities of the United States.

Of all the problems that beset naval supply as a result of neglect between the wars the most serious was the provision of naval aircraft. In 1918 the Royal Navy had lost most of its air-minded officers, and the primary control of naval aircraft procurement, to the RAF. It did not regain full control of the Fleet Air Arm until 1937 – after much bitter inter-service rivalry – by which time it was too late to fully repair the damage that had been done and, for most of the war, the service was reliant for its best and most numerous aircraft on the United States. The Royal Navy's loss of its aircraft enthusiasts produced a lack of vision for the future potential of the naval air arm and generated a bias towards surface and anti-submarine warfare. Both these latter areas were in a relatively advanced state by 1939 but aviation development had been largely directed toward support for the surface fleet rather than direct offensive action. In 1939 British front-line naval aircraft were of a multi-role type that militated against optimum performance in an offensive role and of these only the most recent (the Blackburn Skua fighter/dive bomber) was a monoplane.

At the same time the anti-aircraft weapons and control equipment of the fleet were to prove seriously inadequate in the early years of the war. In the case of the primary high-angle control system (HACS) and close-range AA weapons this resulted from high investment at too early a date. The evolution of long-range AA equipment was, by contrast, somewhat late, subject to indecisive direction of design and generated several over-complex and expensive solutions which placed a heavy burden on available manufacturing facilities in the early years of the war. Other areas were better served – aircraft carriers and their equipment (in contrast to their primary weapon system) were brought to an advanced state and British torpedoes, submarines and anti-submarine equipment were among the best in the world. Electronic warfare was also well served and RDF (radar) development was ahead of the competition until the latter years of the war when Britain was overtaken by the United States.

Ship design, in which there was a strong bias towards fleet surface action and trade protection, was advanced but to some extent limited by a conservative approach in such areas as machinery development and welded construction. The war revealed further problems – particularly inadequate endurance and electrical generating capacity – and, as in the First World War, provided many lessons that were applied to wartime production. At the same time, as the industry geared up its war production, new methods were introduced to streamline the construction process, including prefabricated construction methods and the extensive use of welding. During 1939-45 the ships and equipment of the Royal Navy saw extensive and far-reaching changes but even so never entirely recovered from the retrenchment that took place between the wars.

The naval limitation treaties

One other factor remains to be included amongst the influences on British warship design between the wars, the series of international treaties agreed between the world's major naval powers. Although initially intended as a means of limiting international conflict, these were increasingly used by the countries concerned to gain an advantage in support of their own political, financial or strategic objectives rather than the cause of disarmament. In setting upper limits on the displacement and armament of individual warship types, the treaties exerted considerable influence on the design process and to some extent distorted the natural progress of warship development. For new construction these restrictions tended to become a minimum as well as a maximum requirement as nations, seeking not to be outdone by their rivals, built ships to the limit (and in several cases beyond it). The resulting vessels could be considered either larger or smaller than was desirable,

depending on the view at the time as to the relative balance of size, cost and numbers to meet financial, strategic and tactical requirements. In addition it was often found that the maximums for armament and displacement could not be combined to the satisfaction of naval staff or designers in what would be regarded as a well-balanced ship – ideally requiring either greater size or smaller calibre/fewer guns.

The treaties originated from a desire to stop a potentially dangerous post-war arms race in capital ship construction between Britain, the USA and Japan for which none of the participants were particularly enthusiastic – primarily due to the cost but also for political reasons given the unpopularity of arms production. The large battlefleet with which Britain ended the First World War gave an apparent security to her traditional role as the world's major navy but this secure position was soon under serious threat. Many of the battleships and battlecruisers of the fleet were obsolescent 12in gun dreadnoughts which were soon decommissioned and placed on the disposal list or relegated to subsidiary duties. By 1921 the Royal Navy's front-line capital ships had effectively been reduced to twenty-one vessels armed with 13.5in or 15in guns[5] all of which were less than ten years old. However, even these comparatively recent vessels gave cause for concern as all, with the partial exception of the battlecruiser *Hood* – completed in 1920, were of essentially pre-war design and did not incorporate the lessons of the war with regard to standards of protection against surface, aerial or submarine attack. Added to this both the USA and Japan had substantial new construction programmes either under way or planned which would ultimately give them a capital ship fleet of twenty-seven and twenty-four ships respectively by the end of the decade.[6] Moreover, this quantitative advantage would be enhanced by a qualitative one in that a large proportion of these foreign vessels would be of more recent construction, larger, more heavily armed and in certain cases faster than anything in the British fleet.

While it was clear that some substantial effort was required to maintain the strength of what was regarded as Britain's main arm of defence, it was also clear that the country no longer had either the finance or the will to maintain the Royal Navy at the level it had enjoyed prior to the war. No new construction had been included in the naval estimates since the end of the war and to maintain the new 'one-power standard' in the face of the US and Japanese programmes required the construction of new and substantially more powerful battleships and battlecruisers. Reluctantly, the Government agreed to the provision of four battlecruisers in the 1921 Naval Estimates and to plans for these to be followed by four battleships. These were to have been ships of considerable power that fully incorporated the lessons of the war and potentially outclassed anything afloat, under construction or planned. The battlecruisers (design G3) were 48,400-ton ships, armed with nine 16in guns and capable of a speed of 31kts; the battleships (design N3) were slightly larger at 48,500 tons and, at 23kts, sacrificed speed for

MIDSHIP SECTION

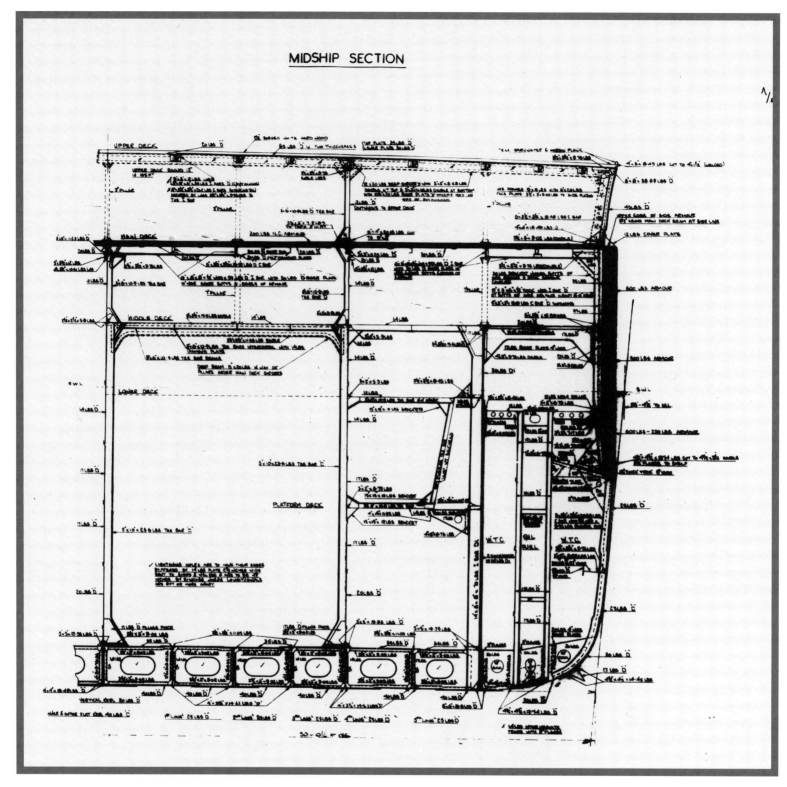

Lion *Class, Midship and Structural Sections, 1938. These two drawings are typical of the transverse structural sections produced by the DNC's department for general reference and as guidance to the* builders. *They were employed in conjunction with the written specification to provide full detail on the materials and fixing methods to be employed in the construction of the hull.* (Admiralty No 615254)

FORWARD SECTION.

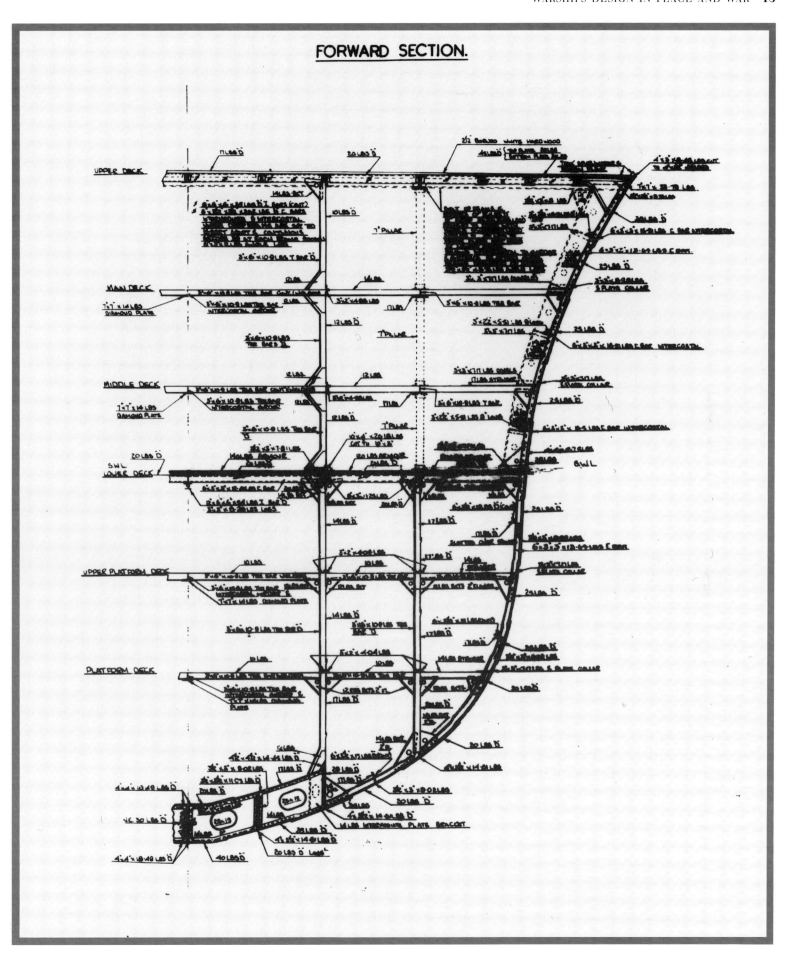

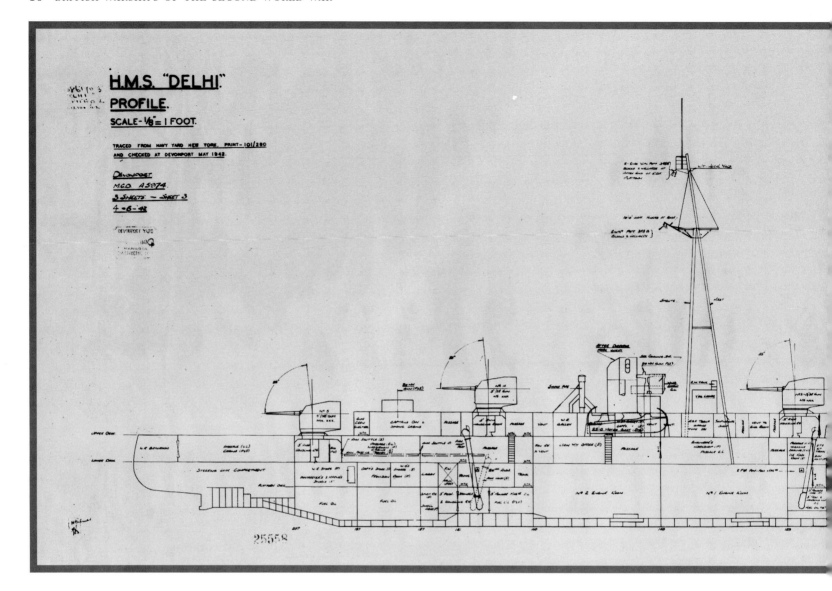

HMS Delhi, *Profile, Devonport Dockyard, 4 June 1942.* *This relatively simple but unusual drawing shows the First World War 'D' class cruiser* Delhi *after her reconstruction and rearmament at New York Navy Yard during 1941-2. The principal purpose was to allow the Admiralty to evaluate the US 5in/38 DP mounting and the Mk37 director control system. The new armament proved very successful but the original request to the US authorities was made before their entry into the war and no further ships were similarly modified. The drawing is not a formal 'as fitted' but a copy of a New York Navy Yard print.*
(Admiralty No 686170/3)

thicker armour and a heavier armament of nine 18in guns. Given the circumstances of the time it seems unlikely that this programme would have been fully implemented. The country could ill afford such vast expenditure and the First World War had generated a strong desire for the peaceful resolution of international conflict. In the event the United States of America provided a solution. Similarly burdened by an unpopular and expensive programme of construction, they invited the major naval powers to Washington to take part in a conference on the limitation of naval armaments.

The Washington Conference took place during November 1921- February 1922 and resulted in a treaty that limited the relative strengths of the capital ships and aircraft carriers of the major navies and placed a ceiling on the size and armament of all new construction warships. The signatories agreed to retain a certain number of their most modern capital ships and to scrap the remainder, while Britain, the United States and Japan also agreed to cancel their new capital ship construction programmes. In the longer term the replacement of existing ships was to result in equal strength in the capital ship fleets of Britain and the United States,

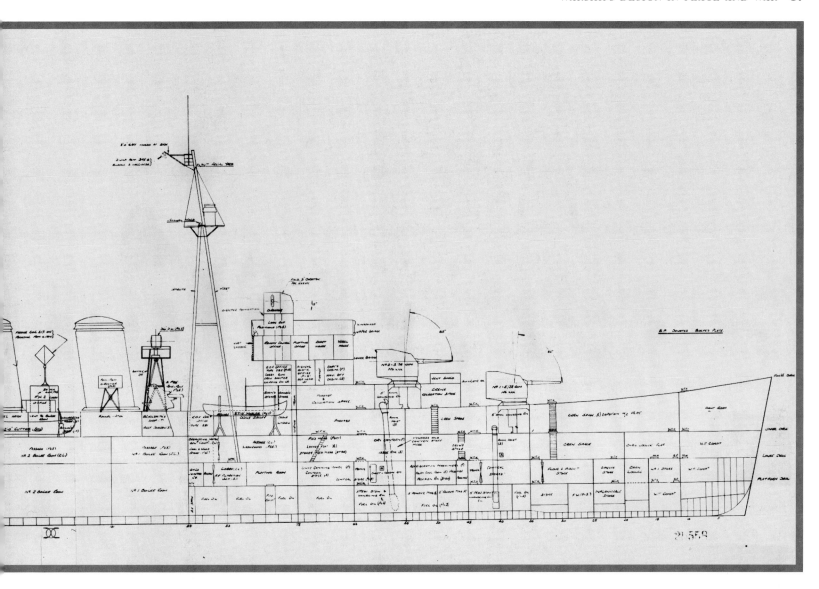

while the Japanese were limited to 60 per cent and the French and Italians to 35 per cent of this strength.[7] The immediate result was that Britain retained twenty-two existing capital ships (including the battleship *Thunderer* which was employed as a seagoing training ship in the early 1920s), the United States eighteen battleships and the other three nations ten ships each. There were, however, some exceptions – two each of the nearly completed 16in gun battleships of Japan and the United States were allowed to be retained– the *Nagato* and *Mutsu* for the former and the *Colorado* and *West Virginia* for the latter.[8] To compensate for this, Britain was allowed to construct two battleships to the new quantitative limits of the treaty – 35,000 tons (36,560 tonnes) maximum displacement[9] and 16in (40.64cm) maximum gun calibre – but had to scrap the *Thunderer* and the three ships of the *King George V* class when these new ships completed, thus reducing her total to twenty ships.

In recognition of the fact that the older capital ships were vulnerable to modern weapons, the treaty allowed for the addition to such ships of enhanced protection against aerial and underwater attack. There was a 3000-ton (3048 tonnes) limit to the weight that could

be added and all additions were to be for defensive purposes only – no increase in offensive qualities being allowed.[10] This was intended to provide for the addition of bulges for defence against torpedoes and additional deck armour as defence against bombs but was also generally interpreted as allowing for the modernisation of anti-aircraft weapons. This was an important concession and, with new construction substantially curtailed, resulted in major reconstructions of the older battleships and battlecruisers in order to extend their useful lives. In the 1930s these reconstructions became extensive and costly and, in all the countries involved, deviated somewhat from the 'for defensive purposes only' requirement by enhancements in ship speed and subtle improvements to the main armament and protection.

In the case of aircraft carriers it was decided to treat all existing vessels of this type as experimental ships which could be replaced at any time. In fact Britain possessed four ships in this category while Japan and the USA had only one small carrier each. The standard displacement limit for new construction carriers was set at 27,000 tons (27,433 tonnes) with an overall limit of 135,000 tons

(137,160 tonnes) each for Britain and the USA, 81,000 tons (82,296 tonnes) for Japan and 60,000 tons (60,960 tonnes) each for France and Italy. The proportions allowed to each country were generally similar to those for battleships but the total tonnage limit is important as there was no restriction on the numbers of carriers provided the total displacement did not exceed the overall limit. As an exception to the 27,000-ton limit, the signatories were allowed to construct a maximum of two carriers each with an upper displacement limit of 33,000 tons. This clause was inserted particularly to allow the United States and Japan to convert two of their uncompleted capital ships into carriers. For all other warship types the only limit was a ceiling of 10,000 tons standard displacement and a maximum gun calibre of 8in which effectively provided the upper limit for cruisers.

With the exceptions mentioned above, it was agreed that no capital ship or aircraft carrier could be replaced by new construction until 20 years after its completion and, to allow for the time of construction, any such replacement ship could be laid down three years before this date was reached. This meant that Britain, the United States and Japan could not begin any replacement capital ships until 1931, while both France and Italy could initiate new construction with single ships in 1927 and 1929. The Washington Treaty was intended to remain in force until 31 December 1936 unless one of the contracting powers gave two years notice of termination.

In case technical developments gave reason for modifying the Treaty a further conference was due to take place approximately eight years after the ratification of the agreement. This conference took place in London in 1930 but was more concerned with the reduction of naval expenditure than with recent developments and produced an extension of the Washington limits for both individual warships and total tonnage. The resulting London Naval Treaty produced an agreement between Britain, the United States and Japan. France and Italy withdrew from the conference but were of course still bound by the original terms of the Washington Treaty. The new treaty extended the 'holiday' in capital ship construction to the full term of the Washington Treaty (*ie* no new ships were to be laid down until 31 December 1936). In addition the scrapping of older ships to bring the respective capital ship strength of the three nations down to the 15/15/9 agreed at Washington was to be accelerated. For the first time restrictions were also imposed on cruisers, destroyers and submarines. Limitations on overall tonnage were to be achieved by 31 December 1936, with Britain and the USA equal and Japan running at 60 per cent of that strength for cruisers, 70 per cent for destroyers and equal in strength for submarines.[11] These restrictions involved a substantial programme of disposal of the older ships in all the fleets concerned. Cruisers were divided into two sub-groups for ships with guns larger or smaller than 6.1in calibre (effectively 8in gun cruisers and 6in gun cruisers) and were allowed a minimum 20-year life before replacement (16 years if completed before 1919). Destroyers were limited to a standard displacement of 1500 tons (16 per cent of the total allowed could be up to 1850 tons provided the overall limit was not exceeded), were not to mount guns larger than 5.1in calibre and were given a minimum life of 16 years. Submarines were limited to 2000 tons, 5.1in guns and a 13-year life.[12]

Neither France nor Italy had exercised their option to lay down new battleships in 1927 or 1929 (France was actually allowed three replacement ships as she had lost the battleship *France* in 1922), but within a few years an escalating naval race was in progress between France and Italy/Germany. In addition as the 1930s progressed, the increasingly aggressive actions of the fascist dictatorships in Europe and the Japanese in the Far East placed a substantial strain on the possibility of continued world peace. The Admiralty, although still keen to retain limits on capital ship construction, was soon pointing out that under these circumstances an extension of the battleship construction 'holiday' could not be accepted in the replacement for the Washington Treaty which was due to be agreed in 1936. The conference to discuss this treaty started in London in December 1935 and the resulting document was signed by Britain, the United States and France in March 1936. Both Japan and Italy withheld their agreement, although Italy eventually ratified the Treaty in December 1938.

The second London Naval Treaty abandoned the controls on numbers of ships but extended the qualitative limits placed on individual ships. In the case of battleships the 35,000-ton limit on size agreed at Washington was retained but the maximum gun calibre allowed was reduced to 14in (35.56cm) – a modification primarily instigated by the British Admiralty who foresaw difficulties in constructing a well balanced 16in gun ship within the 35,000-ton displacement limit. The upper limit on displacement for aircraft carriers was reduced to 23,000 tons while, in contrast, that for destroyers was increased to 3000 tons.[13] A 'holiday' was imposed on the construction of 10,000-ton 8in gun cruisers for the term of the treaty – due to run until 31 December 1942 – and cruiser construction was limited to a maximum displacement of 8000 tons and a gun calibre of 6.1in

However, if Japan failed to agree to the 14in gun limit by April 1937 the maximum allowable calibre was to revert to 16in. In addition the treaty provided an escalator clause which could be invoked by the signatory powers if any nation was found to be constructing ships outside the treaty limits. Both these provisions were invoked as a result of Japan's failure to agree the 14in gun limit and her extreme secrecy regarding her future construction plans. In the case of the escalator clause the displacement limit was raised to 45,000 tons in March 1938 when it became clear that Japan intended to build battleships well above the treaty limit – although it was not realised at the time just how large their new ships were going to be.[14]

In the late 1930s Britain, accepting German intentions to restore her military power, made strenuous efforts to include that country in the international control of naval armaments. This process was

complicated by the French refusal to allow Germany to be represented at the 1936 London Naval Conference and by German con-
cerns about Russian naval construction. The German desire for
naval expansion was initially covered by the Anglo-German Naval
Agreement of 1935 in which Britain agreed that Germany could
increase the size of her navy to 35 per cent of that of the Royal Navy.
This was followed up in 1937 by two naval limitation treaties, one
with Germany and one with Russia, which, with some small exceptions, extended the requirements of the Second London Naval
Treaty to those two nations. Most of these latter-day agreements
were not worth the paper they were written on – Germany, Japan
and Italy were already ignoring the qualitative limits in the Treaties
that they had signed. In the late 1930s Britain and the United States
reluctantly began restoring their navies with the most extensive
naval construction programmes since the First World War but, until
the outbreak of war, continued to restrict their new construction to
the treaty limits.

Rearmament and war production

During the four years leading up to the outbreak of war in
September 1939 the Naval Estimates provided for the construction
of nine battleships, six aircraft carriers, twenty-three cruisers,
forty-nine destroyers and eighteen submarines. To a large extent
these programmes reflected the Admiralty's bias toward planning
for fleet action. They also represented an attempt to build up a battle fleet that was large enough to cope with war in the Far East as
well as in Europe. However, there was some change of emphasis in
the last peacetime Estimates with the addition of a large number of
escort vessels (twenty escort destroyers and fifty-six corvettes).
This subtle change was the first sign of a wartime shift to the construction of large numbers of escorts and merchant ships to support
the battle against the U-boats. This, together with the high pressure
on repair facilities, stretched available building resources to an
extent where substantial delays were generated in the construction
of larger warships. Of the pre-war programmes, four of the battleships ordered were at first suspended and eventually cancelled,
while several other battleships, carriers and cruisers were subjected to delays and occasional suspensions of construction. There was
also a major bottleneck in gun mounting production which resulted in two cruisers and several destroyers entering service with an
extemporised armament. In addition problems with a lack of capacity in turbine manufacture resulted in the majority of wartime-pro-
duced escorts being fitted with steam piston engines.

War construction involved considerable effort and saturated the
shipbuilding capacity in Canada and Australia as well as Great
Britain. The war programmes concentrated on destroyers, submarines, escorts and smaller vessels until 1942 when there was a
substantial increase in the orders for aircraft carriers. It was also
around this time that the design of British ships shifted from the
'wartime utility' types intended for rapid and cheap production to
more sophisticated vessels. These latter ships incorporated many
wartime lessons, were generally larger, better armed and more
capable than their predecessors. However, few of these ships were
to be completed for service before the end of the war and many, still
under construction in 1945, were subsequently cancelled. The
wartime additions to ships were substantial, involving primarily the
enhancement of AA armament and the addition of radar and other
electronic equipment, which created problems with both stability
and accommodation. Despite all these problems, British shipbuilders managed to construct a vast number of ships during the
war and the Royal Navy was substantially larger in 1945 than in
1939 despite heavy war losses. It also benefited from the transfer of
large numbers of ships, mainly escorts, escort carriers and
amphibious warfare vessels of all types, from the shipyards of the
United States whose wartime building capacity outstripped that of
all other nations.

The Admiralty's design department also expanded substantially
between 1939 and 1945 and contributed a great deal to the successful conclusion of the war. It was, and is, subject to much criticism for various supposed or real shortcomings in design. But these
criticisms seldom take account of the departmental overload which
was suffered, nor the shared responsibility for specification and
equipment with the naval staff, ordnance and engineering departments. In addition, comparison with foreign design, a particular
favourite of British naval officers, is often misleading, in failing to
compare like with like. What is often missed is the high standard of
innovative design produced during the war, which provided a
benchmark for others to follow. Among these, the most outstanding
were the introduction of the escort carrier, escort destroyer and
tank landing ship (LST) all of which inspired the production of similar vessels in the United States.

CAPITAL SHIPS

The demise of the battleship as the prime unit of the fleet was predicted by many during the period between the wars. Foremost among these were the air enthusiasts, who tended to confuse the present and future capabilities of aircraft and often spoilt their arguments with a poor understanding of ship technology. The Admiralty held firm in their belief in these ships because, provided they could be adequately defended from air attack, there was no reason to believe they could not continue to maintain their superior position. There were, moreover, precedents for this view – the end of the power of the big gun, armoured ship was predicted on the appearance of the torpedo boat in the 1880s and again at the turn of the century with the development of submarines. In both cases the threat was much less than that predicted and the countermeasures developed were sufficient to allow the battleship to remain the ultimate measure of a nation's sea power. Between the wars it was envisaged that adequate defence against this new aerial threat could be provided by anti-aircraft guns (with advanced fire control equipment) and defending aircraft. The former were to prove less than sufficient, while the latter were eventually revealed as the only adequate means of protection and it was this that proved to be the battleship's undoing. The Admiralty was right in the narrow sense but in the long term the survival of a fleet would become dependent on its aircraft carriers. These vessels could engage each other well outside the range of a battleship's guns and the winner would hold the field – the defeated fleet, battleships and all, would have to retire or suffer the consequences of air attack without adequate defence.

To some extent this is a simplistic view of a fairly complex process. It was not until well into the Second World War that aircraft really gained a true ascendancy. Early losses to aircraft were more a case of inadequate air defence than of proof that aircraft had won the day. Aircraft also had their operational limits in that ships could operate in conditions that would keep aircraft grounded or at least seriously impaired. It is worth noting that, although the Admiralty has been much criticised for its adherence to the battleship, other nations were similarly reluctant to abandon them, including both the USA and Japan. In the latter years of the war battleships were virtually reduced to very expensive shore-bombardment vessels – a role adopted because they happened to be available, although it is debatable if this represented good employment of scarce personnel. The Admiralty continued its interest in battleship construction throughout and after the Second World War – to some extent a reflection of its conservative approach. What seems to have finally caused the abandonment of all such projects, apart from financial considerations, was the development of very powerful guided weapons against which no amount of armour could provide adequate protection.

Rodney and Nelson

Britain was fortunate in being allowed to build two new ships under the terms of the Washington Treaty. Apart from providing an opportunity to produce a modern design incorporating the lessons of the war, in theory it provided the fleet with the two most modern and powerful battleships afloat until 1940 when the first of the new generation of fast battleships began to appear. The design was a cut-down version of the cancelled G3 battlecruiser in which the displacement was reduced by accepting a lower speed and a lower level of protection. The two ships – Nelson and Rodney – completed in 1927 were of unique appearance with all three of their triple 16in turrets mounted forward of the bridge – an arrangement adopted to concentrate the magazines amidships for maximum protection and to save weight.

One of the prime requirements for the two ships was that they should carry guns of the maximum calibre allowed by the treaty. This gave the DNC's department some problems in providing a well-balanced design without exceeding the 35,000-ton displacement limit – a difficulty that was to manifest itself with many treaty-limited ships. In order to get the most from the design a great deal of effort was put into weight control. Particular attention was paid to reducing hull weight by the use of high-tensile steel in place of mild steel and by the careful control of material during construction. Extensive use was also made of lightweight fittings (not always successfully) and some pressure was placed on the E-in-C to minimise the weight of the machinery. In fact the machinery came out slightly heavier than provided for in the design but the savings made in the other areas mentioned more than compensated for this loss. The Rodney completed 1270 tons and the Nelson 1687 tons under the intended standard displacement. Since the design could have been improved if the potential saving had been known in advance, this was something of an embarrassment. However, the experience (also repeated in the first treaty cruisers) was of considerable benefit and served the DNC's department well in the preparation of future designs.

The design had many advanced features resulting primarily from war experience. The protective system was markedly different from earlier British ships in adopting an 'all or nothing system' in which the main armament, magazines, main machinery and conning position were heavily protected by armour while the rest of the ship was either unprotected or defended only against splinters. Two new innovations of this arrangement were the use of thick armour for the protective deck (as opposed to multiple layers of HT plating) to provide defence against bombs and long-range shellfire and the fitting of the side armour internally. The latter was angled at 72° to increase its relative thickness to an approaching shell – an idea

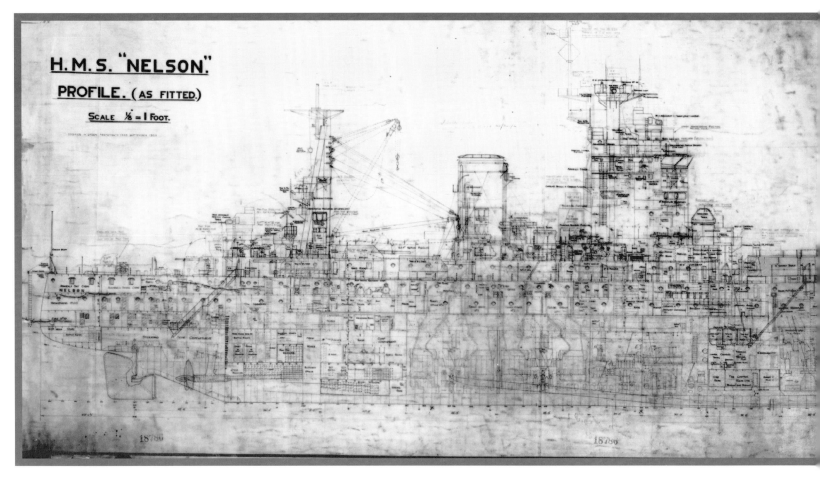

H.M.S. "NELSON."

PROFILE. (AS FITTED.)

SCALE ⅛ = 1 FOOT.

HMS Nelson, *Profile (as fitted), Armstrong Whitworth 8 August 1927. The battleship* Nelson *was completed in June 1927 and, following standard practice, her 'as fitted' set is dated a few weeks later than this – a reflection of the time required to generate the drawings. The stamps in the top left corner include that of the Admiralty Overseer V G Shepheard who was to become DNC in 1951. This set has one recorded set of corrections – 'modified in green Portsmouth Yard, September 1929' – but also has an unusual group of sketchy pencilled changes made in about 1945. These include an incomplete record of the major alterations made to the ship's AA armament up to the end of her 1944-5 refit at Philadelphia and various notes on the differences in this armament between her and her sister-ship* Rodney. *The profile follows standard conventions in having both external and internal detail, the latter primarily a section down the ship's middle line. Most notable is the ship's unusual profile with the*

armament concentrated amidships and 'X' turret approximately on the centre of the overall length. Apart from providing the best protection to the magazines (which unlike earlier British ships are fitted below the shell rooms) and shortening the length of ship required to accommodate them this arrangement had the advantage of reducing the effects of the fire control problems generated by yaw. Among the features of note are the forward submerged 24.5in torpedo tubes, one on each side of the platform deck – angled outward but facing forward as in a submarine. The tubes are in a separate compartment from the torpedo body room with only the breech end of the tubes projecting into the latter. This arrangement greatly simplified the equipment for loading and firing torpedoes and reduced the size of the compartments required. Moving aft, the machinery is the reverse of the standard arrangement with the boiler rooms abaft the engine rooms. The latter compartments are immediately below the bridge structure and sub-divided

into a forward 'turbine' room and after 'gearing' room with the boiler rooms abaft them – all the machinery compartments were further subdivided by a middle-line bulkhead. In the hold between the base of 'X' mounting and the forward bulkhead of the engine room is the Transmitting Station which accommodated the principal fire-control instrument for the main armament – the AFCT MkI. Unfortunately the armour is shown by a double line which makes it considerably less visible than the more standard arrangement of illustrating it in solid black (see King George V *profile). The armoured middle deck runs from the fore end of 'A' barbette to the base of the main mast before dropping down one deck and continuing aft to the after bulkhead of the steering gear compartment. The most visible of the alterations are in the upper works. The original HA control platform on the top of the bridge structure has been overdrawn with the larger HA control tower for two HACS MkIII* directors – the foremost being raised above the second*

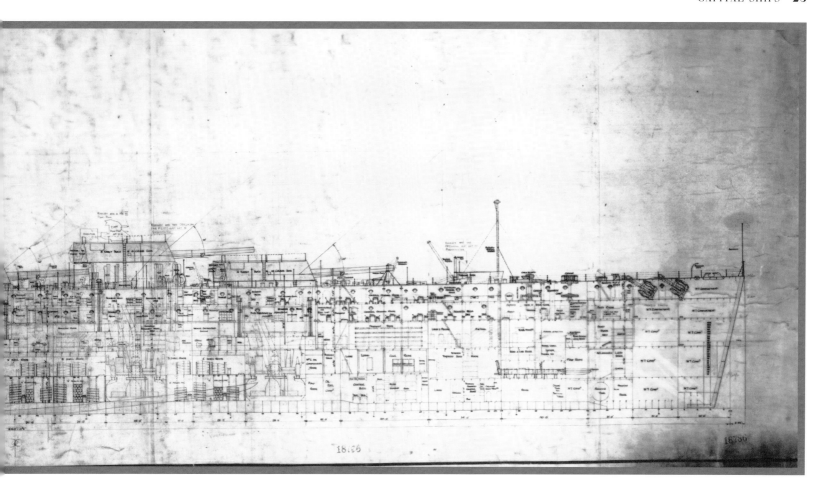

(Rodney *had only one director*). *This alteration was carried out during 1937-8 but the drawing actually shows the arrangement in 1945 as evidenced by the pole mast carrying the FC2 direction finder aerial and the air warning radar Type 279 receiving aerial which were added in 1940 (Type 279 transmitting aerial was on the main mast). The receiving office for the Type 279 is immediately abaft the bridge (on the same level as the armoured director hood) with the D/F office on its roof. Additionally the mainmast starfish platform carries the radar lantern of the surface warning Type 273 aerial with the note* 'Rodney *has larger enclosure'. The multiple pompom mountings MkVIA (8-barrel) on the quarterdeck and* 'B' *turret were fitted in 1940 and 1942 respectively (*Rodney *had a 4-barrel MkVII mounting on* 'B' *turret).*

(Plan No NPB7587, Neg No 467149)

Nelson

Displacement:	As completed – 33,313 tons standard, 38,400 tons deep, 41,250 tons extra deep
	1945 – c37,000tons standard, 44,054 tons extra deep
Dimensions:	660ft (pp), 710ft (oa) x 106ft (max) x 28ft 1in (mean)
Armament:	As completed – Nine 16in MkI (3 x 3); twelve 6in MkXXII* (6 x 2); six 4.7in MkVIII* (6 x 1); eight 2pdr (8 x 1); two 24.5in torpedo tubes.
	1945 – as above except close-range AA = forty-eight 2pdr (6 x 8); sixteen 40mm (4 x 4); sixty-one 20mm (61 x 1)
Armour:	Belt – 14in abreast magazines, 13in abreast machinery; Bulkheads – 12in and 8in forward, 10in and 4in aft; Barbettes -15in-12in; Turrets – 16in face, 11in & 9in sides, 9in rear, 7.25in roof; CT – 14in; Middle deck – 6.25in over magazines, 3.75in over machinery; Lower deck (aft) 4.25in; Torpedo bulkheads – 1.5in
Machinery:	Two shaft, Brown Curtis geared turbines, 45,000shp = 23kts; eight Admiralty 3-drum boilers; 3805 tons oil fuel; range 7000nm at 16kts
Complement:	1314

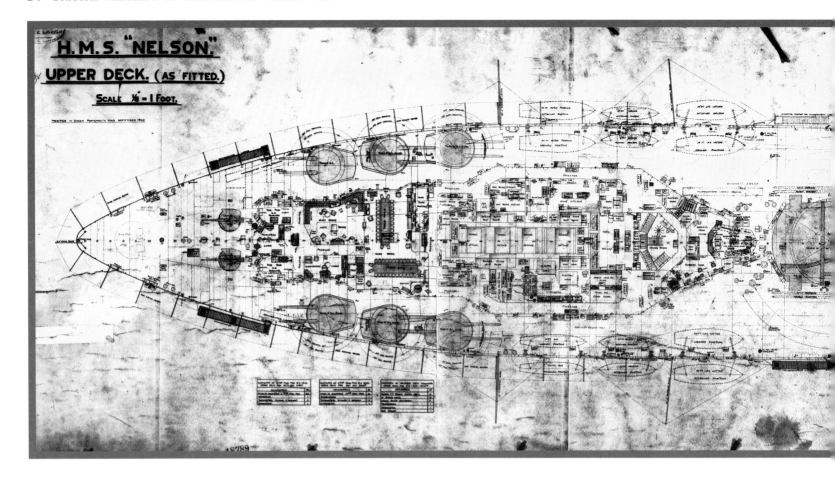

HMS Nelson, *Upper deck (as fitted), Armstrong Whitworth 8 August 1927. The layout of the ship's armament is very clear in this view – particularly the concentration of the secondary 6in turrets aft which, as they only had splinter protection, was the cause of some concern in case the entire battery on one side was wiped out by a single hit. Apart from these and the ship's 16in main armament, two of the ship's six 4.7in AA gun mountings can be seen on the quarterdeck – these were fitted with shields in 1940, a modification not shown on the drawings. Immediately abaft the forward breakwater on the middle line is the torpedo hatch and extending abaft that, in its stowed position, the gantry that was used to embark torpedoes. The rigged position of this gantry, which was used to lower torpedoes into the torpedo compartment in the vertical plane, can be seen in the profile drawing (shown in broken line projecting vertically upward from the upper deck). Either side of this the two rectangular blocks against the breakwater are paravane houses employed to stow both paravanes and their associate gear – paravanes are also stowed on each side at the rear of 'B' barbette. The short booms projecting from the side aft and on the port side forward are for side awnings which were intended to serve as sun-shades – those aft for the officer's accommodation, that forward for the sick bay. The other (longer) booms on each side are from forward – the 50ft guest warp boom, 30ft sounding boom and 30ft swinging boom. The outlines of the boats on each side abreast the bridge are shown in both their inboard and outboard positions. Unfortunately shown very faint the 1945 modifications include the quarterdeck pompom, the centres of both the Nelson's and Rodney's cranes (located to port and abaft 'X' turret) and, somewhat oddly, the locations of the 20mm Oerlikons in Rodney. (Plan No NPB7584, Neg No 467149c)*

already employed in several battlecruisers including the *Hood*, although in these cases the belt was external. The torpedo protection system was built into the hull under the belt armour in such a way that an underwater explosion could vent itself outside the belt and through the ship's side. It was, in effect, an extension of the system employed in *Hood* but with the maximum beam of the bulge carried vertically upward, outside the side armour, to the upper deck. Although the underwater protection followed earlier practice, with an outer air space and inner buoyancy space bounded inboard by a thick torpedo bulkhead, it deviated markedly in having the buoyancy space filled with water rather than steel tubes. This provided equal protection and allowed the tanks to remain empty in peacetime thereby saving on weight and fuel costs and reducing the complexity of the structure. Filling the buoyancy spaces required 2870 tons of seawater and the system, designed for protection against a 750lb torpedo warhead, was later deemed adequate to provide defence against a 1000lb warhead. The system also provided defence against mines and what were referred to as 'B' bombs – bombs exploding in the water alongside or under the bilge – a danger that was seen as very serious by the Naval Staff and Constructor's Department. In the event the torpedo proved to be the most deadly of aircraft weapons so far as battleships were concerned; bombs being much less of a danger until the advent of large guided weapons in the latter years of the war. Finally, as a direct result of war experience, a great deal of detail design went into providing a good supporting structure to the armour including heavy

chocks for the bases of the side armour and barbettes and the use of tongue and groove joints for the armour butts. Despite all this work the system had several areas of weakness, largely resulting from the weight limits of the design. Principal among these was the danger of a shell passing under the belt armour due to its lack of depth and inward slope at the base. There was also concern about the lack of protection to the hull forward of the citadel and the fact that the secondary armament was protected only against splinters.

Other advances in the design were to be found in the main armament and its fire control system and an extensive, for the time, AA capability – the latter to some extent compromised by the lack of the four 8-barrel pom-pom mountings provided for in the design but not available at the time of completion. However, the main armament was to prove troublesome in service, partly due to a move away from well-tried practice in the design of both the 16in gun and the loading system of the mounting and partly to an excessive requirement for safety interlocks. Both the gun and the mounting had teething problems, which took several years to correct and even then did not reach the efficiency and rate of fire that Britain enjoyed with its earlier 15in twin mounting.

Rodney and *Nelson* were the only battleships designed and built by any nation during the 1920s and were unfortunate in falling between two design periods. By the standards of the First World War they were very advanced and powerful ships but they were outclassed by later vessels primarily because of their comparative lack of speed but also because subsequent ships benefited from

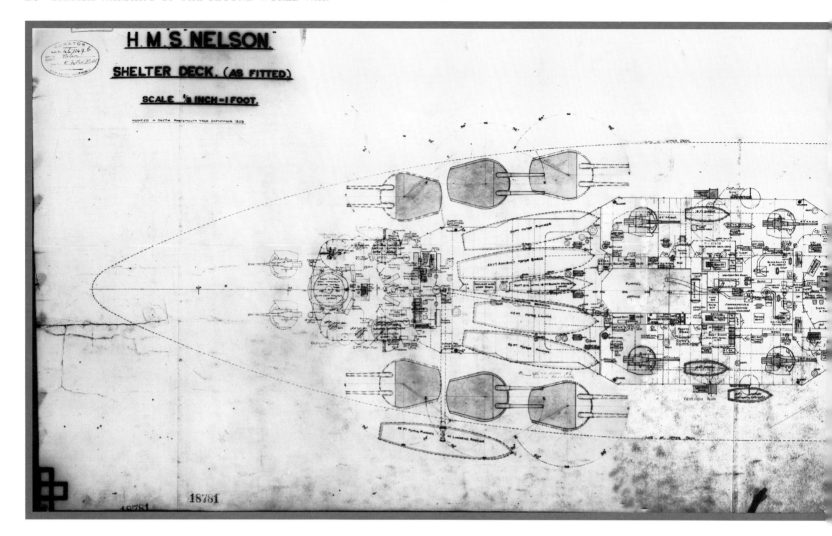

HMS Nelson, *Shelter deck (as fitted), Armstrong Whitworth 8 August 1927.* All six of Nelson's 4.7in AA guns can be seen in this plan – the four on the shelter deck being grouped abreast the funnel and after side of the bridge. The only other AA guns carried at the time of completion were eight single pom-poms, four of which were fitted at the after end of the shelter deck, here shown deleted (the other four were fitted on the conning tower platform). The design provided for four 8-barrel pom-pom mountings but these were not available at the time of completion and neither Nelson nor Rodney were so equipped until 1933-4 when two mountings were fitted in each ship on platforms abreast the fore side of the funnel. The training angle shown for 'X' turret is 150° on each side but the peacetime training angle was restricted to 118° to avoid damage to the bridge structure when the guns were fired abaft the beam – particularly at high angles of elevation. The cramped boat stowage arrangement illustrates the difficulty of finding sufficient space for these craft on what was a comparatively small superstructure – although the fitting of the main armament forward eliminated the other standard problem of finding a position clear of gun blast. The original fit from port to starboard was a 50ft motor pinnace (these were similar to the earlier steam pinnace but were fitted with diesel engines), 50ft Admiral's motor barge, 30ft gig with 16ft dinghy inside, 45ft motor launch and 50ft motor pinnace. By the end of the war the Admiral's barge had been replaced by a 45ft motor launch, with a 35ft motor boat inside, and the two 50ft boats had been removed to provide space for five single 20mm Oerlikons on each side.
(Plan No NPB7591, Neg No 467149b)

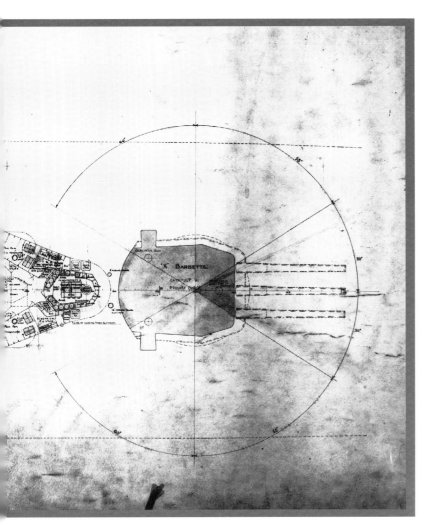

nautical miles at cruising speed. Although coast defence was without doubt intended as one of their functions, the general features of the design, particularly their high endurance, made it obvious that they were also intended to serve as commerce-raiding cruisers. Weight saving and long range were obtained principally by the employment of diesel engines and welded construction but the designers were unable to keep to the specified limits and the completed ships were nearly 2000 tons in excess of their published displacement.

This first sign of the re-emergence of German naval power reactivated France's interest in her allowable replacements under the Washington Treaty. In 1932 she laid down the 26,500-ton battlecruiser *Dunkerque* which, with a speed of 29.5kts and a main armament of eight 13in (33cm) guns, was intended as a direct reply to the German ships. She was followed by a sister-ship – the *Strasbourg* – in 1934, the two ships entering service in 1937 and 1938 respectively. This, in turn, prompted a reaction from Germany, which by this time had renounced the Treaty of Versailles, in the shape of the battlecruisers *Scharnhorst* and *Gneisenau*, laid down in 1935 and completed in 1938.[16] These ships were larger, faster and better protected than their French rivals. To add to French woes, in 1934 Italy laid down the first of the true fast battleships of the period – the *Littorio* and *Vittorio Veneto* – to which France replied in the following year with the commencement of the battleship *Richelieu*. In 1936 Germany laid down the battleships *Bismarck* and *Tirpitz*, in 1938 Italy followed with the next pair of the *Littorio* class and in 1939 France commenced two sister-ships to *Richelieu*. These battleships were, in theory, originally restricted by the 35,000-ton displacement limit but both the German and Italian vessels were of over 40,000 tons.

Britain, which viewed these developments with increasing anxiety, joined the battleship construction race with the rearmament programmes of 1936 and 1937 and laid down the five ships of the *King George V* class in 1937. A glance at the accompanying table illustrates the escalating situation in capital ship construction during the 1930s. Noteworthy is the general adoption of high speeds, which, once established, left little choice to Britain but to follow suit. Although the improvement of machinery design allowed the production of such ships without excessive sacrifices in protection the Admiralty would have preferred a lower speed to allow more weight for armour and guns. This in spite of the fact that British battleships were generally fitted with thicker armour than their foreign contemporaries – a reflection of the traumatic experiences of the First World War. Also worthy of note is the adoption by France and Italy of gun calibres below the 16in maximum allowed to them by Treaty.

additional technical developments.[15] Their protection system was complex and expensive – both in terms of construction and repair – and they carried a main armament which never reached peak efficiency. Nevertheless, they provided the naval and design staffs with valuable lessons for the future, were a substantial addition to the fleet and served with distinction in the Second World War.

Move and counter move

In 1929 Germany laid down the first of three 'armoured ships', more popularly known as 'pocket battleships', which were to enter service between 1933 and 1936. Ostensibly these were coast defence vessels intended primarily for service in the Baltic and were built to replace the ageing pre-dreadnoughts, which Germany had been allowed to retain under the terms of the Treaty of Versailles. According to this treaty such replacement ships were limited to 10,000 tons and 11in (28cm) guns. The application of ingenious design produced vessels substantially at odds with the intention of these limits. They possessed a speed greater than any existing battleship and an armament superior to any existing cruiser, were moderately well protected and had a range of 20,000

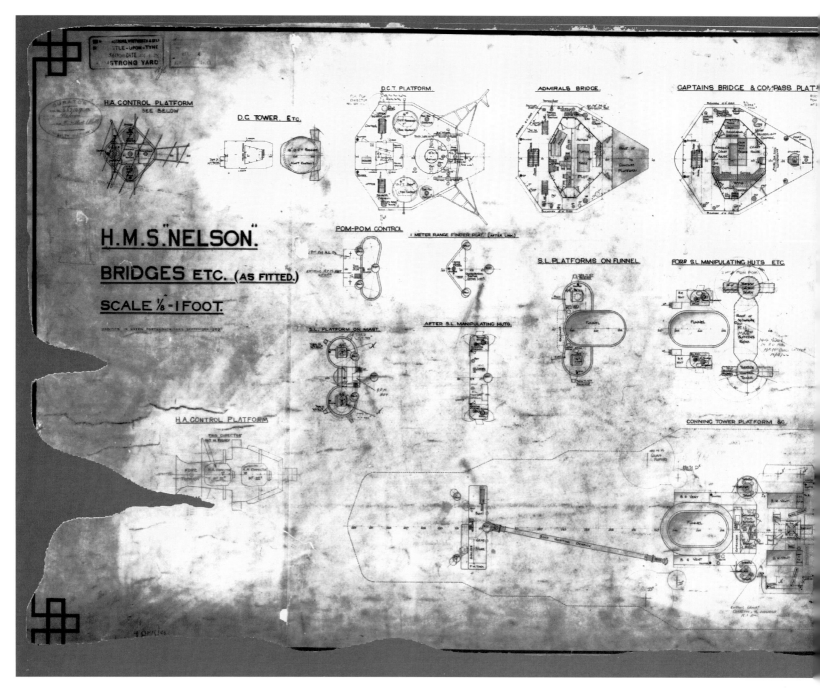

HMS Nelson, *Bridges etc (as fitted), Armstrong Whitworth 24 January 1928.* This drawing, which was not stamped by the builders until five months after the other drawings of Nelson *that are reproduced here, shows the bridge, funnel and mainmast platforms (this drawing may be from a different set of 'as fitted' drawings hence the different date). The tower bridge structure was one of the ship's more notable features and set the pattern* for future British bridge designs. It was intended to provide a solid, vibration free, structure for the main and secondary armament directors, give improved shelter to the bridge personnel and more space than was available from the earlier tier type bridge. Rodney *and* Nelson *were the last British battleships fitted with a heavily armoured conning tower – fitted forward of the bridge and directly accessible from its base. The armoured director on its roof was* also the last such item fitted in a new battleship – unlike earlier versions the hood was not fitted with a range finder. At top left the original (deleted) HA control platform contains a simple AA director on each side, a HA range-finder on the centre line aft, a Dumaresque instrument on the centre line forward and an Evershed bearing indicator at the centre. The final HA control platform with its two directors is shown at bottom left. The drawing shows

faintly most of the positions of the additional close-range AA mountings added to the superstructure up to 1945. These include four quad 40mm fitted during her 1944-5 US refit (two abaft the funnel and two on the conning tower roof) and the two 8-barrel pom-pom mountings that replaced the torpedo control towers abreast the fore side of the funnel in 1933-4.
(Plan No NPB7592, Neg No 467149a)

The King George V class

The problems encountered with the main armament of *Nelson* and *Rodney*, particularly the difficulties with the loading cycle, generated a desire on the part of the Gunnery Branch to return to the well-tried twin mounting. As a result the Staff Requirements for the 1931 capital ships called for the mounting of four twin 16in mountings in the conventional two forward/two aft disposition. The DNC was quick to point out that this would involve a longer ship with consequent increase in hull weight and reduction in the allowable thickness of the armour. In addition the level of underwater protection to the magazines would be reduced due to them being in a narrower part of the ship. These difficulties of balancing the requirements of protection and armament within treaty limits were to be a constant source of concern throughout the remaining period of treaty restrictions.

Although the Staff Requirements were written to meet the existing treaty limits, the Admiralty also considered the designs of smaller vessels armed with 14in, 12in, 11in and 10in guns.[17] The primary purpose in this was the reduction of costs; not only for construction but for operation and manning. However, such a reduction could not be contemplated without the international acceptance of lower limits. The Admiralty therefore proposed a reduction of the treaty limits to 25,000 tons and 12in guns but the extension of the holiday in battleship construction agreed at the 1930 London Conference rendered this proposal irrelevant.

The Requirements for battleships were reconsidered again during 1933-5 as a preliminary to the Second London Conference. Initially these were generally similar to the earlier requirements except that the *Nelson* armament arrangement was stated as being acceptable if a satisfactory design with four twin mountings could not be produced and provided that a new triple mounting design gave improvements in rate of fire and loading cycle. Suggestions were again put forward for a reduction to 12in guns but these were abandoned in 1934 when preliminary approaches to the USA made it clear that such a reduction would not be acceptable. A further complication then arose with the commencement of the construction of fast battleships in Europe. This forced the Admiralty into accepting a higher speed than 23kts which complicated still further the problem of producing a well-balanced design, as the increase in machinery weight would require reductions in the protection and/or armament. An extensive Staff study into this problem was supported by the production of several sketch designs for 16in, 15in and 14in gun ships with speeds of 27kts or 30kts. To limit ship length, all these designs had three turrets, triples in the 15in and 16in gun ships (one 16in sketch had two triples and one twin) and quad mountings or combinations of twins and quads in the 14in gun ships. The Staff concluded that a 35,000-ton ship of at least 29kts, armed with nine 15in guns in three triple turrets was best suited to meet British requirements. However, in October 1935 it became known that the USA was willing to consider a reduction in

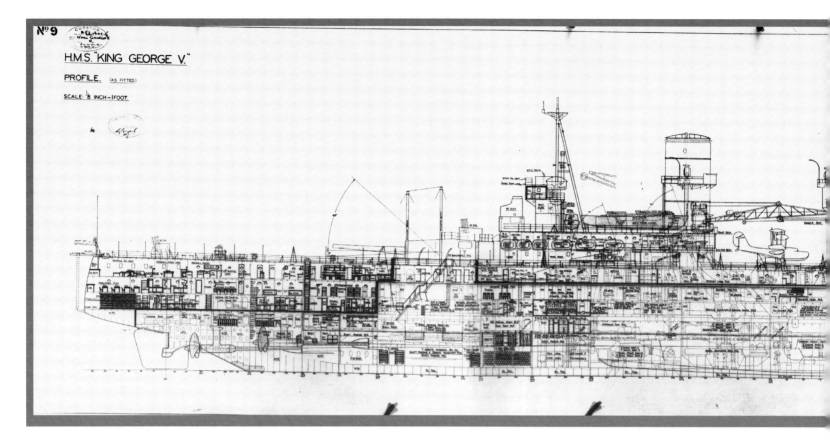

H.M.S. "KING GEORGE V."

PROFILE. (AS FITTED)

SCALE: 8 INCH = 1 FOOT

gun calibre to 14in at the forthcoming naval limitation conference. As a result the accepted design was modified to a 28kt ship armed with three quadruple 14in mountings. The Admiralty was by this time desperate to get the battleship construction programme under way and was willing to risk proceeding with the existing design without awaiting the outcome of the 1936 conference. This was driven primarily by the need to counter the construction plans of Germany and Italy for which the chosen design was considered an adequate match – although this was based on the assumption that the *Bismarck* and *Littorio* were actually 35,000-ton ships. Design work on the quadruple 14in mountings – the item with the longest lead-time – began in October 1935, two months before the conference started and the finalisation of the preliminary design for the ships continued while the conference was taking place. In the final stages the design was subjected to changes aimed primarily at improving the ship's protection. Early in 1936 it was decided to move the armour deck up one level from the middle to the main deck thereby increasing the armoured volume of the hull and reducing the amount of vulnerable structure above the citadel. This increase in armoured area necessitated a reduction in the thickness of deck and belt armour which was seen as a serious deficiency by the Naval Staff which they were unwilling to accept. Restoration of the armour thickness was achieved by changing 'B' 14in turret to a twin, which meant accepting a delay in the manufacture of the main armament but saved 770 tons on the armament weight. The Board approved the modified design in May 1936 and in the same month the 14in mountings for the first two ships were ordered. The

King George V

Displacement:	As completed – 36,727 tons standard, 42,076 tons deep.
	1945 – c39,100tons standard, 44,460 tons deep
Dimensions:	700ft (pp), 745ft (oa) x 103ft (max) x 29ft (mean).
Armament:	As completed – Ten 14in MkVII (2 x 4, 1 x 2); sixteen 5.25in MkI (8 x 2); thirty-two 2pdr (4 x 8); four UP mountings.
	1945 – as above except close-range AA = sixty-four 2pdr (8 x 8); ten 40mm (2 x 4, 2 x 1); thirty-six 20mm (6 x 2, 24 x 1).
Armour:	Belt – 15in abreast magazines, 14in abreast machinery; Bulkheads – 12in forward, 10in and 4in aft; Barbettes -13in-11in; Turrets – 12.75in face, 9in & 7in sides, 7in rear, 6in roof; Main deck – 6in over magazines, 5in over machinery; Lower deck 5in-2.5in; Torpedo bulkheads – 1.75in.
Machinery:	Four shaft, Parsons geared turbines, 110,000shp = 28kts; eight Admiralty 3-drum boilers; 3700 tons oil fuel; range 6000nm at 14kts.
Complement:	1422

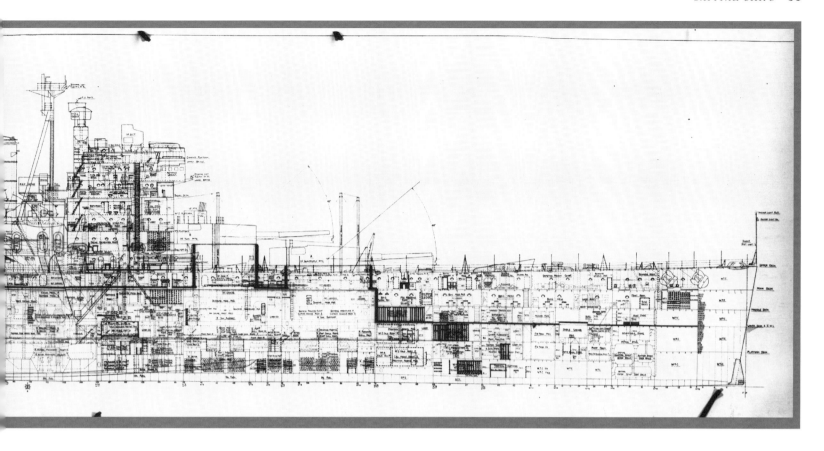

HMS King George V, *Profile (as fitted), Vickers Armstrongs 12 July 1941.* This set of 'as fitted' drawings were stamped several months after the ship's completion and in general are slightly less detailed than pre-war drawings – a reflection of the pressure on wartime resources. They also have some minor items missing, the siren platforms on the fore funnel and the external de-gaussing coil for example, although the omission of the upper sections of the masts is common as this detail was covered by the rig drawings. The National Maritime Museum has at least one other 'as fitted' set (dated 13 June 1941) and it is possible that these two sets were among the last to be produced. This profile shows clearly the armour on the decks, bulkheads and barbettes by virtue of being shown in thick black lines (the 13 June set shows the armour by double line as in the Nelson). Less obvious is the armoured conning position below the

Admiral's bridge (described as the Admiral's lookout on this drawing) shown as a shaded box to indicate its relatively light protection (4.5in sides, 3in ends, 2in floor and roof). The thick lines surrounding the compartments on the platform deck below the bridge and the lower deck below the mainmast are not indications of armour but the sound-proofing around the 14in Transmitting Station and HA control position (forward) and the central communication office (aft). The drawing includes a couple of unusual features – the machinery being shown in broken line (indicating that this was not on the middle line) and the illustration of the ammunition derricks in the rigged position (extending vertically from the upper deck abreast the turrets) when this was normally left to be shown on the rig drawing. The odd-looking features on the roofs of 'B' and 'Y' mountings and at the after end of the quarterdeck are four UP mountings (two

fitted abreast on 'Y' turret). These were 20-barrelled rocket firing AA weapons, the UP being an abbreviation of unrotated projectile, introduced as a stop-gap due to the shortage of multiple pom-pom mountings. They were not a success and the quarterdeck mounting was removed in June 1941 to be replaced by a 20mm Oerlikon (ex-Rodney – a second 20mm from the same source was temporarily fitted on 'B' turret in front of the UP mounting) while those on the turrets were replaced with multiple pompom mountings in December 1941. The oval features on the sides of the superstructure are Carley life rafts. The drawing illustrates well the exposed nature of the propeller shafts, the 'Achilles heel' of the battleship, which was to be the cause of extensive damage and flooding to the King George V's sister-ship Prince of Wales *when she was lost in December 1941.*
(Plan No NPB5308, Neg No A661601/9)

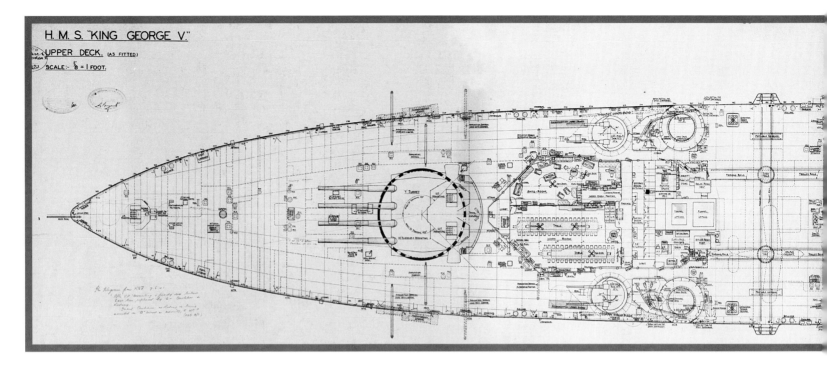

H.M.S. "KING GEORGE V."

UPPER DECK. (AS FITTED)

SCALE :- ⅛ = 1 FOOT.

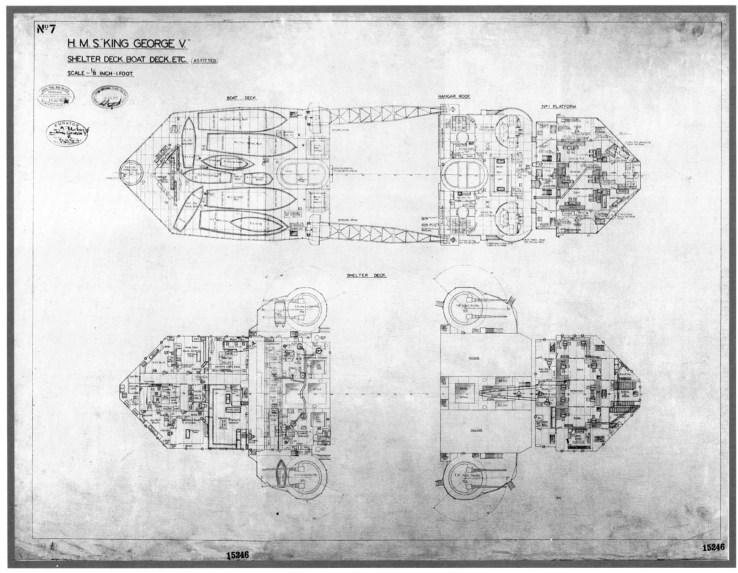

№ 7

H. M. S. "KING GEORGE V."

SHELTER DECK. BOAT DECK. ETC. (AS FITTED.)

SCALE - ⅛ INCH - 1 FOOT

BOAT DECK

HANGAR ROOF

№ 1 Platform

SHELTER DECK

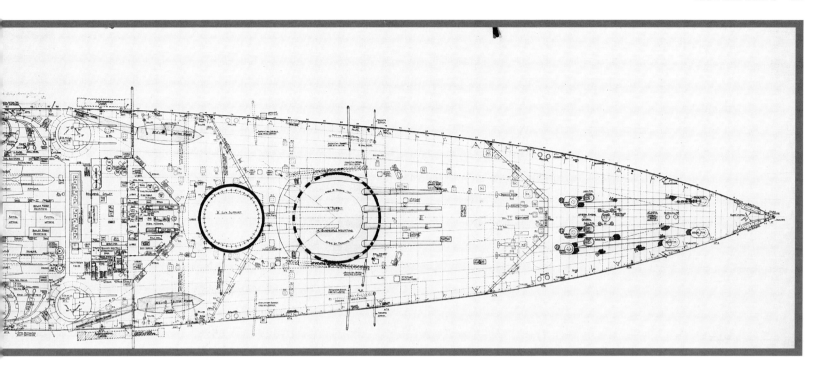

Above: *HMS* King George V, *Upper deck (as fitted), Vickers Armstrongs 12 July 1941. The layout of the upper deck makes an interesting comparison with* Nelson, *with a distinct impression of neater layout and more space. To some extent this is an illusion created by the fact that the superstructure and secondary armament now occupies the wider part of the ship although* King George V *also had the advantage of being 35ft longer (but with 3ft less beam). The major disadvantage over the* Nelson *arrangement was the greater difficulty in accommodating the magazines, particularly those aft, which were more vulnerable to damage due to their position in a narrower section of the ship. However, there were also considerable gains in the improved layout of the secondary armament into four separate groups and the ability to provide a unit machinery layout with alternate engine and boiler rooms. Both these also assisted in the provision of a clear space amidships for the cross-deck aircraft catapult. The drawing shows the two aircraft hangars with a Walrus amphibian (wings folded) in each. The rails for transporting the aircraft to the catapult and the turntables to turn them though 90° are also clearly shown. The tracks extending from the bottom of the* superfiring 5.25in mountings are the shell and cordite chutes which carried the ammunition from the tops of the dredger hoists to ammunition rings at the base of the mounting from where they could be loaded into the mounting's hoists. The split chute was for an alternative HA and LA shell supply for which there were separate main hoists from the shell room; the third hoist was for the cordite charge which fed a separate ring.
(Plan No NPB5309, Neg No A661601/6)

Left: *HMS* King George V, *Shelter deck, boat deck, etc (as fitted), Vickers Armstrongs 12 July 1941. Although having a greater area in which to accommodate the ship's boats when compared to* Nelson, *the boat deck still looks crowded, partly because more of the ship's pulling boats have been accommodated in the available space. The only boats on the upper deck being the two 32ft life cutters located abreast the fore end of the bridge. However, it has still been found necessary to accommodate a 16ft dinghy and a balsa raft under the guns of S3 and P3 5.25in mountings respectively. The two cranes abreast the after funnel served both the boats and the aircraft. The* boat deck represented a substantial loss of available space for close-range AA weapons and the ship's four 8-barrel pom-poms had to be crowded around the fore funnel where they had reasonably good arcs of fire from forward to abaft the beam but were limited to a single mounting on each side when firing aft. This situation improved somewhat with the addition of mountings on 'B' and 'Y' turret roofs, which not only increased the firepower but also allowed for aircraft to be tracked across bow and stern. The irregular dark tracks visible in the superstructure between P3 and S3 mountings are additional ventilation trunks to the engineering workshops – implying a serious problem with high temperatures in these compartments. Hardly a surprising situation as they straddle the after boiler uptakes and contained the blacksmith's and engineer's forges as well as the boiler room vent trunks.
(Plan No NPB5315, Neg No A661601/7)

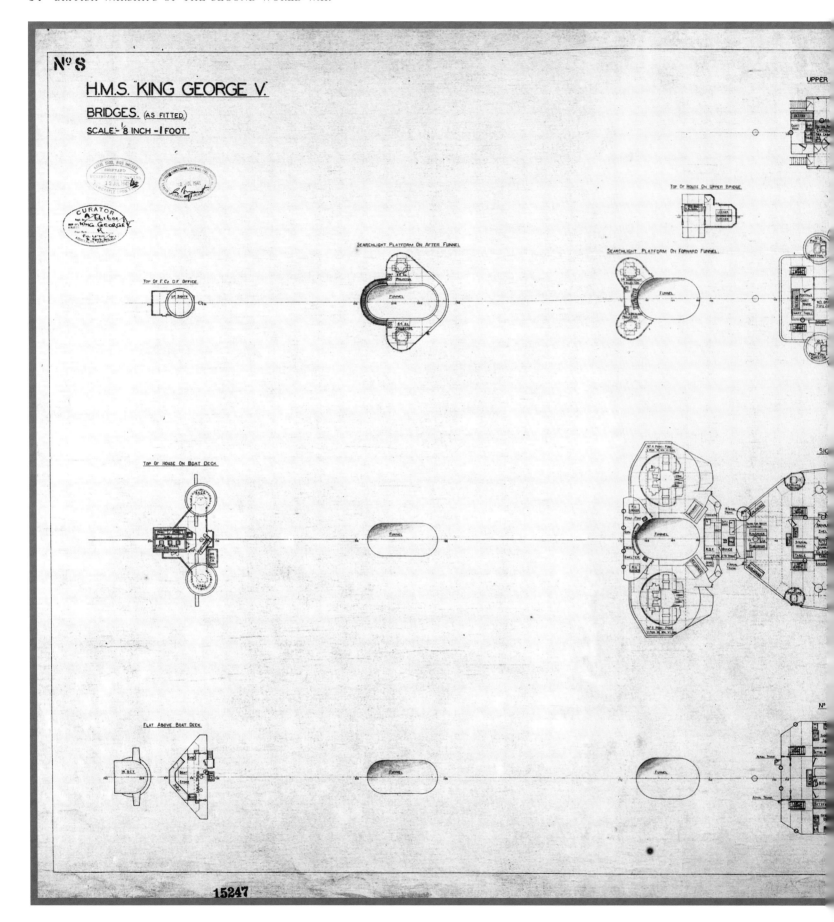

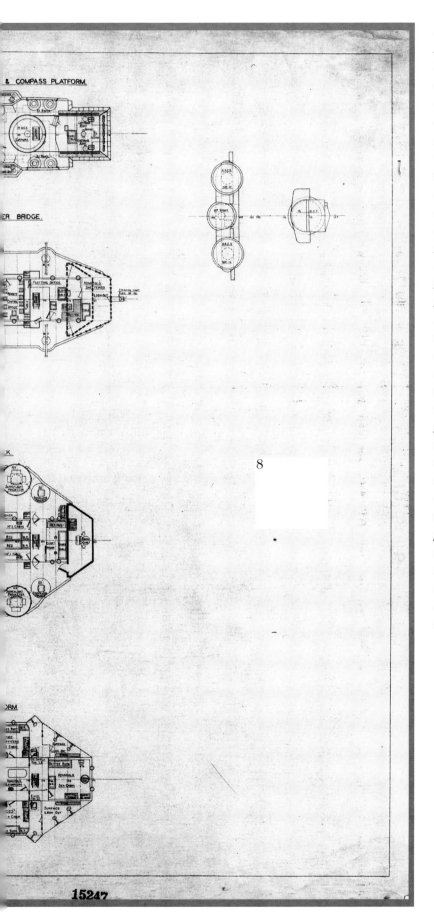

HMS King George V, *Bridges (as fitted), Vickers Armstrongs 12 July 1941.* The platforms within the bridge tower below the signal deck were primarily employed for accommodation and recreational facilities. The upper platforms were the ship's principal areas of command and control. The signal deck was largely occupied with facilities for flag signalling but also had the armoured steering position at its fore end, the chart house and two officers' sea cabins. The lower bridge accommodated the fully enclosed Admiral's lookout (or bridge) at its fore end, abaft which were various offices including that for the wireless and Type 284 main armament radar. The two circular tubs on each side of this platform contained the directors for the pom-pom mountings grouped around the fore funnel. The upper bridge and compass platform provided the primary conning position at its fore end with a roof over, the remainder of the platform being open. The large central circle is the base of the main 14in director and the deckhouse abaft it, containing the Captain's sea cabin and chart room, is the base of the tower supporting the two forward MkIV HACS directors. The latter are shown at top right (together with the roof of the 14in director) with the director sight for the UP mounting on 'B' turret fitted between them (this was later replaced by a pom-pom director). The enclosed areas projecting outward on each side are the air look-out positions, while the three circular objects inboard of the screens on each side are target bearing sights (that inboard of the air look-outs was for starshell). The drawing also shows the positions of the ship's six 44in searchlights – two on the signal deck (together with four smaller signalling searchlights) and two on each of the funnel platforms. The detail on the left shows the after main and HA directors and their supporting structure. At top left the small rectangle and circle represent the roof of the FC2 D/F office with the after UP sight mounted on its roof (the office itself was on the after HA tower between the two directors).
(Plan No NPB5316, Neg No A661601/8)

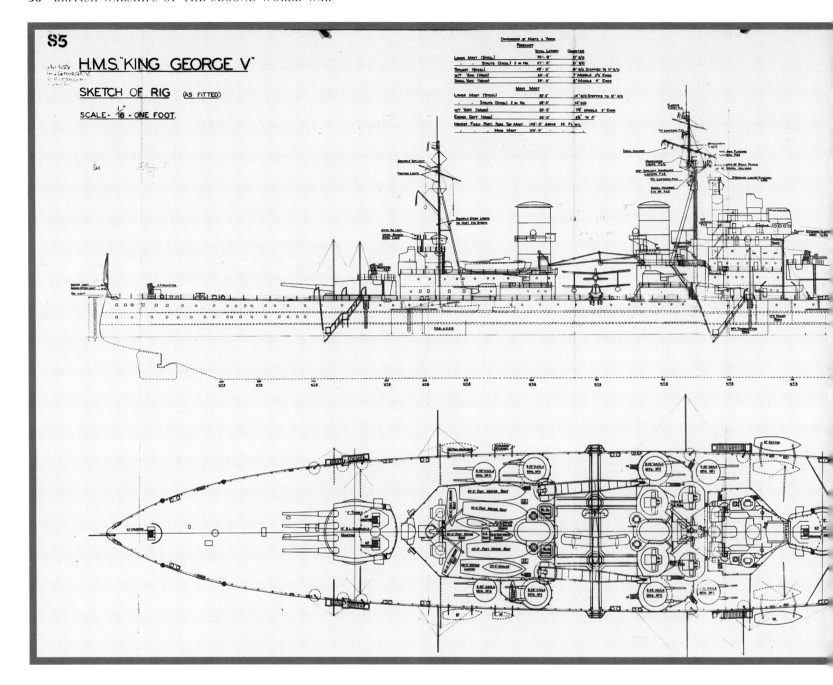

HMS King George V, *Sketch of Rig (as fitted).* Although rig drawings are usually fairly simple, this version for King George V is much less detailed than normal and contains little text relating to the rig apart from indicating the various navigation lights. It does, however, provide a list at top centre of the dimensions of the masts and yards. Strangely, it does provide text to indicate the various gun and UP mountings and the ship's boats, neither of which have direct links to the arrangement of the rig. The boats shown in broken line outboard, abreast the after superstructure, are harbour positions for the 25ft fast motor boats and dinghies normally stowed on the boat deck.
(Neg No A661658)

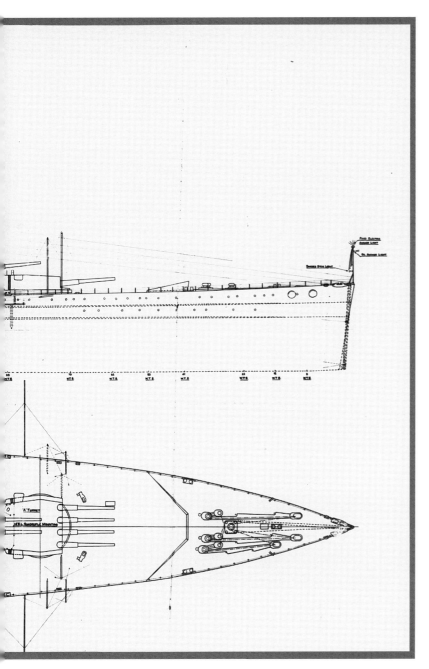

ships themselves, *King George V* and *Prince of Wales*, were ordered in July 1936 with completion anticipated in 1940.

At this point the Admiralty found itself with yet another dilemma. Having progressed the two 1936 ships it was now desired to place early orders for the three battleships of the 1937 Programme. Although the 1936 Treaty had accepted the 14in gun as an upper limit it also contained escalator clauses which (a) provided for a return to the 16in gun if Japan did not accept the treaty limits by April 1937 and (b) allowed for an increase in the displacement if any nation began to construct ships outside the treaty limits. Unfortunately the Admiralty were not willing to wait until April as, apart from the initial delay, any change in circumstances would require the development of new ship and gun mounting designs which would add still further to the delay in the start of construction. In November 1936 the Board decided that the three 1937 Programme ships should be repeats of the existing design – all five ships of the class were laid down between January and July 1937.[18]

In general the design was a marked advance on the *Nelson* apart from the greater underwater vulnerability of the main magazines. On the same designed displacement the *King George V* had a significantly higher speed and had armour which was both thicker and covered a larger area. The internal sloped belt of *Nelson* was abandoned in favour of a conventional external, vertical belt fitted flush with the ship's side. This was in part due to the conclusion that external venting of the torpedo protection compartments was of limited value and in part to simplify the structural arrangements and increase the armoured reserve of buoyancy. The depth of the belt was 23ft 6in, compared with 13ft in *Nelson*, of which 8ft 6in extended below the load waterline. Although protection outside the citadel was still limited, the addition of waterline protection forward and aft and the raising of the armoured deck greatly reduced the unprotected volume of the ship. However, heavy conning tower armour was abandoned in order to save weight and control and command positions aloft were, like the secondary armament, provided only with splinter protection. The torpedo defence system was further developed from that in *Nelson* by the provision of an air

European Capital Ship Construction 1929-39

Class (no of ships)	Country	Laid down	Displacement (tons)	Main Armament	Speed (kts)
Deutschland (3)	Germany	1931-4	11,700	Six 11in (28cm)	27
Dunkerque (2)	France	1932 & 34	26,500	Eight 13in (33cm)	29.5
Littorio (2)	Italy	1934	40,000	Nine 15in (38cm)	30
Scharnhorst (2)	Germany	1935	32,000	Nine 11in (28cm)	32
Richelieu (1)	France	1936	35,000	Eight 15in (38cm)	30
Bismarck (2)	Germany	1936	40,000	Eight 15in (38cm)	29
King George V (5)	Britain	1937	35,000	Ten 14in (35.6cm)	28
Littorio (2)	Italy	1938	40,000	Nine 15in (38cm)	30
Richelieu (2)	France	1939	35,000	Eight 15in (38cm)	30
Lion (2)	Britain	1939	40,000	Nine 16in (40.6cm)	30

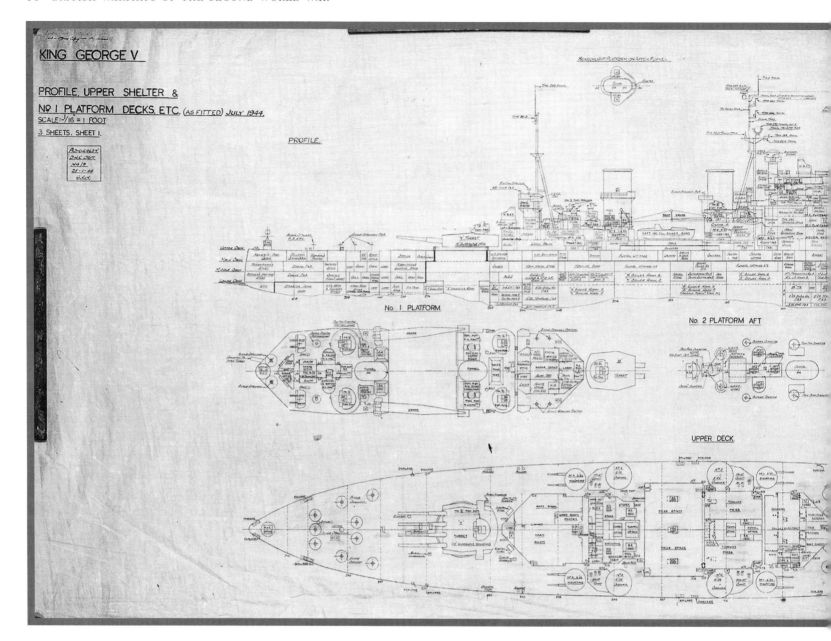

HMS King George V, *Profile, Upper, Shelter and No1 Platform Decks, etc (as fitted), July 1944. This flysheet to the original 'as-fitted' drawings shows the modifications made to* King George V *during a major refit of February-July 1944 at Liverpool. These alterations were primarily related to the improvement of her close-range AA armament, fire control gear, radar and communications equipment prior to her transfer to the Far East and Pacific. Similar refits were carried out on her sister-ships –*Howe *at Devonport (December 1943 – May 1944);* Duke of York *at Liverpool (September 1944 – April 1945); and* Anson *at Devonport (July 1944 - March 1945). The most obvious change is the omission of the aircraft equipment which cleared the centre section of the upper deck for additional crew space and a new stowage area for the boats. The hangars were utilised for accommodation and recreational facilities, including a cinema. The clearing of the original boat deck provided additional space for AA guns and this area was rearranged to accommodate two 8-barrel pom-pom, two quad 40mm, four twin and two single 20mm mountings together with their ready-use ammunition and, in the case of the four larger mountings, their directors. The remaining 20mm armament included eighteen singles on the upper deck – equally divided between forecastle and quarterdeck – four singles on the forward shelter deck, two singles on the fore funnel platform and a twin mounting on each side of the flag deck. Also included in the refit was the replacement of the quad pom-pom on 'Y' turret with an 8-barrel mounting. Among the array of radar, IFF and TBS aerials on the fore mast are the newly fitted dish aerial of Type 277*

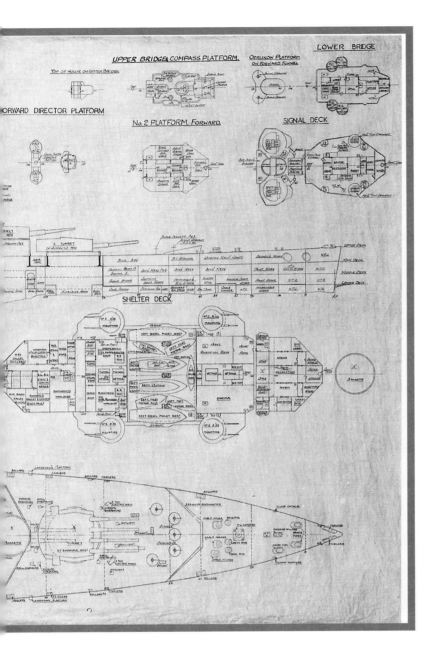

combined air and surface warning radar on the starfish platform and the cheese aerial of Type 293 surface warning radar at the head of the fore topmast. At the top of the main top mast is the single aerial of Type 281B long-range air warning radar – replacing the earlier Type 279 which had separate transmit/receive aerials – one on each mast. The small deckhouse at the after end of the quarterdeck is the RH2 direction finder office with the associated aerial on its roof.

(Plan No NPA4167, Neg No E0712)

space between the buoyancy space and the protective bulkhead, giving an air/water/air sandwich. In order to reduce the full load under war conditions the buoyancy spaces were arranged to serve as fuel oil tanks – the oil being displaced by seawater as it was used in order to maintain the protective value of the system.

Despite the care taken to avoid the problems of the 16in triple mounting, the 14in quad and twin suffered from a number of teething problems on entering service. However, these were almost entirely due to problems with the mountings' complex system of safety interlocks and these were corrected within a comparatively short time, although not before they had caused some embarrassment to *Prince of Wales* during her short action with *Bismarck* in May 1941. The weight limits of the original design had led to a decision to abandon the mixed secondary armament in favour of a combined HA/LA armament of ten twin 4.5in gun mountings. However, the naval staff considered that this weapon lacked the stopping power required to deal adequately with surface attack by destroyers and cruisers. Initially no larger weapon with a rate of fire suitable for use against aircraft was available but the development of the twin 5.25in mounting for the AA cruisers of the *Dido* class provided an answer and this mounting was adapted for use in the *King George V* and her sisters. The close-range AA armament followed the standard of the time with four 8-barrel pom-pom mountings and four quad 0.5in mountings. The number of pom-pom mountings was later increased to six (not initially fitted in first two ships) and the 0.5in guns were never carried, being replaced by other weapons in the completed ships.

The fitting-out of the class was progressively delayed by wartime shortages. Only *King George V* actually completed in 1940, and then only just, she was followed by *Prince of Wales* and *Duke of York* in 1941. The last two ships, *Anson* and *Howe*, had their construction suspended for 3 and 6 months respectively in 1940 and did not complete until 1942. The ships of the class were the best-protected treaty battleships of the period; in fact it might well be argued that too much emphasis was placed on heavy armour at the expense of other design features. However, the Second World War provided little evidence for the advantages of armour versus gun power in a straight action with modern battleships. The *Prince of Wales* and *King George V* fought *Bismarck* and *Duke of York* the *Scharnhorst* but only in the first case did the British ship receive any significant damage and even then this was largely superficial. The significant points of the damage to the *Prince of Wales* were the vulnerability of unprotected structure and the danger from underwater diving shell –

neither of which would have come as a surprise. One of *Bismarck*'s projectiles went very deep and hit the ship at the turn of the bilge about 30ft below the waterline and 16ft below the bottom edge of the belt. The shell came to rest against the lower edge of the torpedo bulkhead 12ft inboard fortunately without detonating. The *Prince of Wales* proved to be a very unlucky ship being sunk by Japanese aircraft off Malaya in December 1941. The loss of such a modern ship caused considerable concern and resulted in an extensive investigation. Apart from the obvious cause (that she was operating without air cover) she was hit by six torpedoes one of which distorted the port outer propeller shaft causing flooding to run forward through the shaft passage to the port outer engine room. The extensive flooding caused by this one torpedo was well beyond anything that might normally be expected and virtually crippled the ship. There were also problems with the electricity supply, which seriously reduced the effectiveness of the AA armament and the pumping and flooding system. Thus, in her short career *Prince of Wales* managed to provide examples of the two forms of attack that were most difficult to defend against – diving shell and damage to the vulnerable steering and propulsion areas at the stern.

The end of the line

The failure of Japan to accept the terms of the 1936 Treaty initially and the consequent return to the 16in gun limit in April 1937 initiated the production battleship designs to this new limit for the 1938 Programme. Achieving a satisfactory balance of features for such a ship within 35,000 tons gave the DNC's department and the Staff considerable problems but this straightjacket problem was soon alleviated. The Japanese were becoming more and more uncooperative and secretive but it was clear to both the British and Americans that Japan was planning to build ships totally unconstrained by treaty limits. In March 1938 Britain, the USA and France invoked the escalator clause of the Naval Treaty and raised the maximum displacement limit to 45,000 tons. The Admiralty had attempted to limit this increase to 40,000 tons, which it saw as quite sufficient for a 16in gun ship, but the USA would not except anything less than 45,000 tons. Consequently the Admiralty, in an attempt to avoid what it regarded as 'monster ships', decided to self impose the lower limit for its new battleships and communicated this information to the European naval powers with the hope that they would also accept 40,000 tons as an upper limit!

The final design produced for the 1938 Programme was essentially an enlarged 16in gun version of the *King George V* design with the speed increased to 30kts. The first two ships of the class, *Temeraire* and *Lion*, were laid down in June and July 1939 respectively, while the second pair, *Conqueror* and *Thunderer* of the 1939 Programme, were due to be ordered in late 1939. At this time it was anticipated that in the event of a war with both Germany and Japan,

the *King George V* class, two of the *Lion* class and the three battle-cruisers (*Hood*, *Renown* and *Repulse*) would be retained in home waters while the other two *Lion* class ships, *Nelson*, *Rodney*, five *Queen Elizabeth* class and three *Royal Sovereign*s would form the core of the British Fleet in the Far East. This, however, was on the basis that war would not begin for some years (the first two *Lion*s were expected to complete in 1942 and the second pair in 1944). In the event Britain found herself at war on an escalating basis, first with Germany, then with Italy and finally with Japan. Although this represented the pre-war vision of 'worst case' the fact that the involvement was spread over two years and eventually provided Britain with a powerful ally in the shape of the USA, allowed what amounted to a holding war in the Far East until the conflict in Europe was under control. By that time there was little need for battleships and the fact that the construction of the *Lion* class was suspended shortly after the outbreak of war had little effect on British naval power. Their construction was originally halted on the basis that resources could be better employed in destroyer production and that they were unlikely to be completed in sufficient time to take part in the war in any case. As the war progressed the demands on British shipbuilding, particularly in relation to the production of escort vessels and merchant ships, ensured that they were never restarted, despite an Admiralty desire to do so. The *Lion* design was reworked and reconsidered at various times during the war to incorporate improved equipment and war lessons but was eventually abandoned altogether when it was concluded that a completely new design was required. The Staff Requirements were redrafted in 1942 and again in 1944. Some idea of the improvement demanded as a result of war experience can be seen from the fact that the standard displacement considered necessary to meet these requirements was 48,000 tons and 67,000 tons respectively – and this whilst still retaining the nine 16in gun main armament and with no major change in speed or armour. Various additional designs were generated with the intention of reducing the size of the ships but none of these was more than a paper exercise and plans for battleship construction were eventually abandoned after the war when it was realised they no longer served a function that could justify their cost.

The *King George V* class should, therefore, have been the last British battleships to enter service but early in 1939 a suggestion was put forward for the production of a battleship intended to circumvent the delays caused by the bottleneck in armament production. This involved building a new ship utilising four existing 15in twin mountings held in store as spares.[19] Work began on a design for a 30kt, 40,000-ton ship which, apart from the main armament, was generally similar to the *King George V* but this was stopped shortly after the outbreak of war. In December 1939 Winston Churchill became aware of the existence of this design and, impressed by the idea of obtaining a new battleship at an early date, initiated the revival of the design process. The design was approved in May 1940 but circumstances conspired to delay the ship's construction and she was not laid down until October 1941 and took $4^{1}/_{2}$ years to build. The last and largest battleship of the Royal Navy was, somewhat inappropriately, named *Vanguard*. As with the *Lion* class she was modified as the war progressed to incorporate hard won lessons and new equipment but she had little real function in the post-war fleet and saw very little service before being placed in reserve.

Modernisations

The Washington and 1930 London Naval Treaties effectively extended the front-line service of the older capital ships of the fleet for much longer than would otherwise have been the case. While, in theory at least, this kept the major battleship fleets in a state of technical equality, the vulnerability of the older ships to aerial and underwater attack considerably reduced their acceptability for modern conditions. This problem was addressed by the Washington Treaty allowance of 3000 tons per ship for 'defensive only' modernisation. The British ships for which modernisation was considered essential were the 15in gun battleships and battlecruisers, the older 13.5in gun ships having a limited expected life. The prime requirements were for the provision of bulges and deck armour but financial limits meant that both could not be provided simultaneously. Because the ships concerned required the higher stability provided by the addition of bulges in order to accommodate the extra topweight of deck armour it was essential to bulge the ships first and leave the armour for fitting at a later date as and when the funds became available. This had the additional financial advantage that the bulging process was cheaper than fitting deck armour. In addition to these measures, improvements were required in AA defence and modifications to provide protection against gas (known as collective defence). The ships given highest priority for modernisation were the five *Queen Elizabeth* class battleships, the remaining ships having already been fitted with bulges except for *Royal Oak* and *Renown* whose refits were already under way. The principal bulging refits of this period were as follows:

Royal Oak	1922-4
Renown	1923-6
Warspite	1924-6
Queen Elizabeth	1926-7
Malaya	1927-9
Valiant	1929-30
Barham	1931-4

Apart from bulging, the standard modernisation for the period included enhancement of the AA armament to bring ships to an outfit of four single 4in AA guns and a HA control system (initially an interim version and later the new HACS MkI as equipment became available). In addition ships were fitted to provide protection against gas shells and bombs, and detailed changes were made to bridge structures. The *Queen Elizabeth* class also had their fore funnels trunked into the after funnel to reduce smoke interference with the bridge and spotting top. These and other, less extensive, changes were carried out piecemeal, as and when convenient, and did not necessarily coincide with the major bulging refit.

The next stage of the modernisation process became increasingly more involved and expensive as the 1930s progressed. The relatively simple improvements originally envisaged being replaced by extensive rebuilds prompted in part by similar reconstructions of foreign battleships – particularly those of Italy and Japan. The *Royal Sovereign* class were not included because they were relatively slow and, being shorter than the *Queen Elizabeth* class, lacked space amidships (they were also due to be replaced by the *King George V* class). All of the remaining ships (*Queen Elizabeth* class and the three battlecruisers) were due for modernisation but the outbreak of war halted the plans for *Barham* and *Hood*. Of the remainder, two (*Malaya* and *Repulse*) were subjected to intermediate reconstruction and the other four (*Warspite, Renown, Queen Elizabeth* and *Valiant*) to full reconstruction. In chronological order the major refits were as follows:

Repulse	1933-6
Malaya	1934-6
Warspite	1934-7
Renown	1936-9
Valiant	1937-9
Queen Elizabeth	1937-41

The principal improvements carried out were progressively more extensive, the primary changes being described below.

Deck Protection: *Barham*, being the last ship of the *Queen Elizabeth* class to undergo the initial bulging refit and therefore into the period when more capital was available for modernisation, was fitted with 4in armour over her magazines. In *Repulse* and *Malaya* this protection was extended to the engine rooms (2.5in) and in the later *Queen Elizabeth* class ships to the boiler rooms (2.5in). The increasing weight of the deck armour provided was a reflection of weight savings made elsewhere (see below). In *Renown* deck armour had been fitted during her 1923-6 refit and additions during her major reconstruction involved extending the armour already present.

Machinery: The extensive reconstructions of *Warspite, Renown, Valiant* and *Queen Elizabeth* were made possible to a large extent by the substantial savings in weight generated by fitting them with new machinery. In *Warspite* the machinery weight was reduced by 1390 tons and in the *Queen Elizabeth* and *Valiant* by 1485 tons. This also saved a considerable amount of space which was utilised for other purposes and the need to virtually rebuild the machinery compartments provided the opportunity to substantially enhance

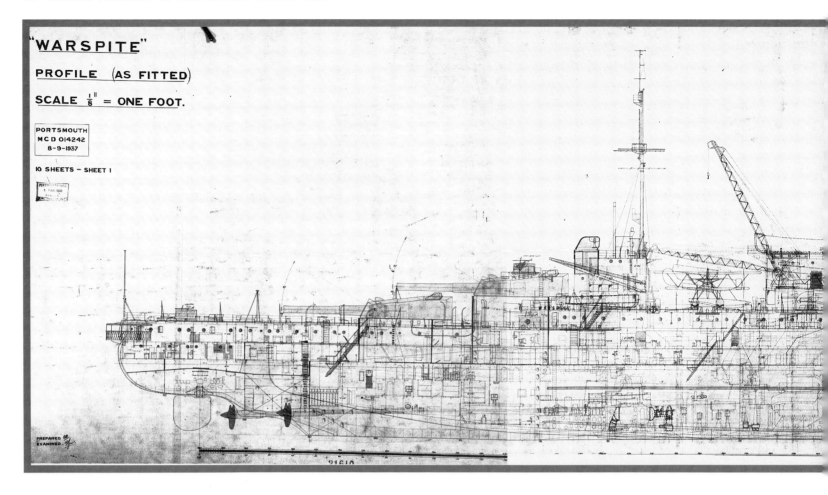

HMS Warspite, *Profile (as fitted), Portsmouth Dockyard 8 September 1937.* One of the Royal Navy's most famous battleships, the Warspite *saw much more action than the majority of her contemporaries. She ended the war as a much-scarred veteran having been extensively damaged at various points in her career. Her first baptism of fire was at the Battle of Jutland in 1916 when she came under the concentrated fire of a large section of the German Fleet. In the Second World War she was hit by a 550lb bomb during the Battle for Crete in 1941, very seriously damaged by a 3000lb radio-controlled bomb off Salerno in 1943 and finally detonated a ground mine in the North Sea in 1944 while returning from the Normandy beaches. She was returned to service with minimum repairs in August 1944 to provide shore support for the landings on Walcheren with one boiler room, one 15in mounting and one propeller shaft out of action. These drawings are a new set generated as a result of the ship's reconstruction at Portsmouth during 1934-7 when the main machinery was replaced together with practically all the superstructure above the forecastle deck. As the new boiler installation occupied less space, the original forward boiler room was not required so this was converted to other purposes. The remaining main machinery compartments were retained much as they were except for the addition of a middle line bulkhead in the boiler rooms and a transverse bulkhead in the engine room between the turbines and their gearing. The grey stripe running the length of the machinery spaces just below the level of the lower deck is a wood fender attached to the ship's side. The aircraft (shown in both end view and profile on the catapult and again in profile in the hangar) is a Blackburn Shark TSR. These aircraft were replaced with Swordfish floatplanes shortly after completion of the* Warspite's *modernisation and were in turn replaced by Walrus amphibians in 1940. Although the drawings have no annotation indicating alteration they include changes that show the additions made to the ship up to mid-1943. The items of this type visible in the profile include the direction finding aerial projecting from the fore side of the compass platform; the gunnery radar aerials for Type 284 (rectangles on front and top of DCT) and Type 285 (on the bridge HA director); the relocated fore topmast to allow for the fitting of the surface warning Type 271 radar office and lantern on the starfish platform; and the additional height to mainmast with the receiving aerial for the Type 281 long range air warning radar at its head (transmitting aerial at top of fore top mast).*

(Plan No NPC5161, Neg No 595901)

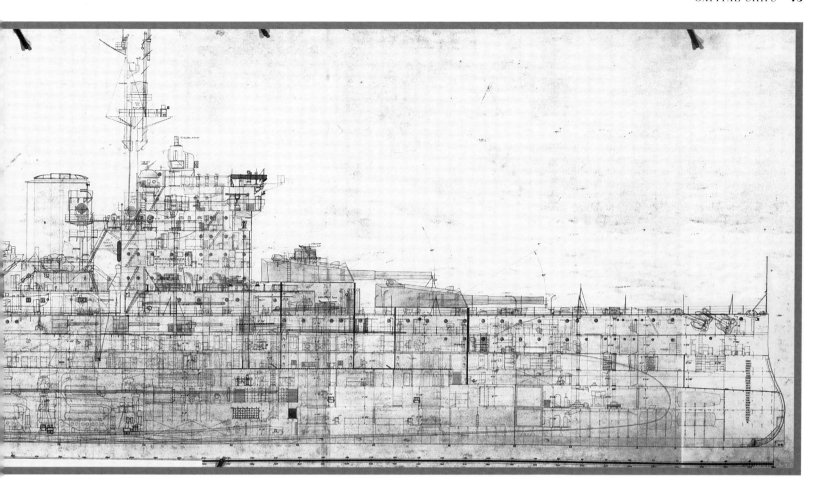

Warspite (1937)

Displacement: 31,315 tons standard, 36,450 tons deep

Dimensions: 600ft (pp), 639ft 5in(oa) x 104ft (max) x 28ft 9.5in (mean)

Armament: Eight 15in MkI (4 x 2); eight 6in MkXII (8 x 1); eight 4in MkXVI (4 x 2); thirty-two 2pdr (4 x 8); sixteen 0.5in (4 x 4)
1945 – as above except 6in and 0.5in guns removed and thirty-five 20mm (27 x 1, 4 x 2) added

Armour: Belt – 13in lower, 6in upper; Bulkheads – 6in and 4in; Barbettes -10in-7in; Turrets – 13in face, 11in sides, 4.25in roof; Middle deck – 5in over magazines, 3.5in over machinery; Torpedo bulkheads – 2in

Machinery: Four shaft Parsons geared turbines, 30,000shp = 23.5kts; six Admiralty 3-drum boilers; 3500 tons oil fuel; range 7500nm at 12kts

Complement: 1124

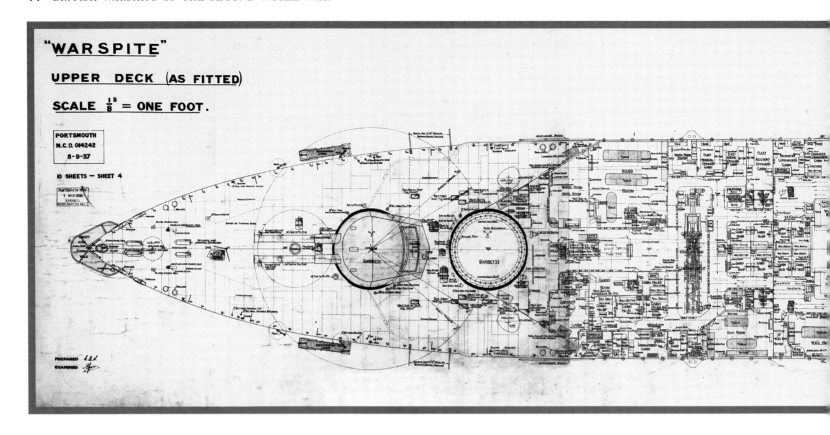

HMS Warspite, *Upper Deck (as fitted), Portsmouth Dockyard 8 September 1937.* The interior areas of this deck were largely employed for accommodation with the principal exception of the 6in gun battery. The latter, reduced from the original six to four guns on each beam, have had their 6in side armour replaced by 2in splinter protection as a weight-saving measure. The batteries also have internal splinter protection in the shape of 2in screens between the gun bays, 2in end bulkheads and a 2in middle line bulkhead separating port and starboard batteries – all are indicated by slightly thicker lines. Abreast 'Y' turret can be seen the double broken lines which indicate the position of 6in armour bulkheads immediately under the deck. These bulkheads were originally fitted to protect an after 6in battery which was omitted prior to the ship's completion in 1915. The armour was retained originally, and at the time of modernisation, because it added to the security of the after magazines. Located athwartships about half way between the after end of the 6in battery and 'X' barbette is the aircraft catapult machinery. The quarterdeck, otherwise unaltered since the ship's completion, shows the positions of three 20mm Oerlikons fitted in December 1941– one on the middle line near the stern and two mounted abreast 'X' barbette. (Plan No NPC5162, Neg No 595901c)

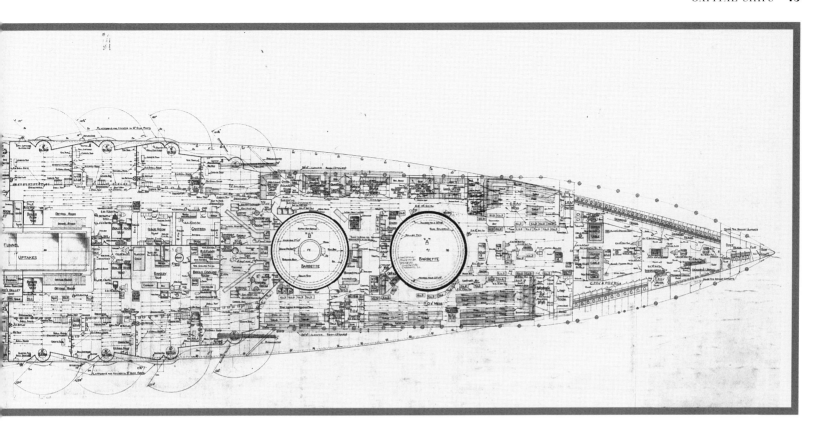

water-tight subdivision. In the case of *Warspite* the boiler pressure was limited by the retention of original steam powered auxiliaries but in the other three ships the fitting of new auxiliary machinery allowed in an increase from 285 to 400psi.

Long Range AA Armament: In the mid-1930s the twin 4in HA/LA mounting began to replace the single 4in in both reconstructed and non-reconstructed ships, all battleships and battlecruisers being so fitted by the outbreak of war except for the *Renown*, *Queen Elizabeth* and *Valiant*. These last three ships were equipped to a higher standard with the newly introduced twin, between-decks, 4.5in HA/LA mounting (twenty guns in each ship). In each case these guns replaced the original secondary armament (4in triples in the *Renown* and the 6in casemate guns and their armour – which saved considerable weight – in the other two). Control of the AA armament remained the HACS which passed through various modifications from MkI to MkIV up to 1939. By 1939 all ships had been fitted with two such systems (four in the case of *Queen Elizabeth*, *Valiant* and *Renown*). It proved inadequate under war conditions, even after the addition of radar, being too simple in principle to cope with the complex fire control problem of engaging modern aircraft.

Close Range AA Armament: Two weapons were developed between the wars for close range AA defence – the multiple (8-barrel and 4-barrel) pom-pom and the quad 0.5in machine gun mountings. The former was a very advanced weapon at the time it was conceived in the early 1920s but was delayed in introduction and was due for replacement by 1939. It did nevertheless prove reasonably effective during the war, particularly against dive bombers.

The 0.5in MG mounting on the other hand was close to useless. As the war progressed these two mountings were superseded by the 40mm Bofors and the 20mm Oerlikon but, whereas the 0.5in mounting had virtually disappeared from the fleet by the middle of the war, the pom-pom continued in service throughout the war and beyond.

Aircraft: The limited availability of carrier aircraft during the 1930s lead to a substantial development programme for the fitting of aircraft in both capital ships and cruisers. These aircraft were primarily intended to serve in the reconnaissance and spotting roles, although they did have a very limited offensive capability. At the end of the 1920s the crude flying-off platforms fitted on capital ship turrets began to be replaced by aircraft catapults, initially fitted on the quarterdeck but soon moved to a turret roof position when the former was found unsatisfactory.[20] A desire to carry more aircraft (stowed in hangars for weather protection and maintenance) and for improved aircraft handling led to a more sophisticated approach for both the new and reconstructed ships of the 1930s. This consisted of a fixed cross-deck catapult amidships and two hangars fitted abreast the forward superstructure. The first such arrangement was fitted in the *Malaya* and with little variation was followed in all later modernisations.

Main Armament: The modernisations from *Warspite* onward included an increase in the elevation of the 15in guns from 20° to 30°. This modification was accompanied by the introduction of improved 15in projectiles and the combined effect of both changes was to increase the maximum range from 23,700 to 32,200 yards. This, needless to say, was not in the spirit of 'for defensive purposes

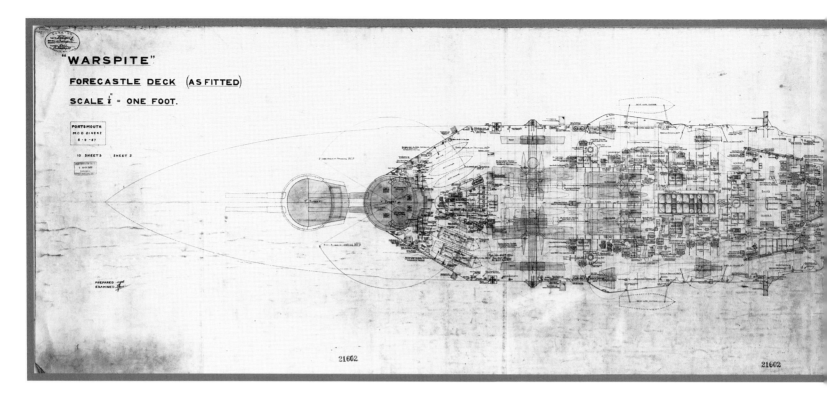

Below: *HMS* Warspite, *Shelter Deck and Bridges (as fitted), Portsmouth Dockyard 8 September 1937.* The larger ship's boats grouped on the hangar roofs were originally drawn as two 45ft motor boats to port and one 45ft motor launch to starboard. The outer position on the starboard side was unoccupied being shown without an outline for a boat and a note stating that it was 'stowage for 45ft motor launch, bow pointing forward', although why such an alternative was necessary when space was limited is not clear. The boat shown in this position, a 35ft motor boat, and the 20ft motor whaler abaft it are later additions to the drawing. The ship's four 8-barrel pom-poms – her main close-range AA weapons and the only such mountings she ever carried – are grouped around the funnel in similar fashion to the forward group in King George V. *Also similar to* King George V *is the bridge layout although in this case the HA directors are mounted on the after corners of the Admiral's bridge below the level of the main DCT rather than above it on the compass platform. Forward of the HA directors, the circular objects on each side, are the ship's original 6in gun directors – retained to control the secondary

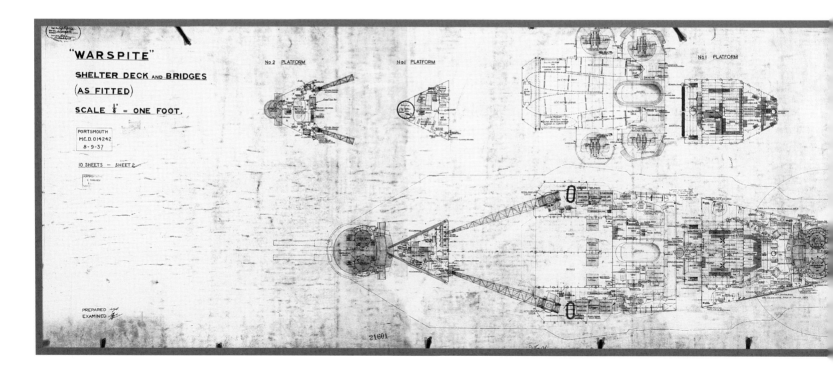

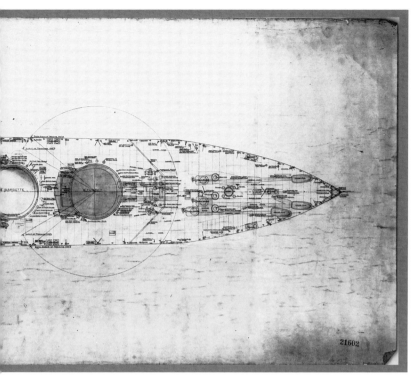

Left: *HMS* Warspite, *Forecastle Deck (as fitted), Portsmouth Dockyard 8 September 1937.* The plan of Warspite's *forecastle shows a standard general layout for the new and modernised capital ships of the period apart from the fact that she is the only such vessel where the aircraft hangars are side by side and not separated by a funnel. The Shark aircraft, of which she carried two, are shown both in the hangars (with wings folded) and on the catapult in their 'harbour position'. The effect of limited space for boat stowage on the superstructure and the need to keep the catapult deck clear is illustrated by the location of several of the ship's boats abreast the after superstructure where they were vulnerable to gun blast damage. This problem was substantially eased when the aircraft equipment was removed in 1943. Note the sponsons on each side of the forecastle abreast the hangars, which allowed for the after twin 4in mountings being fitted further outboard where they had improved arcs of fire – particularly on after bearings. The only substantial additions shown in this plan are for six single Oerlikons – two abreast 'B' barbette added in late 1941, two abreast 'X' barbette added in 1943 and two which replaced the quad 0.5in MG mountings on 'X' turret roof in 1942. (Plan No NPC5170, Neg No 595901b)*

battery. Also retained from the original fire control gear is the armoured gun control tower and its revolving director hood. This was transferred from the original armoured conning tower to the after end of the superstructure to serve as the secondary control position for the main armament. The remainder of the additional Oerlikons can be found in these plans – four added on the forward shelter deck (added late in 1941) and two, which replaced the quad 0.5in MG mountings on 'B' turret in 1942. Other visible alterations include the extension of the signal deck at its after end, the Type 281 radar office at the after starboard side of No 2 bridge platform and the two Type 285 radar offices at the after end of the Admiral's bridge, close to the HA directors with which they operated. (Plan No NPC5169, Neg No 595901a)

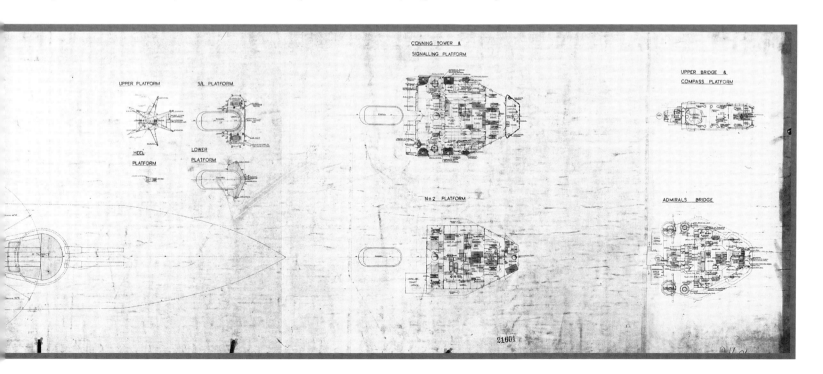

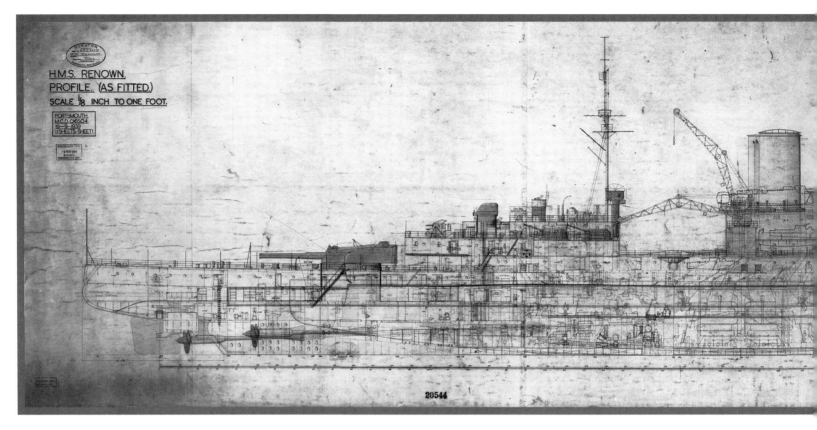

HMS Renown, *Profile (as fitted), Portsmouth Dockyard 19 September 1939. This profile is from the new set of as-fitted drawings produced at the end of the* Renown's *major reconstruction at Portsmouth Dockyard during 1936-9. This rebuild followed the pattern set by* Warspite *but included further machinery and armament improvements which were also adopted in the reconstruction of* Warspite's *sisters,* Queen Elizabeth *and* Valiant. *The major advance was the adoption of the twin 4.5in BD mounting as a dual-purpose secondary armament, arranged in four* 'cornered' groups with a HA director for each – two above the bridge in similar fashion to those on King George V *and two abreast the mainmast. As in* Warspite *the original gun-control tower and its revolving director-hood were reinstalled on the after superstructure to serve as a secondary main armament control position. She has three, rather than the more usual four, 8-barrel pom-pom mountings – one on each side on raised platforms between the funnels and one at the after end of the superstructure. The replacement of the machinery has generated an even greater* saving in this high powered ship, only four of the original six boiler rooms being required. The space saved was employed for 4.5in magazines, a HA control position, an auxiliary boiler room and additional oil fuel tanks. Like the drawings for Warspite, those for Renown *include some unrecorded additions but in this case they are very sketchy and incomplete. The additions mainly relate to the fitting of radar Types 273, 281, 282, 284 and 285 during a refit at Rosyth in 1941.*
(Plan No NPC0019, Neg No 632509)

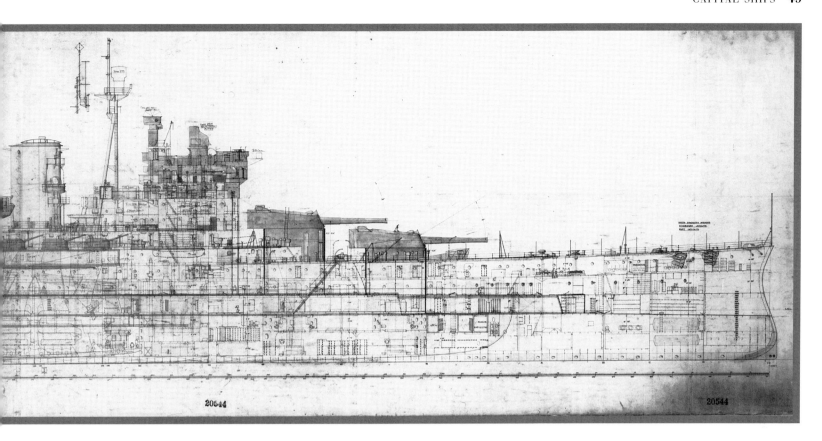

only' but it followed similar enhancements in the battleships of other navies. At the same time the fire control system was updated to the latest standard, including a DCT and AFCT in place of the old director and Dreyer table dating from the First World War.

The later modernisations proved very effective and the ships remained in front-line service until the end of the war. They were not of course as valuable as new ships but, while the money might well have been better spent in this way, the limited resources for new construction, particularly the supply of a main armament, made any such idea impractical.

Renown (1939)

Displacement:	30,750 tons standard, 36,800 tons deep. 1944 – *c*31,300tons standard, 38,395 tons deep
Dimensions:	750ft (pp), 794ft 1.5in(oa) x 102ft (max) x 26ft 6in (mean)
Armament:	Six 15in MkI (3 x 2); twenty 4.5in MkIII (10 x 2); twenty-four 2pdr (3 x 8); sixteen 0.5in (4 x 4). 1945 – as above except close range AA = twenty-eight 2pdr (3 x 8, 1 x 4); sixty-four 20mm (20 x 2, 24 x 1)
Armour:	Belt – 9in; Bulkheads – 4in and 3in forward, 10in and 4in aft; Barbettes -7in-4in; Turrets – 9in face, 7in sides, 11in rear, 4.25in roof; CT – 14in; Main deck – 4in and 5in over magazines, 2.5in over boiler rooms, 3in over engine room
Machinery:	Four shaft, Parsons geared turbines, 120,000shp = 30.75kts; eight Admiralty 3-drum boilers; 4613 tons oil fuel
Complement:	1200

AIRCRAFT CARRIERS

British naval aviation was in a position of pre-eminence at the close of the First World War. Between the wars this advantage, so far as aircraft development and the operational employment of carriers was concerned, was gradually eroded. The reasons, as already noted, were the loss of the majority of air-minded personnel to the RAF, the control of the Fleet Air Arm by the RAF and, of course, the ever-present financial limitations. The major effects showed in a general, but not universal, lack of vision in the naval staff and the relatively low-performance aircraft with which the Fleet Air Arm began the war. In contrast the development of the aircraft carrier itself was maintained in a fairly advanced state although their design was affected by the limited expectations of naval air power. To some extent this was justified by the need to accommodate treaty and financial restraints and the apparently limited threat from the air which existed in the 1930s. The only European country with an aircraft carrier was France, which had one (the *Bearn* completed in 1927), and the major threat was from land-based aircraft – particularly in the restricted waters of the Mediterranean. The fact that the carriers' prime functions were seen as fleet support in providing reconnaissance, spotting and air strike capabilities against enemy ships left little capacity for air defence fighters. Those fighters that were provided were primarily intended as escorts for the carrier's other aircraft rather than the fleet which,

rather optimistically, was to defend itself with its AA weapons. This also applied to the carriers themselves which were expected to strike down their aircraft and clear their hangars of aircraft munitions and fuel when under threat from shore-based aircraft. This was not unreasonable given that British naval aircraft lacked the performance of land planes and would in the majority of cases be outnumbered by the attacking force.

To some extent this doctrine was self-fulfilling in that carrier design was directed at providing a high level of passive defence which in turn led to the limitation of aircraft numbers. In contrast US and Japanese carriers tended toward maximising their air complement at the expense of safety and carried substantially more aircraft than their British contemporaries even though in several cases they were of smaller size. To some extent this resulted from the British reluctance to accept a permanent deck park for aircraft – a restriction which disappeared during the war with a consequent increase in aircraft carried. In the event, British pre-war carrier policy was to a large extent justified while the war was restricted to a European conflict but from 1942 onward there was a marked change in the operational use of fleet carriers and consequently in the type of aircraft they carried. A change which was primarily lead by events in the Pacific and which, for the Royal Navy, was substantially aided by access to the modern carrier aircraft of the USA via Lend-Lease.

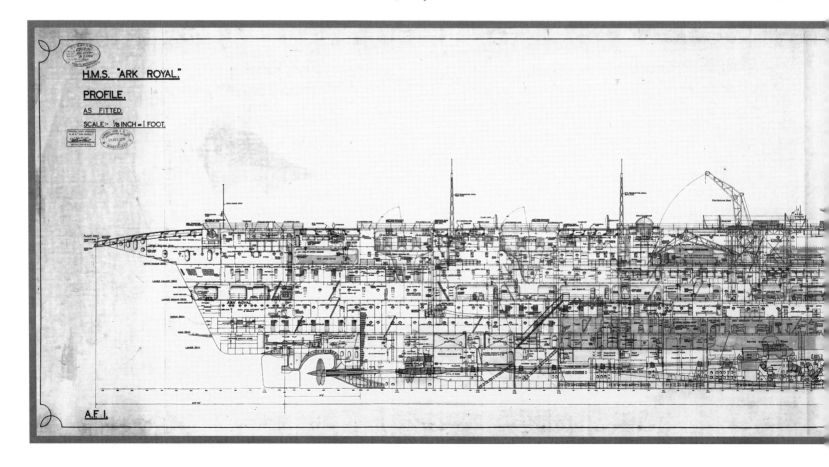

The carrier fleet of the 1920s

By 1919 Britain's wartime carrier development had produced a group of experimental vessels with varying degrees of utility and in varying stages of completion. Of these the most important were *Argus*, *Furious*, *Eagle* and *Hermes* all of which were to survive until, and serve in, the Second World War. The *Argus*, a converted liner of 15,000 tons, was completed in 1918 as the world's first aircraft carrier with a full-length flight deck. The *Hermes*, the world's first purpose-built carrier, was laid down in 1918 and completed in 1923. The first carrier with an island superstructure, she was small (10,850 tons), of moderate speed (25kts) and carried twenty-one aircraft. The *Eagle* was a converted battleship completed as a carrier in 1924. Like *Hermes* she had an island superstructure but, although substantially larger (22,000 tons), she was no faster (24kts) and carried only three more aircraft. The *Furious* had been converted from a battlecruiser and, in two construction stages, ended up with a forward and after flight deck divided by a central

HMS Ark Royal, *Profile (as fitted), Cammell Laird, Birkenhead, 15 August 1939. The draughtsmen of Cammell Laird produced some of the most detailed of the 'as fitted' drawings in the Admiralty Collection and this superb set of Ark Royal is no exception. The ship's distinctive profile, with its remarkable flight deck overhang, illustrates well the complexity of the ship and the remarkable quality of the drawings. The more easily distinguishable features include the side armour – seen as a dark area on the ship's side – and the multitude of fittings extending above the level of the flight deck. Much of the latter are items that would be unshipped or lowered during flying operations. Of these the more obvious are the guardrails, ensign and jack staffs and the hinged lattice W/T aerials (that forward for receiving and the three aft for transmitting were matched by a similar group on the port side). Less obvious is the telescopic (navigation-light) mast shown immediately forward of the bridge but actually located on the middle line of the flight deck. There is some sign of economy in the drawing in that only the foremost twin 4.5in MkIII, multiple pom-pom MkVI and quad 0.5in MG mountings are drawn – the remainder being indicated purely by position – a style followed in the plan views. However, their inclusion would merely be repetition and the omission assists in the clarity and visibility of other features in the drawing. Notable in the internal detail is the relatively small length occupied by the main machinery – in part due to the adoption of a compact installation of three double boiler rooms arranged abreast to minimise the area occupied by the funnel uptakes and the weight of armour to protect them. The latter contributed to the late introduction of the unit machinery arrangement in British carriers although the Illustrious class did have an intervening compartment between the engine and boiler rooms.*
(Plan No NPA5905, Neg No 624570/1)

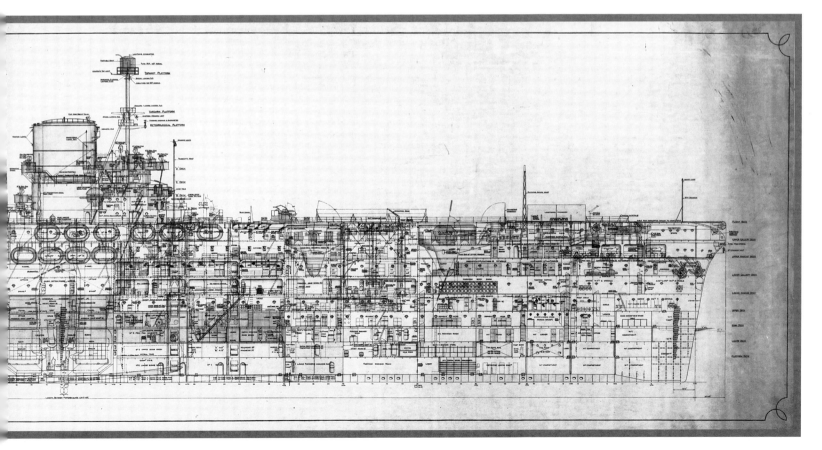

superstructure. She was used extensively for experimental work and both proved the utility of carrier-based aircraft and the need for a clear flight deck. She was completely reconstructed between 1921 and 1925 and emerged with a full-length flight deck and a double-storey hangar which could accommodate thirty-five aircraft. The upper hangar opened at the fore end onto a short, secondary, flying-off deck. Her two half-sisters, *Courageous* and *Glorious*, were similarly converted into carriers during 1924-8 (*Courageous*) and 1925-30 (*Glorious*). They emerged generally similar to *Furious* except that they were fitted with an island superstructure which increased the available internal space, mainly because the extended funnel trunking to the after end was no longer required, allowing an increase in the air complement to fifty aircraft. The high speed of *Furious*, *Courageous* and *Glorious* and their relatively large aircraft capacity made them the primary units of the Royal Navy's carrier force until the completion of *Ark Royal* in 1938.

Ark Royal

Displacement:	22,000 tons standard, 27,700 tons deep
Dimensions:	685ft (pp), 800ft (oa) x 112ft (extreme), 94ft 9in(wl) x 27ft 4in (mean). Flight deck: 797ft x 96ft (max), 50ft (min). Hangars: 568ft x 60ft x 16ft (upper), 452ft x 60ft x 16ft (lower)
Armament:	Sixteen 4.5in MkI (8 x 2); forty-eight 2pdr (6 x 8); thirty-two 0.5in (8 x 4)
Aircraft:	60
Armour:	Belt – 4.5in: Bulkheads – 2.5in; Deck over citadel – 3.5in; deck over steering gear 3.5in & 2.5in; Magazines 3.5in crowns, 2.5in sides; Torpedo bulkheads 1.5in
Machinery:	Three shaft, Parsons geared turbines, 102,000shp = 31kts; six Admiralty 3-drum boilers; 4620 tons oil fuel
Complement:	1781

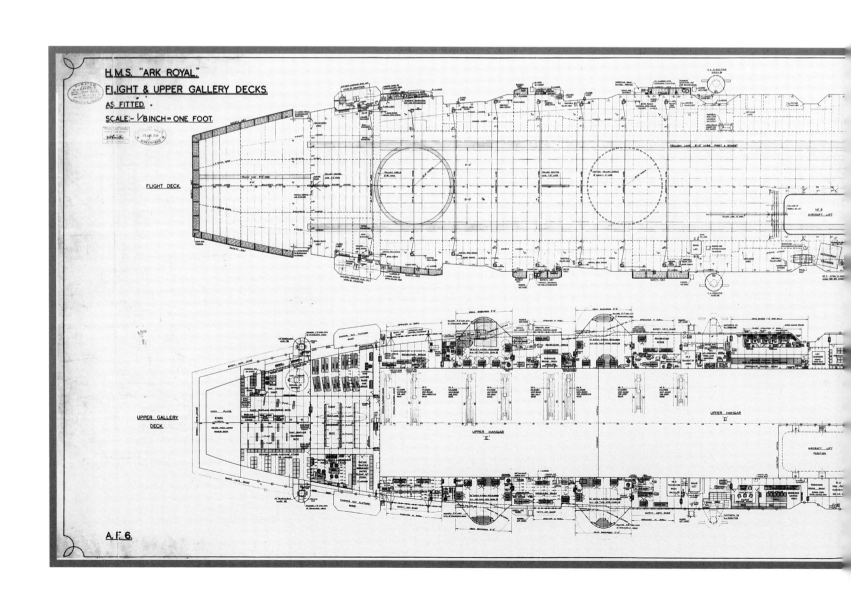

HMS Ark Royal, *Flight and Upper Gallery Decks (as fitted), Cammell Laird, Birkenhead, 15 August 1939.* One of the more interesting features of the flight deck plan is the inclusion of the deck markings together with their colour (yellow) and dimensions. These include the two circles aft, the broad bands running though the tangents of each, the off-centre band right aft and the taxi lines running aft from the three aircraft lifts and the two forward catapults. Other flight deck features include the windscreens (shown laid flat) at the rear and after sides of the catapults, the eight arrester wires, the crash barrier (laid flat abreast the after end of the island) and the tops of the two bomb lifts – one just inboard and slightly abaft of the after starboard 4.5in gun director and the second between the two pom-pom mountings forward of the island. The upper gallery deck clearly shows the extent of the upper hangar. The lines bridging the hangar, including those at the ends of the lifts, are fire curtains, while the boundary on the inboard sides of the lifts are solid longitudinal bulkheads. The lower hangar was shorter; terminating forward at the position of the forward fire curtain of the upper hangar and aft about mid-way between the 4.5in gun platforms. The items shown on the port side of the hangar aft are the cylinders for the arrester gear, which were fitted immediately under the flight deck. The area aft of the hangar was primarily employed for storage but also includes a compartment for a Link trainer (noted as supplied by the Admiralty) which can be seen just inboard of the port after searchlight platform. Noteworthy is the provision of deck planking on the 4.5in gun platforms – indicated by being partly drawn at the outer edges. (Plan No NPA5906, Neg No 624570/6)

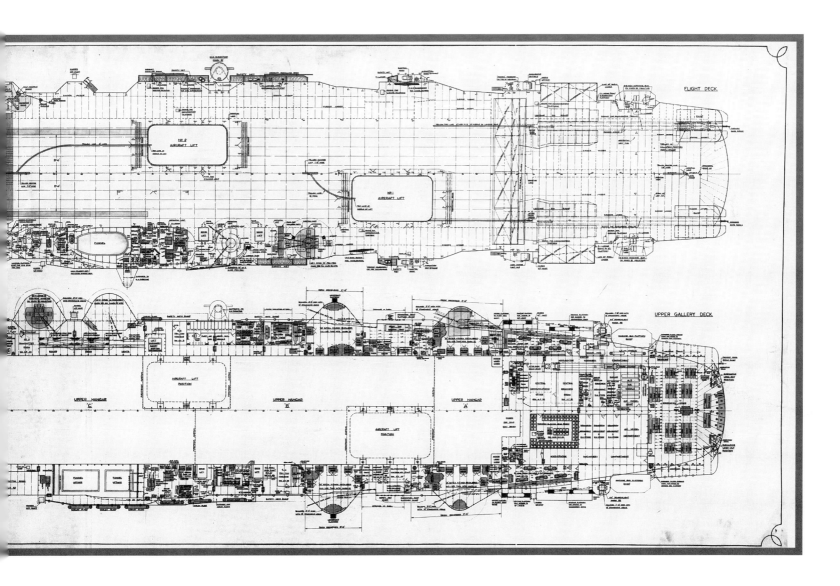

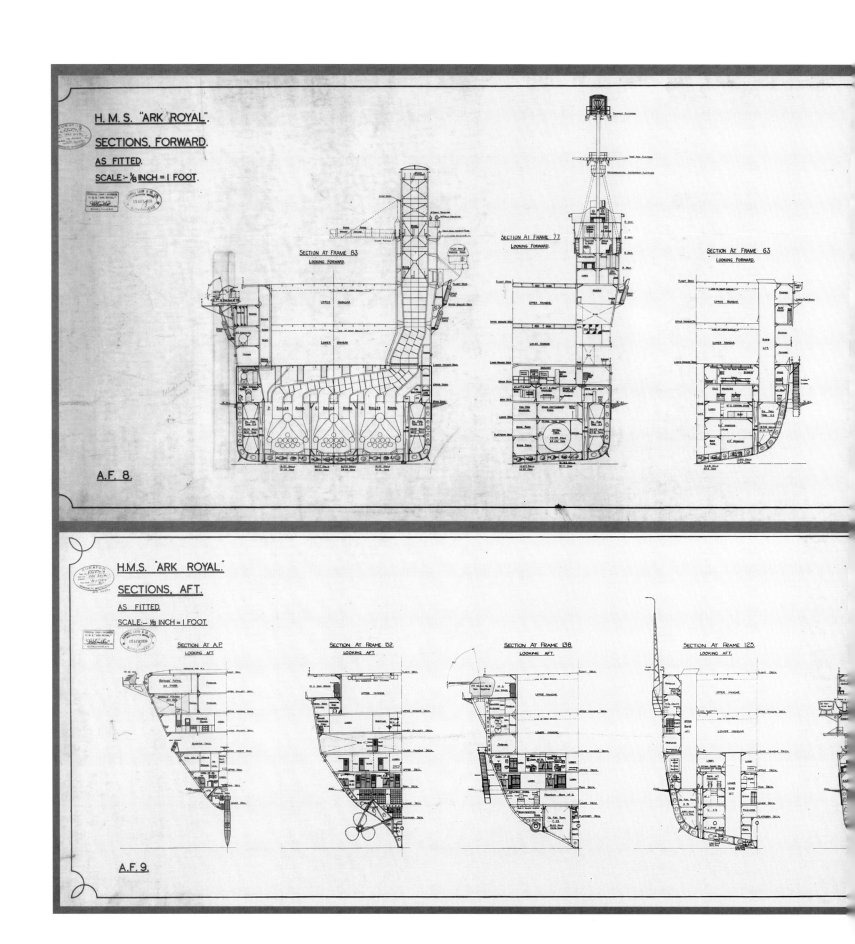

HMS Ark Royal, *Sections forward and section aft (as fitted), Cammell Laird, Birkenhead, 15 August 1939.*

These drawings serve as an example of the transverse sections which formed part of the as-fitted set. As with most of those for large ships they are divided between two drawings, one for the forward and one for the after sections. Following standard convention they employ half sections for the starboard side, the fore sections being viewed looking forward and the aft sections viewed looking aft, with the exception of that at frame 83 where, more unusually, the full width of the ship is shown. As in the other drawings of Ark Royal, *there are so many points of interest that it is difficult to isolate those most worthy of mention. The high level of detail is particularly noticeable at two points. Firstly the full section at frame 83 shows much more detail of the boiler uptakes than is usual – in particular the support frames and platforms within the funnel. It also illustrates well the arrangement of trunking that contributed to the ship's loss, when flood water spread across the ship from one boiler room to the next until she lost all steam power. Secondly the section at frame 77 shows at the head of the mast not just the drum shaped enclosure of her Type 72X aircraft homing beacon but the W/T aerial within it (also visible in the profile as hidden detail). Other items of interest include the aircraft fuel stowage, an arrangement of cylindrical tanks divorced from the ships structure and surrounded by seawater for reasons of safety. The starboard forward tank, mounted horizontally fore and aft is visible in the hold at frame 77 and the after starboard tanks, mounted vertically, in the hold at frame 118. The aircraft lift shown at frame 109 reveals that there were two platforms, one for the upper and one for the lower level which moved as a unit. In the same section can be seen one of the two cranes that served the principle ship's boats – visible in the sections immediately fore and aft at 96 and 118 frames respectively. The forward bomb lift is shown at frame 63 and that aft (divided between upper and lower lifts) at frame 125.*
(Plan No NPA5903 and 5904, Neg No 624570/8 and /9)

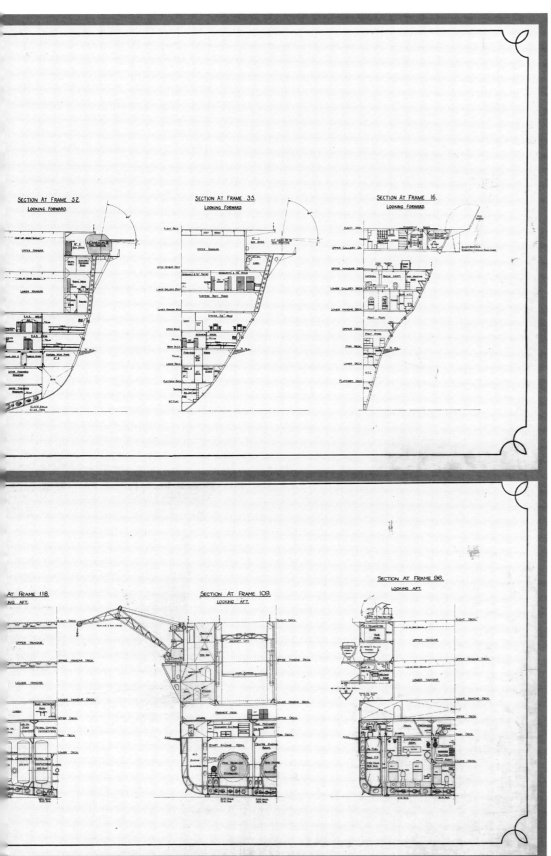

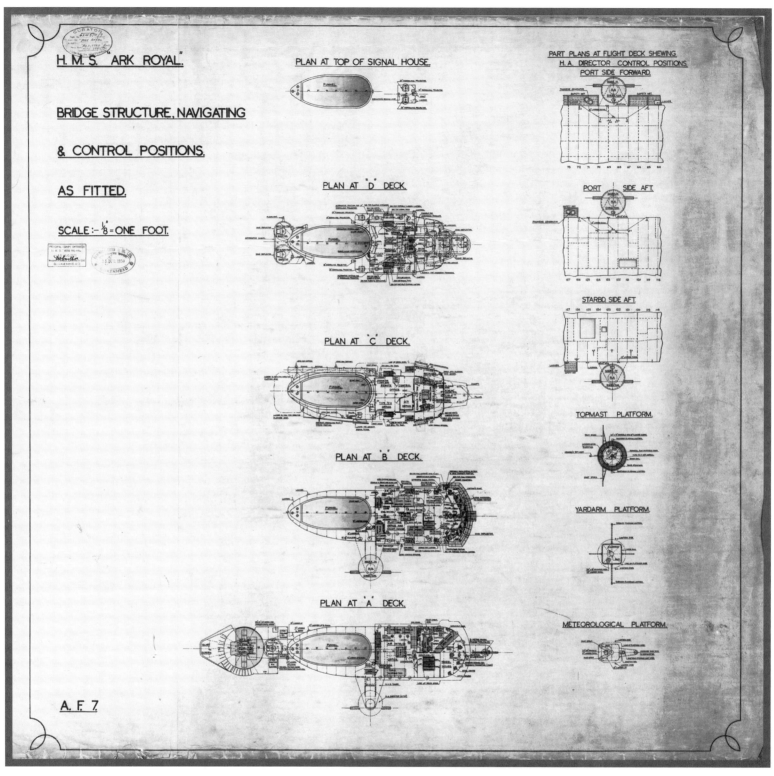

HMS Ark Royal, *Bridge structure, navigating and control positions (as fitted), Cammell Laird, Birkenhead, 15 August 1939. The internal areas of the island forward of the funnel are almost entirely taken up with command and control functions apart from the Captain's sea cabin on 'A' deck and the* Admiral's sea cabin on the flight deck. Externally the bridge carried all of the ship's pompom directors – three forward in a tiered arrangement on 'D' deck (shown more clearly in the profile), two abreast at the aft side of the funnel, also on 'D' deck and one abaft the funnel on 'A' deck. This drawing also includes plan views of all four of the ship's MkIV HA/LA directors – one on the starboard side of the bridge and the others shown in part views of the flight deck edges.

(Plan No NPA5902, Neg No 624570/7)

Ark Royal

The total carrier tonnage allowed by the Washington Treaty was sufficient to give Britain five 27,000-ton aircraft carriers. However, the Admiralty wished to maintain a fleet of six such ships and, having established that a smaller vessel would meet anticipated needs, accepted a lower requirement of 22,500 tons when the construction of a new carrier came up for consideration in the early 1930s. Initial designs resembled the *Courageous* with upper and lower flight decks but the development of catapults for launching aircraft over the fore end of the flight deck combined with arrester gear aft to reduce the length required to bring landing aircraft to a halt, allowing simultaneous take-off and landing operations from a single flight deck, resulted in the early abandonment of the lower take-off deck and the extension of the principle flight deck to the stem. The flight deck was initially required to be 900ft long to accommodate the new mode of operation but when it was realised that this would cause difficulties with docking and manoeuvrability it was reduced to 800ft and even that required a considerable overhang at the stern. The new design, which became HMS *Ark Royal*, was approved in 1934 by which time the displacement had been reduced to 22,000 tons. She was Britain's first 'large', purpose-built carrier and combined the collected experience of the existing carrier fleet with the latest British thinking on carrier design and operation. One of the principal features was the adoption of closed hangars which provided improved fire safety but limited the numbers of aircraft (seventy-two later reduced to sixty) that could be carried and prevented aircraft engines being run for warm up or maintenance until they were on the flight deck.

The hangars and flight deck formed an integral part of the hull structure, rather than just being superstructure, which reduced the hull stresses and substantially improved the general hull strength whilst providing some saving in weight. Structural weight was also reduced by the extensive use of arc-welding for about 65 per cent of the hull structure – primarily for internal and upper hull construction. The skin plating from the upper deck down (excluding the foremost 100ft) and the flight deck were riveted as these were the principal strength members of the hull structure and welding was not as yet fully trusted. This was estimated to have saved 500 tons but, although experimentation with welding continued, primarily in cruisers, facilities for this type of construction remained limited until well after the outbreak of war and *Ark Royal* was an exception to the general rule. She was laid down in September 1935 and completed in November 1938 and proved a very successful and popular ship.

Air operations generally required a greater degree of freedom for carriers than for other ships while operating with the fleet, which had to be allowed for in high endurance, combined with good speed and manoeuvrability plus defensive protection in case of interception by enemy cruisers or destroyers while outside the protection of the main fleet. High speed was also required to generate a wind speed over the deck for the launch and recovery of aircraft, although the use of catapults and arrester wires allowed much greater freedom in this respect. *Ark Royal*'s machinery provided for a maximum speed of 31kts, adequate to keep pace with the battlecruisers and cruisers of the fleet and later its fast battleships but not sufficient to give a reasonable margin under battle conditions. It was a three-shaft arrangement which, with the centre shaft immediately behind the rudder, gave the ship the required manoeuvrability, while 4370 tons of oil fuel gave an endurance of 11,000 nautical miles at 16kts – well above that provided in the fleet's capital ships. The machinery and magazines were protected against 6in shell fire, 500lb bombs and 750lb torpedo warheads. The upper hull structure had protection against small bombs and strafing attacks by virtue of the relatively thick flight deck, although this was thick for reasons of hull strength rather than defence. She was lost to a single torpedo hit on the starboard side amidships in November 1941 as a result of an inherent problem of layout in adopting double hangars. The lower hangar required the routing of the funnel uptakes across the ship at a comparatively low level. The flooding extended via these uptakes and eventually caused a complete power failure making the adequate control of further flooding impossible. She capsized after a 12-hour struggle to keep her afloat.

The armoured carrier

The rearmament programme initiated in 1936 included two carriers under each of the Programme years 1936 and 1937, and one in each of the 1938 and 1939 Programme years. It was originally intended that all these ships should form a single class but changes to requirements resulted in the production of one class of three and two sub-groups. The first three, *Illustrious*, *Victorious* and *Formidable* were laid down in the first half of 1937 and completed during 1940-1. The fourth ship, forming the first sub-group, was *Indomitable*, laid down late in 1937 and completed in 1941. The second sub-group comprised *Implacable* and *Indefatigable*, laid down in 1939 and, due to wartime delays and shortages, not completed until 1944. These ships formed the backbone of the British carrier force during the Second World War.

The British view that carriers would be vulnerable to land-based aircraft and surface ships, combined with concern over the vulnerability of carrier hangars which were likely to contain bombs, torpedoes and highly inflammable aviation spirit, led British designers to seek high levels of security against both enemy action and accidents. This took the shape of very stringent controls on the distribution of aircraft fuel and munitions, which could be rapidly cleared from the hangar and restowed below in the event of any emergency. However, even this combined with *Ark Royal*'s closed hangar was deemed insufficient for the new carriers of the rearmament programme which were to be provided with fully armoured hangars, proof against 6in gunfire and 500lb bombs. In general the

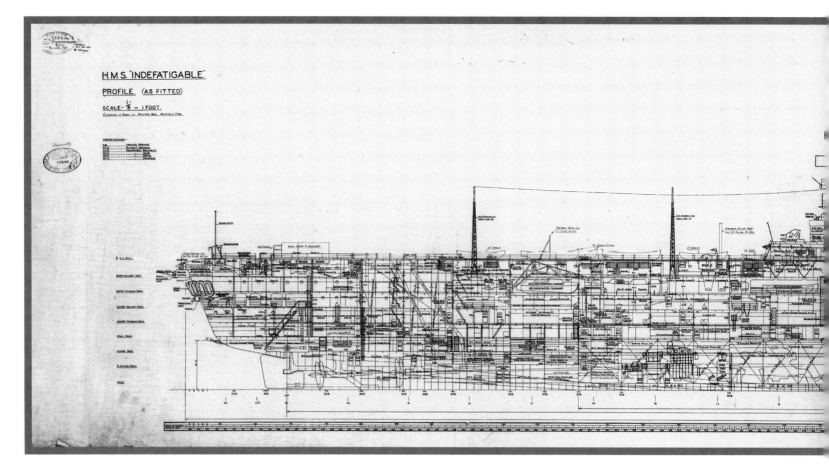

new design followed the layout of *Ark Royal* but, in order to accommodate the additional top weight and maintain stability, it was necessary to substantially reduce freeboard which, in turn, required the omission of the lower hangar and a reduction in deck head clearance in the hangar that remained. The hangar became an armoured box with 4.5in sides, 3in roof (flight deck) and 4.5in bulkheads. Outside the area of the hangar the flight deck was 1.5in thick while the hull proper was protected on the same scale as *Ark Royal* except that the deck protection was omitted from the hangar floor. The main penalty for this high level of passive defence was a reduction in the air complement to thirty-six aircraft – half that originally provided in *Ark Royal*.

The next ship, *Indomitable*, was originally to have been the same as the *Illustrious* group but was modified as a result of design changes under consideration for the 1938 Programme carrier (*Implacable*). The height from upper deck to flight deck was increased by 6ft and a short lower hangar fitted under the main hangar from just aft of amidships to the after lift. Compensation for the additional weight was provided by reducing the thickness of the hangar sides from 4.5in to 1.5in and reducing hangar height. The changes increased the hangar capacity to forty-five aircraft but when the employment of a deck park was accepted the ship's overall capacity increased to sixty-five. The same arrangement was adopted in *Implacable* and *Indefatigable* but, being of new rather than modified design, had a slightly larger aircraft capacity –

Indefatigable

Displacement:	23,460 tons standard, 28,970 tons deep
Dimensions:	690ft (pp), 766ft 2in (oa) x 141ft 5in (extreme), 95ft 9in (wl) x 26ft 8in (mean) Flight deck: 760ft x 102ft (max), 58ft 9in (min) Hangars: 456ft x 62ft x 14ft (upper), 208ft x 62ft x 14ft (lower)
Armament:	Sixteen 4.5in MkIII (8 x 2); fifty-two 2pdr (6 x 8, 1 x 4); sixteen 20mm (7 x 2, 2 x 1)
Aircraft:	72
Armour:	Hangar – 3in roof (flight deck), 1.5in sides; Belt – 4.5in: Bulkheads – 2in; Deck over citadel – 2.5in and 1.5in; deck over steering gear 3in; Magazines 3in & 2in crowns, 4.5in sides; Torpedo bulkheads 1.375in
Machinery:	Four shaft, Parsons geared turbines, 148000shp = 32kts; eight Admiralty 3-drum boilers; 4800 tons oil fuel
Complement:	1585

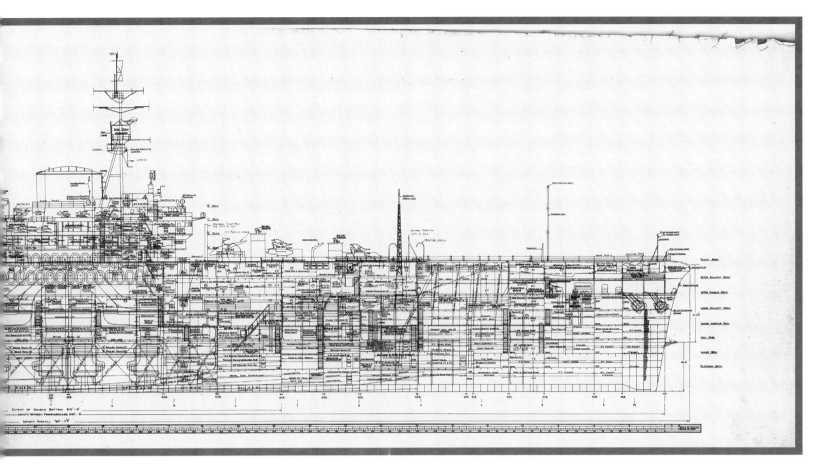

HMS Indefatigable, *Profile (as fitted), John Brown, Clydebank, 5 February 1945. Revealing a much lower profile than* Ark Royal, *as a result of the need to reduce topweight for the provision of an armoured hangar,* Indefatigable *has one less deck than the earlier ship. From top down these decks are flight, upper gallery, upper hangar, lower gallery, lower hangar, main, lower and platform decks (*Ark Royal *also had an upper deck between the lower hangar and main decks). Although this drawing appears at first glance as complex as that for* Ark Royal *it is in fact much simpler – the clutter being enhanced by a high degree of text indicating the location of internal compartments. The 'as fitted' set was modified at Devonport in December 1952 following the ship's conversion to a training vessel during 1949-50. This involved the removal of the majority of her close-range AA weapons (including all her pom-pom mountings apart from the single quad on the port side) the main HA directors and much of her aircraft equipment including the homing beacon on the foremast. The ship has four double boiler rooms, arranged two on each side divided by central oil fuel compartments. Immediately abaft these were the wing engine rooms, with an aircraft fuel tank compartment between them, and abaft these the centre shaft engine rooms. Aircraft fuel compartments were also located forward and abaft the machinery spaces. (Plan No NPB4403, Neg No 744402/1)*

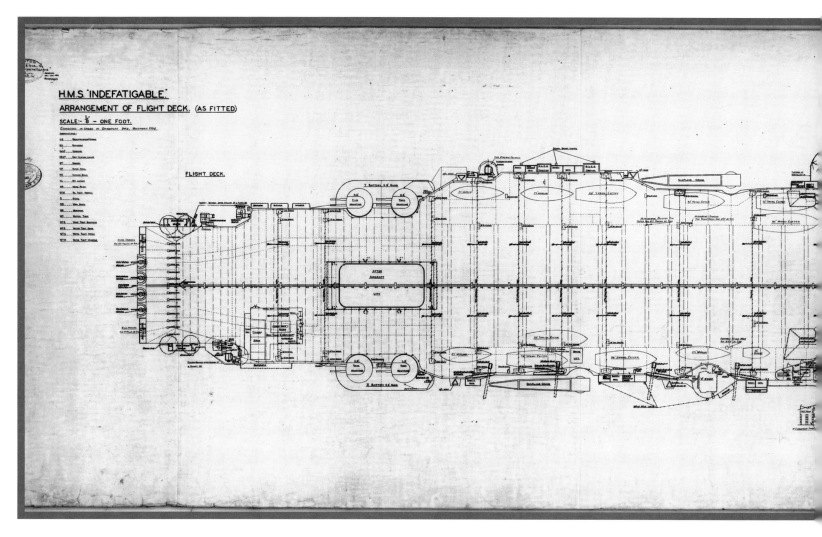

HMS Indefatigable, *Flight deck (as fitted), John Brown, Clydebank, 5 February 1945.* Indefatigable *shows a reduction in the flight deck equipment when compared with* Ark Royal, *having only one aircraft catapult, on the port side forward, and two lifts. However, she still has eight arrester wires and an increase in the* number of crash barriers from one to three (all fitted abreast the island). The larger lift forward could accommodate Seafires, which did not have folding wings, and served the upper hangar only. The after lift gave access to both upper and lower hangars. The 1952 alterations include the large number of boats carried on each side of the flight deck, a deck house on the starboard side aft (boat store and workshop) and the deletion of the arrester wires, multiple pompoms, Oerlikons, searchlights and directors.
(Plan No NPB4404, Neg No 744402/12)

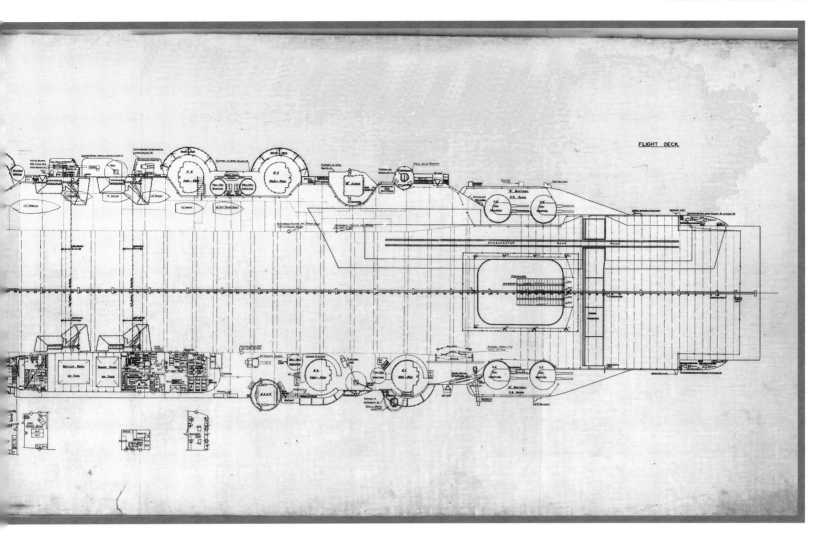

forty-eight in the hangars and twenty-four in the deck park. They were also faster than the earlier ships of the group, having a four-shaft machinery arrangement of higher power, which increased their maximum speed from 30kts to 32kts in the deep condition.

War construction

The inability of the British shipbuilding industry to accommodate an increase in large ship construction during the war meant that no new fleet carriers were completed during the war apart from those of the pre-war programmes. Four 36,800-ton armoured hangar carriers of the *Eagle* class were laid down in 1942-3 but only two were to be completed – the *Eagle* in 1951 and the *Ark Royal* in 1955. These were to have been followed by the four 46,900-ton *Malta* class – none of which were laid down, the entire project being cancelled at the end of the war. However, the need for increased numbers of carriers was such that less ambitious projects were set in train to make up the shortfall. This took the form of designing a carrier with no armour, structural arrangements in line with merchant practice, standard destroyer type machinery and a simple gun armament of close-range AA weapons only. The result was the

13,000-ton, 25kt light fleet carriers of the *Colossus* class – effectively a very much simplified version of the *Illustrious* class. Ten of these ships were constructed, although only six entered service before the end of the war. Despite their small size they could accommodate forty-eight aircraft – a measure of the difference made by the less severe requirements of armour, armament and speed. These ships were followed by an improved version of the type, the *Majestic* class, of which eight were begun but only four completed, all post-war. At the cost of an additional 5000 tons displacement they were capable of 29.5kts but were otherwise generally similar in principle to the earlier ships.

War service

During 1939-42 British carriers were employed more or less as anticipated before the war. The battlefleet support role was demonstrated by the attacks of *Formidable* on the Italian fleet in March 1941 (Matapan) and of *Victorious* and *Ark Royal* on *Bismarck* in May 1941. In both cases the carriers enabled battleships to close and successfully engage an enemy that would have escaped had they not been damaged by air attack. They also demonstrated an

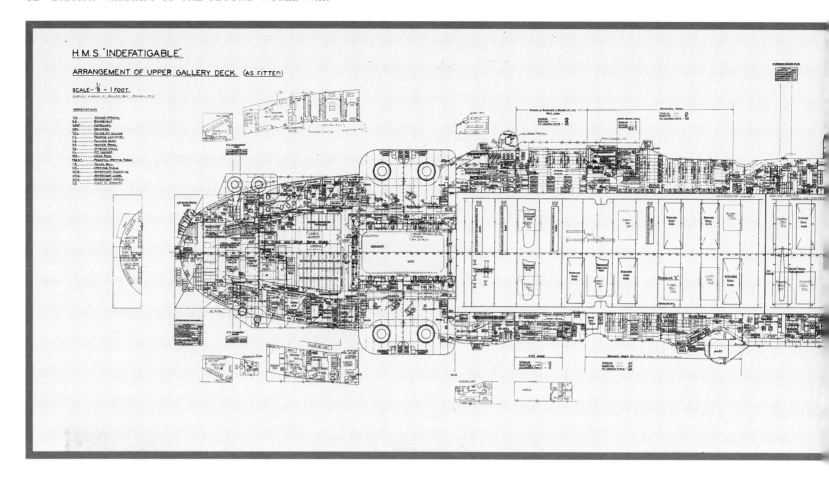

Above: *HMS* Indefatigable, *Upper gallery deck (as fitted), John Brown, Clydebank, 5 February 1945. Note that the lifts are kept clear of the hangar, feeding it from each end to maximise the aircraft stowage area. The hangar is divided into three by two fire curtains – shown as slightly thicker lines bridging the full width of the compartment. The large number of items shown within the hangar are located on its roof and include the arrester gear cylinders, stowage racks, spare aircraft fuselages (Seafires with tail planes and Barracudas without) and spare Barracuda main planes. The isolated compartment drawings located outside the main view are redraws of individual compartments as modified during the 1952 changes.*
(Plan No NPB4408, Neg No 744402/9)

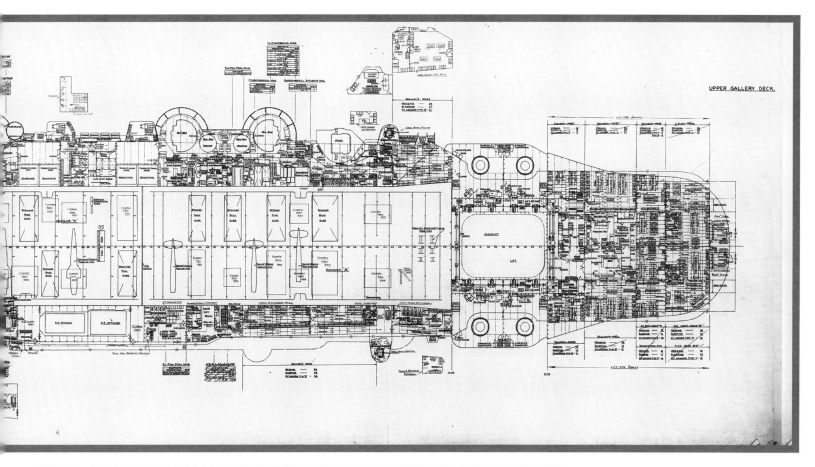

UPPER GALLERY DECK.

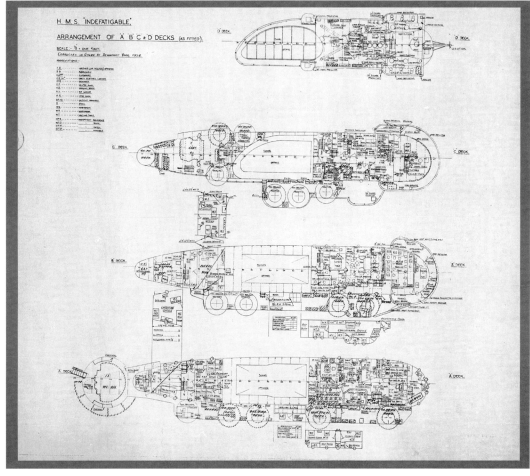

H. M. S. 'INDEFATIGABLE'

ARRANGEMENT OF 'A' 'B' 'C' & 'D' DECKS (AS FITTED)

Left: HMS Indefatigable, Arrangement of 'A', 'B', 'C' and 'D' decks (as fitted), John Brown, Clydebank, 5 February 1945. These four platforms were the principle decks of the island superstructure, which in plan view reveal the streamline form adopted for both the bridge and funnel to minimise the effect of interference with the airflow over the flight deck. The widely distributed circles on all but 'D' deck are the positions of twin or single Oerlikons several of which were removed from the drawing in 1952. However, like all changes to the 'as fitted' drawings the information provides only the details of the outfit as completed and as at the time of alteration and does not give any detail of modifications made in the meantime. Also shown as deleted are the pom-pom mounting on 'A' deck and the main and pom-pom directors at the after end of 'C' deck.
(Plan No NPB4388, Neg No E07013)

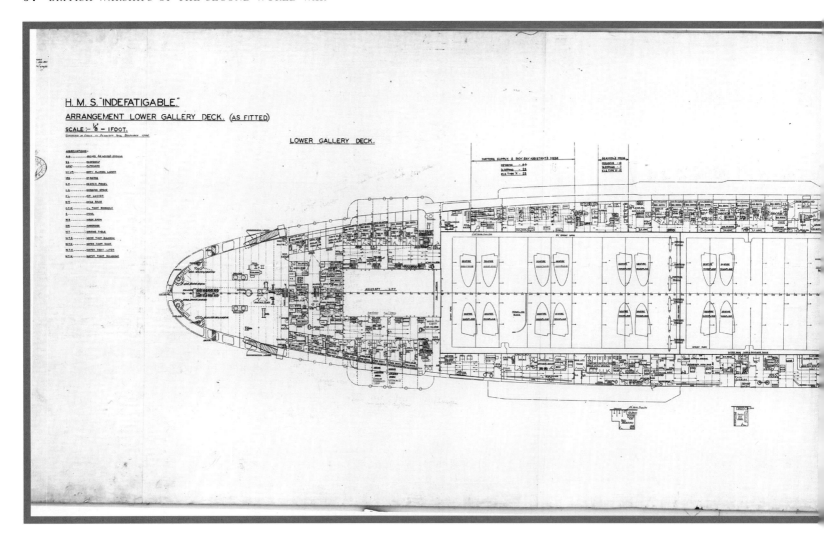

HMS Indefatigable, Lower gallery deck (as fitted), John Brown, Clydebank, 5 February 1945. The shorter length of the lower hangar is clearly seen in this drawing – the area is divided by a single fire curtain and the items stowed against the roof are spare main planes for Seafires. Also visible, at the after end, is one of the few open areas of deck not related to air operations, the officer's quarterdeck which also accommodated four single Oerlikon positions (deleted 1952) and the after mooring facilities. The majority of the area forward of the hangar is for accommodation but also includes the capstan machinery (driving the capstan and cable holders on deck above) and the boiler uptakes and vent trunks. *(Plan No NPB4408, Neg No 744402/9)*

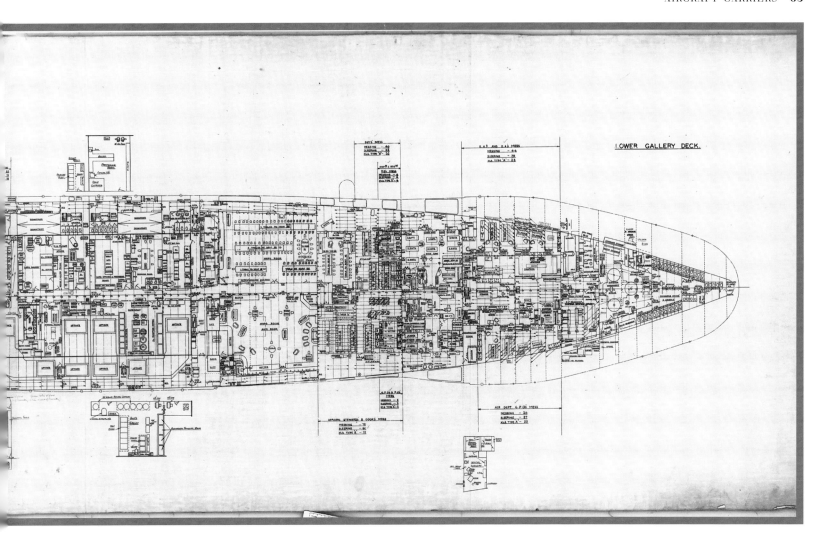

independent air strike capability, although always against targets in harbour. For maximum gain at minimal cost the most spectacular Fleet Air Arm strike of the war was on the Italian fleet at Taranto in November 1940. Eleven Swordfish torpedo bombers from *Illustrious* sank the battleship *Conti di Cavour* and seriously damaged the battleships *Littorio* and *Caio Duilio* for the loss of only two aircraft. This event is said to have had a considerable impact on the Japanese and to have substantially influenced their plans for the attack on the American Fleet at Pearl Harbor. The last major seaborne air attack in home waters was made against the German battleship *Tirpitz* in Norway in April 1944. The attack was carried out by dive bombers from *Victorious*, *Furious* and four escort carriers; fourteen hits were scored which put the battleship out of action for three months.

The advantages of the armoured hangar were demonstrated in

January 1941 when *Illustrious* was subjected to sustained dive-bomber attack by a German elite anti-shipping squadron of Ju87 Stuka dive bombers. She was severely damaged by hits from six 500lb armour-piercing bombs, together with underwater damage caused by three near-misses and was damaged further during air attacks while undergoing temporary repairs at Malta. An unarmoured carrier would not have survived. These advantages were to reveal themselves again in the Pacific where the British armoured carriers demonstrated the ability to continue operations after being hit by Kamikaze aircraft while their US counterparts usually had their flight decks so badly damaged that they had to retire to base for repair. It must be said, however, that US carriers, with their open hangars, had considerable advantages in aircraft stowage and operation and that both navies made choices in carrier design which well suited their own circumstances.

CRUISERS

During 1919-23 Britain disposed of nearly all her pre-war cruisers, the majority being either obsolete or worn out. This left the Royal and Australian Navies with about fifty (including some still under construction) of modern design. Of these only the five ships of the *Hawkins* class (9750 tons, seven 7.5in guns) and a few of the pre-war 'Town' classes were suitable for deep ocean work.[21] Most of the remainder were war-construction fleet cruisers intended for operations in the North Sea which lacked the endurance and seakeeping qualities required of a trade defence cruiser. The 'Town' group were also the oldest cruisers in the fleet and therefore of limited long-term value.[22] Not only was the Navy short of big cruisers, it was also short on numbers as it was estimated that seventy cruisers were required to provide adequate defence for the empire.

The Washington Treaty limit of 10,000 tons and 8in guns was the result of the combined requirements of the British and US navies. In the former case because it was desired to retain the *Hawkins* class and in the latter case because large cruisers were required for the deep seas of the Pacific and Atlantic Oceans. This set the pattern of cruiser construction for the following decade but neither Britain nor the USA were particularly satisfied with the situation that subsequently developed. Britain, France and Japan initiated the con-

Kent

Displacement: As completed – 9850 tons standard, 13,520 tons deep

1938 – 10,430 tons standard

Dimensions: 590ft (pp), 630ft (oa) x 68ft 5in x 16ft (mean)

Armament: As completed – Eight 8in MkVIII (4 x 2); four 4in MkV HA (4 x 1); four 2pdr (4 x 1); eight 21in torpedo tubes (2 x 4)

1945 – Eight 8in MkVIII (4 x 2); eight 4in MkXVI HA (4 x 2); sixteen 2pdr (2 x 8); twelve 20mm (6 x 1, 3 x 2)

Armour: Machinery 1in belt, 1.4in deck; Steering gear 1.5in deck; Magazines 4in sides, 3in crown and bulkheads; 'A' and 'Y' shell rooms 1in sides and crowns; Barbettes and gunhouses 1in

Machinery: Four shaft, Parsons geared turbines, 80,000shp = 31.5kts; eight Admiralty 3-drum boilers; 3425 tons oil fuel; range 13,300nm at 12kts

Complement: 784

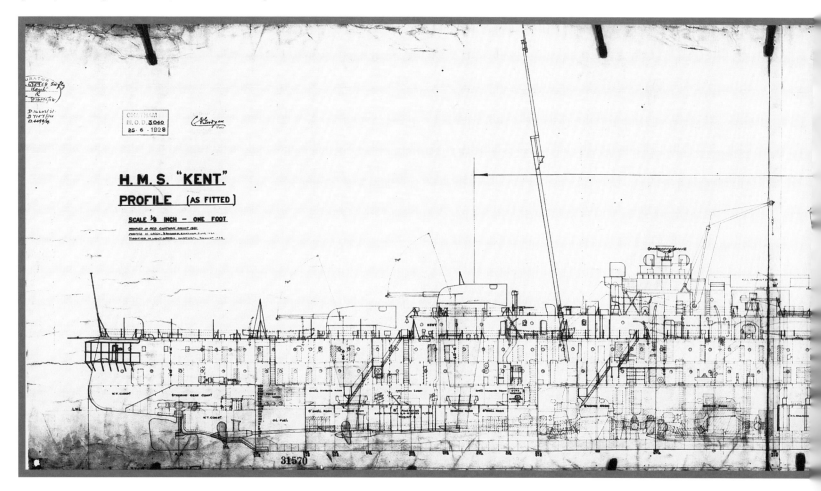

H.M.S. "KENT."

PROFILE (AS FITTED)

SCALE ⅛ INCH - ONE FOOT

struction of ships to the full treaty limit in 1924, while Italy and the USA followed in 1926. By the end of 1927 Britain had thirteen 10,000 ton, 8in gun cruisers under construction or just completed, while Japan had six, France four and Italy and the USA two each. The apparent advantage to the British was not seen as such by the Admiralty. Treaty cruiser construction had begun with a grand plan to build seventeen such ships as a first step towards achieving the seventy-ship ideal laid down in 1919 but as the 1920s progressed the programme was gradually whittled down by Government restrictions on naval spending. The Admiralty, desiring to reduce costs and increase numbers, very soon turned its attention to small-

er ships and no further cruisers of this type were to be built for the Royal Navy.

In the USA funds for new construction were even scarcer which did not balance too well with a strong naval lobby demanding a 'navy second to none' – in other words equal to the Royal Navy. The US authorities attempted to resolve this internal political problem by promoting an international limit on cruiser numbers – in effect reducing the number of cruisers in the British fleet to a level they stood some chance of matching. Both sides resolutely avoided seeing the other's point of view which came to a head in an abortive limitation conference at Geneva in 1927 – the failure of which was

HMS Kent, *Profile (as fitted), Chatham Dockyard, 25 June 1928.*
This profile of Britain's first 8in gun Treaty cruiser shows clearly the distinctive high freeboard and triple funnel arrangement of the type. In other respects the layout is conventional, following the distribution of armament, machinery, accommodation and stores that are common to the vast majority of warship designs. The limited level of protection for these ships is not immediately obvious but the box protection to the magazines can be seen as the thicker lines

over and at the ends of the magazines and shell rooms fore, aft and amidships. The drawing has been subjected to three sets of modification, all made by Chatham Dockyard, and dated August 1931, June 1934 and August 1938. The 1931 alterations include the replacement of the HA rangefinder on the after searchlight tower with a HACS MkI director and the addition of a crane and FIL (folding MkI light) aircraft catapult abaft the third funnel. The 1934 changes include the fitting of two quad 0.5in machine gun mountings abreast

the foremast on the shelter deck. Other changes made during 1933-4 are not recorded on this drawing – principally the addition of two 4in AA guns abreast the funnels and the replacement of the FIL catapult with an SIIL (slider MkII light). The 1938 change is a somewhat simpler affair as it refers to the production of a fly sheet (also reproduced here) for the centre section of the drawing following the ship's major refit of 1937-8. The area concerned is indicated by the lines running from the centre of 'B' to the centre of 'X' turrets and

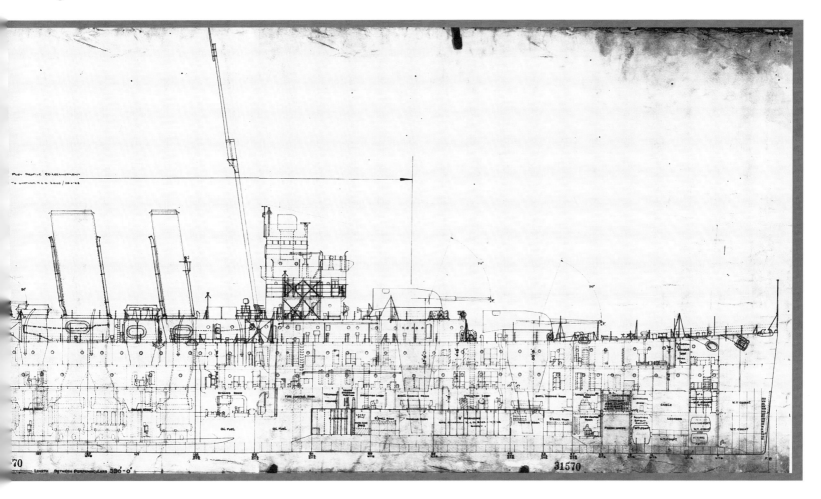

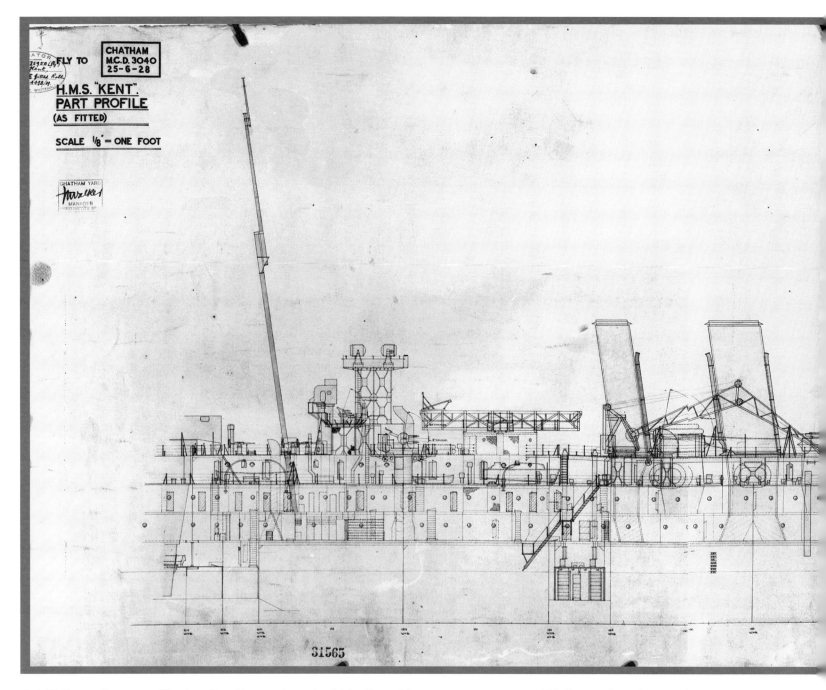

HMS Kent, *Part profile (as fitted), Chatham Dockyard, 1938. This fly to the* Kent's *original 'as fitted' profile shows the changes in the ship's appearance following her reconstruction of 1937–July 1938. The aircraft catapult has again been changed – to an EIVH (extending MkIV heavy) which allowed her to operate a Walrus amphibian – and two new, heavier-duty cranes have been fitted abreast the after funnel. The main director on the bridge has been replaced with a modern DCT and relocated aft – just forward of the mainmast. The after control position and HA director have been replaced by a searchlight tower and the lower bridge platform has been extended aft. The changes to the AA armament, although visible in this drawing, can be more clearly seen in the plan views.*

(Plan No NPB5159, Neg No 475958fly)

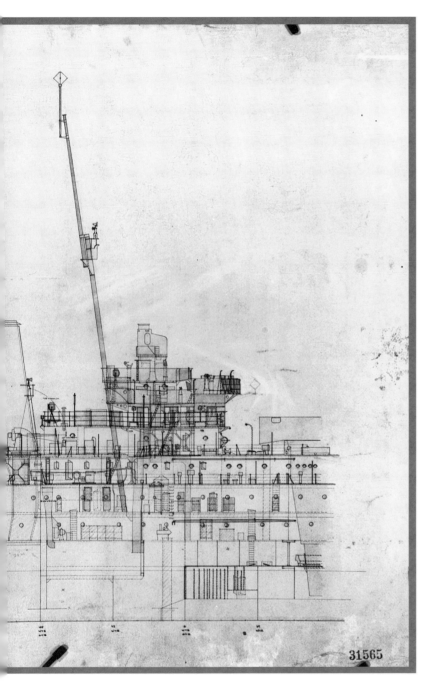

31565

Cruiser Construction 1924-45

Programme Year	Class (no of ships)	Type
1924	*Kent* (7)*	10,000 ton/8 x 8in
1925	*London* (4)	10,000 ton/8 x 8in
1926	*Dorsetshire* (2)	10,000 ton/8 x 8in
	York (1)	8000 ton/6 x 8in
1927	*Exeter* (1)	8000 ton/6 x 8in
1929	*Leander* (1)	7000 ton/8 x 6in
1930	*Leander* (3)	7000 ton/8 x 6in
1931	*Leander* (1)	7000 ton/8 x 6in
	Arethusa (2)	5500 ton/6 x 6in
1932	*Amphion* (3)**	7000 ton/8 x 6in
1933	*Arethusa* (1)	5500 ton/6 x 6in
	Southampton (2)	9000 ton/12 x 6in
1934	*Arethusa* (1)	5500 ton/6 x 6in
	Southampton (3)	9000 ton/12 x 6in
1935	*Southampton* (3)	9000 ton/12 x 6in
1936	*Edinburgh* (2)	10,000 ton/12 x 6in
	Dido (5)	5000 ton/10 x 5.25in
1937	*Dido* (2)	5000 ton/10 x 5.25in
	Fiji (5)	8000 ton /12 x 6in
1938	*Dido* (3)	5000 ton/10 x 5.25in
	Fiji (4)	8000 ton/12 x 6in
1939	*Fiji* (2)	8000 ton/12 x 6in
	Dido (1)	5000 ton/10 x 5.25in
	Modified *Dido* (5)	5000 ton/8 x 5.25in
1941	*Swiftsure* (3)	8800 ton/9 x 6in
	Tiger (2)	8800 ton/9 x 6in
1942	*Tiger* (2)	8800 ton/9 x 6in

* Including two for the Royal Australian Navy
** The *Amphion* class were transferred to the Australian Navy and renamed during 1935-9.

almost entirely due to disagreement over the cruiser question. The problem was more-or-less resolved at the 1930 London Conference where cruisers were limited under two classes – effectively 8in gun cruisers and 6in gun cruisers – and an overall tonnage limit was accepted by Britain which more or less limited her cruiser fleet to fifty ships. The agreement allowed the USA to build her strength up to eighteen 8in gun cruisers while Japan and Britain accepted their existing twelve and fifteen ships respectively. This left the Admiralty free to concentrate on constructing smaller 6in gun ships – a policy to which it was already committed – for which 90,720 tons was available from the tonnage limit for new ships completed up to 31 December 1936. Cruisers completed after this date were for the replacement of ships becoming over-age up to the end of 1939.

The early 1930s proved even more difficult in financial terms than the 1920s and orders were restricted to three cruisers each of the programme years from 1930 to 1935 except for four included in the 1934 Programme. The problem of cruiser numbers remained, as the older ships were nearing the end of their useful lives and required replacement while the foreign construction of large 6in gun cruisers was pushing up the displacement requirement and reducing the numbers that could be constructed under the existing maximum limits. This again was resolved by the 1936 London Naval Treaty which removed all restrictions on cruiser construction except for a maximum displacement limit of 8000 tons. This, combined with the rearmament programme, initiated a substantial expansion of cruiser building – seven being ordered in each year from 1936 to 1938. Four cruisers were included in the 1939 Programme but on the outbreak of war an Emergency War Programme increased this to eight ships and in 1941-2 nine additional cruisers were ordered.[25] Of these seventeen vessels, ten were completed prior to the end of hostilities and one very soon after. All were delayed to varying degrees by the need to concentrate on other areas of construction with higher priorities and, as with battleships and fleet carriers, the cruiser programme suffered accordingly. Several design studies were undertaken, a number of which were for very ambitious big cruisers, but few went beyond the general discussion stage, as the resources to build these ships were simply not available. Of the remaining six cruisers ordered during the war, three were cancelled (two were never laid down) and three (the *Tiger* class) were initially suspended and then completed during 1959-61 to a much modified design. The full cruiser programme for ships actually laid down during the period 1924-45 was as shown in the table.

The 'County' classes

The Staff Requirements for the first of the 10,000-ton Treaty cruisers called for ships with high endurance, a speed of 33kts, good seakeeping qualities and an armament of eight 8in guns in four twin turrets capable of elevating to 70° to provide long-range AA defence. Investigation of the design soon revealed that meeting these requirements would leave little weight available for armour,

even after the requested speed was dropped to 31kts (later increased to 31.5kts) to make more weight available. The best that could be achieved was little more than limited protection against splinters and destroyer gunfire for the machinery (1in deck and 1.5in belt) combined with box protection to the magazines. The magazine 'box' protection, which was internal and therefore minimised the area to be covered, consisted of 4in sides and 3in crowns – sufficient to protect the magazines against 6in guns but barely adequate against 8in. This minimal protection was reluctantly accepted on the grounds that the other features of the design could not be further reduced. Even then, the design required strict weight control and no Board Margin was provided in the legend for additions. As with the battleships *Nelson* and *Rodney*, a great deal of effort was put into the control of material and fittings weights during construction and the ships actually came out slightly light (130 to 250 tons in the standard condition) despite their main armament being above design weight. The five ships of the class (reduced from a programme of eight by the newly elected Labour Government), *Kent, Suffolk, Cumberland, Cornwall* and *Berwick*, were laid down in 1924 and completed in 1928. Their two Australian sisters, *Australia* and *Canberra*, ordered and paid for by the Dominion, were laid down a year later but also completed in 1928.

The *Kent* class was followed by three sub-classes, one of which was never built. The first was the *London* class (*London,*

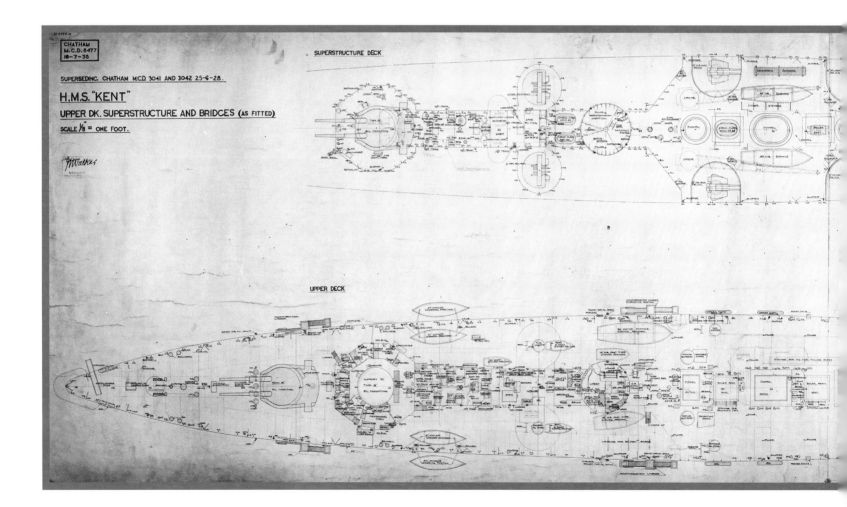

HMS Kent, *Upper deck, superstructure and bridges (as fitted), Chatham Dockyard, 16 July 1938. Unlike the profile drawing this new set for the weather decks was drawn up in 1938 as a replacement for the original 'as fitted' plans. The shelter deck has been extended to the full width of the upper deck abreast the funnels and now accommodates four twin 4in MkXIX mountings, controlled from two HACS MkI directors, one on each side of the upper bridge. Two 8-barrel pom-pom mountings have been fitted on platforms abreast the after searchlight tower and the quad 0.5in mountings have been relocated just abaft and above them. There has also been a redistribution of the ship's boats and the torpedo tubes have been removed. This drawing also includes some very faint changes, which indicate that the drawings were again modified by Chatham following alterations to the ship in September-October 1943. These include the positions of three twin 20mm which were added at this time (one on quarterdeck and one on each side of the upper deck abreast the funnels) and six single 20mm (two each on the roofs of 'B' and 'X' turrets and one on each side of the upper deck abreast the fore funnel) fitted earlier. Also shown are the deletion of the catapult and it support, the replacement of the 0.5in mountings with pom-pom directors, the addition of struts to the masts and the location of various radar offices. (Plan No NPB5150, Neg No E0719)*

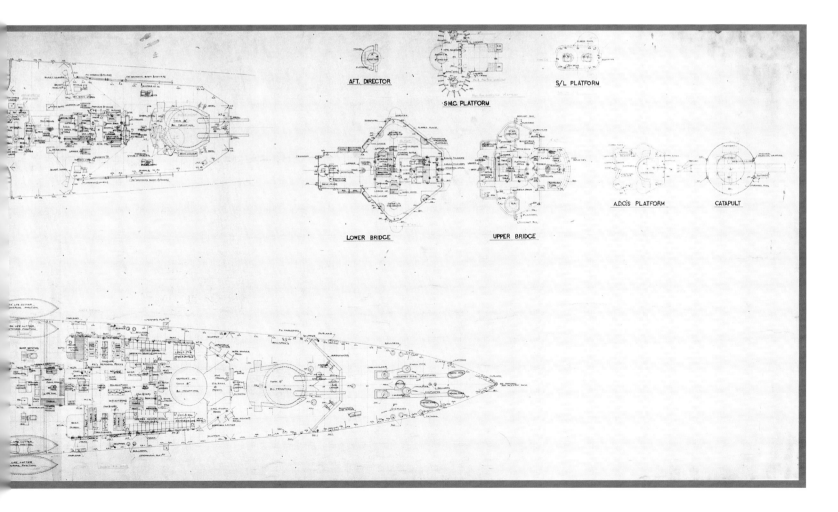

Dorsetshire, Sussex and *Shropshire*) laid down in 1926/27 and completed in 1927/28. Their only major difference from the *Kent*s was a modified hull form. The original class had an integral but external bulge of essentially similar form to that employed in the *Hawkins*. In the *London* class this arrangement was abandoned in favour of a standard, vertical-side hull that allowed an improvement in form and a consequent $^3/_4$kt increase in the maximum design speed. The ships were designed to carry an aircraft catapult and seaplane amidships, a modification also extended to the *Kent* class during construction, but this equipment was not actually ready at the time the ships completed and was not fitted until the early 1930s. The next class consisted of only two ships (*Dorsetshire* and *Norfolk*) which were repeats of the *London* except that they carried their 8in guns in modified (MkII) mountings. These latter had an improved loading system for the hoists and were expected to be lighter than the MkI mounting – in fact they turned out heavier. In addition the box protection to the magazines was extended to cover the 8in shell rooms, previously protected only by 1in crown and sides (except for 'B' mounting which had the same protection as the magazines). The last of the 'County' class cruisers, *Northumberland* and *Surrey*, were to have been included in the 1928 Programme but were deferred until the 1929 Programme when con-

HMS Leander, *Sketch of W/T rig (as fitted), Devonport Dockyard, 7 March 1933. Sometimes included in the standard rig and sometimes produced as a separate drawing, as here, the W/T rig showed the location of aerial wires, their supporting yards and halyards, together with their associated blocks and insulators. It was also common practice to indicated the location of the wireless offices, although that has not been done in this drawing. The main transmitting aerials are those spread between the two 30ft W/T yards at the tops of the main and fore masts – their height above water being directly linked to the obtainable range. The connection to the main office is via the fan of wires descending to the after superstructure while that to the second office extends from the ends of the fore yard to the funnel and then to the aerial trunk just forward of the fore mast. The main receiving aerials consist of wires running from the main topmast head and main yardarms to the after deckhouse. The wires immediately above the bridge, rigged to a jackstay running to the head of the fore topmast, are for direction finding and the two aerials running from the trunk at the side of the bridge to the ends of the lower yard are for the Type 45 short range fire control set.*
(Plan No NPB5648, Neg No 529620)

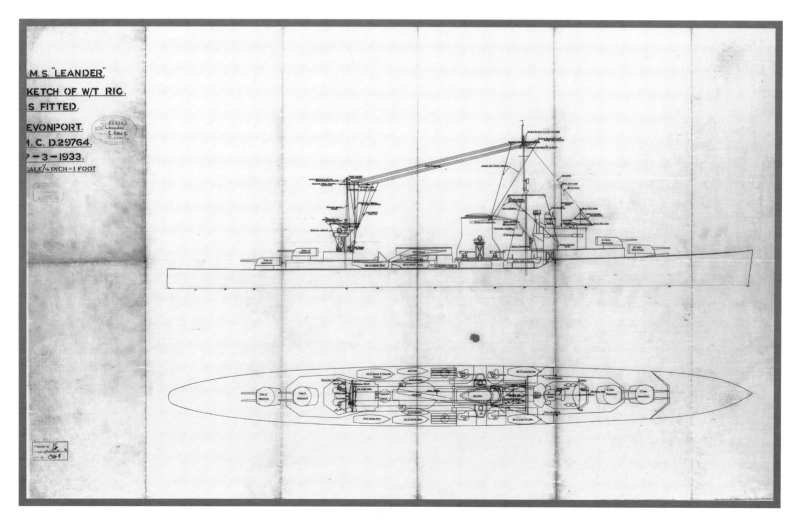

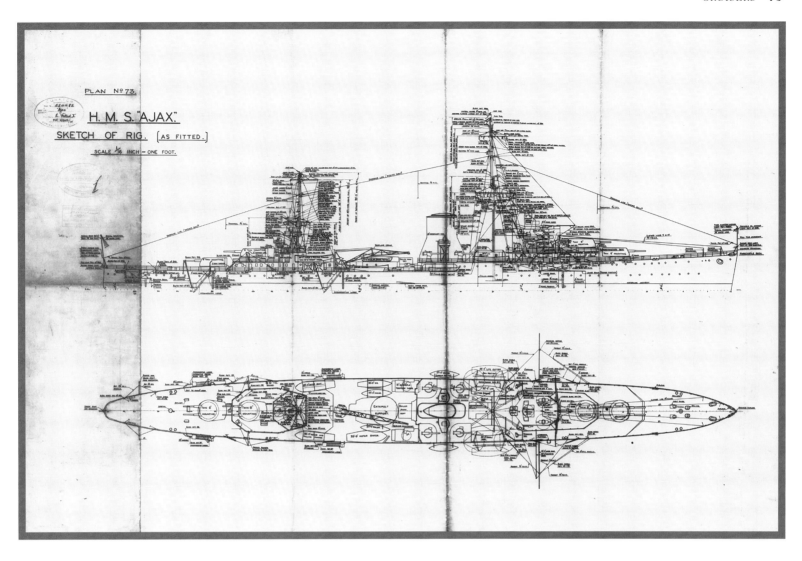

***HMS** Ajax, Sketch of Rig (as fitted), Vickers Armstrongs, 6 April 1935. This rig of* Leander's *sister-ship* Ajax *illustrates well the usual arrangement and level of detail to be found in a rig drawing. It is crowded with text indicating the type and size of masts, spars, booms, cables, ropes, blocks, swivels, insulators and their associated features. It also includes details of the Jacob's ladders, accommodation ladders, navigation lights and sounding gear. As already noted for the rig drawing of* King George V, *they can be less detailed but it is also common to find rigs in which the ship itself is show in considerable detail, although this is more common in smaller vessels than large ones. For modelmakers the rig is an essential part of the 'as fitted' set as the main drawings seldom show much detail of the rig and often omit the upper masts altogether.*
(Plan No NPA4923, Neg No 554482)

Leander

Displacement:	As completed – 7289 tons standard, 9350 tons deep
Dimensions:	522ft (pp), 554ft 6in(oa) x 55ft x 16ft 3in(mean)
Armament:	As completed – Eight 6in MkXXIII (4 x 2); four 4in MkV HA (4 x 1); twelve 0.5in (3 x 4); eight 21in torpedo tubes (2 x 4)
	1945 – six 6in MkXXIII (3 x 2); eight 4in MkXVI HA (4 x 2); eight 40mm (2 x 4); ten 20mm (4 x 1, 3 x 2)
Armour:	Machinery 3in belt (+ 1in side),1.25in deck, 1.5in bulkheads; Steering gear 1.5in sides, 1.25in deck; Magazines 3.5in sides, 2in crown and bulkheads; Turret roofs and ammunition trunks 1in
Machinery:	Four shaft, Parsons geared turbines, 72,000shp = 32.5kts; six Admiralty 3-drum boilers; 1785 tons oil fuel; range 8000nm at 12kts
Complement:	627

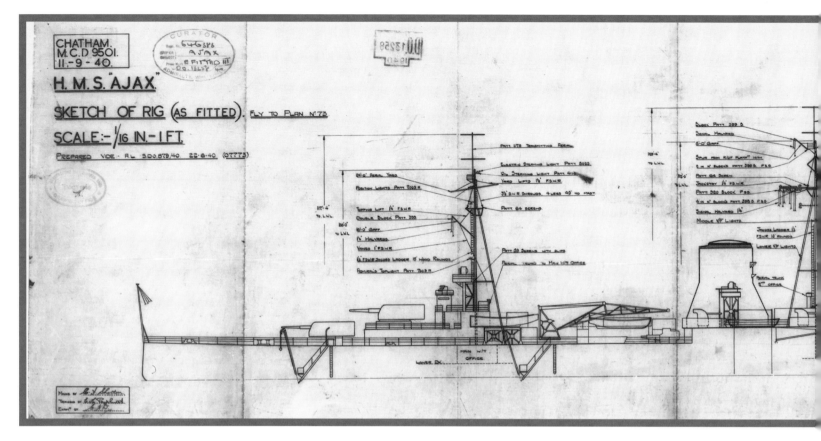

HMS Ajax, *Sketch of Rig (as fitted), Chatham Dockyard, October 1940.*
This drawing is a fly to the rig of Ajax produced after repair and refit at Chatham during December 1939 – July 1940 following action damage received during the Battle of the River Plate. As the drawing is intended for use in combination with the original rig it does not include a plan view or many of the details. However, the comparative simplicity is not just a case of omission as the rig has been much simplified by the provision of tripod masts making the original mast stays unnecessary. The tripods were provided to give better support to the aerials of Type 279 long range air warning radar at the heads of the main (transmitter) and fore (receiver) masts. Unusually, the positions of the main, second and auxiliary W/T offices, omitted from the W/T rig of Leander, are shown in this drawing despite the fact that the W/T aerials are not included. The new fore mast also carries the diamond frame of the direction finder, the office for which, together with that for Type 279, is located at the rear of the bridge. The refit also included the provision of a heavier catapult so the ship could operate a Walrus aircraft. (Plan No NPA4922, Neg No 646383)

Foreign Light Cruisers

Class (No of ships)	Built	Displacement (tons)	Armament	Speed (kts)
France				
Duguay Trouin (3)	1922-6	7250 tons	8-6.1in (4 x 2)	33
Germany				
Emden (1)	1921-5	5600 tons	8-5.9in (8 x 1)	29
Koenigsberg (3)	1926-30	6650 tons	9-5.9in (3 x 3)	32
Leipzig (1)	1928-31	6500 tons	9-5.9in (3 x 3)	32
Italy				
Giussano (4)	1928-31	5100 tons	8-6in (4 x 2)	36.5

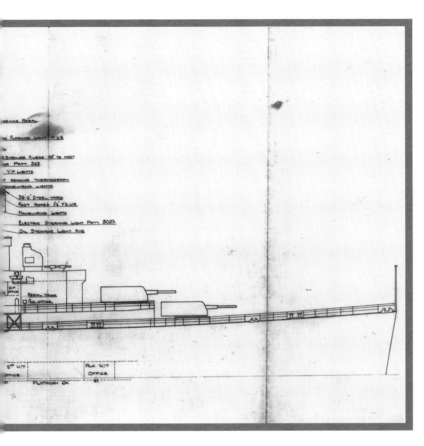

sides, 1.5in deck) and a reduction in complement, showed little to recommend it. In effect the ship fell between the large trade cruiser and small fleet cruiser without showing any major advantage in either role. *York* was followed by a half-sister, the *Exeter*, of essentially the same design but of markedly different appearance due to the adoption of vertical (instead of raked) masts and funnels and the fitting of a large 'box'-like bridge in place of the tiered platform type employed previously. The latter became a standard feature of future British cruisers and, on a larger scale, in British battleships as well.

While the majority of the major navies had concentrated their efforts on the 8in gun cruiser during the 1920s there was some interest in the light cruiser type. The light cruisers laid down up to 1930 by foreign powers were as shown in the table opposite.[24] The Italian vessels were lightly protected high-speed ships designed primarily as an answer to large, fast French destroyers of recent construction.

The Admiralty began consideration of a 6in or 5.5in gun cruiser design in the mid-1920s but final Staff Requirements were not complete until the end of 1928. A preliminary design for a ship of 6500 tons, armed with four twin 6in turrets and having a speed of 32kts was adopted in 1929 but, as the detailed design developed, improvements to the machinery and protection eventually pushed the displacement up to 7150 tons. Two ships were intended for inclusion in the 1929-30 Programme but this was reduced to one by the new Labour Government and that ship, the *Leander*, was not laid down until September 1930; she completed in 1933. Compared with the 'Counties' the result was a better balanced design which with the same armament layout and speed but much improved protection for the machinery – provided by a 4in side and 1.25in deck. *Leander* was followed by four sister ships, *Achilles*, *Orion*, *Neptune* and *Ajax*, built during 1931-5. These differed from the prototype in having a 6in increase in beam, to give a higher reserve of stability, and detail improvements in the machinery and aircraft arrangements. Three more ships of the type, the *Amphion* class, were constructed to a modified design, which adopted a unit machinery arrangement. This had been employed in the last of the light cruisers of the War Construction Programme, *Emerald* and *Enterprise*, completed in 1926, in which the aftermost boiler room was placed between the two engine rooms. This wide separation of engine and boiler rooms added substantially to the survivability of the machinery in the event of damage but was not repeated in post-war cruiser designs. In the *Amphion* the two boiler rooms and two engine rooms were arranged alternately which necessitated the provision of two widely-spaced funnels and, with little variation, this arrangement became standard in all future British cruiser construction. The three ships of the class, *Amphion*, *Apollo* and *Phaeton* were laid down in 1933 and completed in 1935-7. *Phaeton* was transferred to the Australian Navy before completion and renamed *Sydney*, while *Apollo* and *Amphion* followed in 1938 and 1939 respectively being renamed *Hobart* and *Perth*.

struction was initially delayed and then cancelled in 1930 as an economy measure. These vessels were a substantial modification of the earlier ships, having a profile somewhat similar to the cruiser *Exeter* with two funnels and a 'box' bridge structure. Their main advantage was a 5.75in armour belt and a 2.5 - 3in deck, an improvement bought primarily at the cost of reducing the speed to 30kts.

The small cruiser

The Admiralty soon became disillusioned with the 8in-gun 'County' classes - they were big, expensive and lacking in defensive qualities. Although they might well serve effectively on the trade routes, they were not viewed as good fleet cruisers where smaller, faster-firing guns and better manouverabilty were required for scouting and for defence against, and support of, destroyers. This role was filled to a large extent by the light cruisers constructed during the First World War but by the late 1920s there was a serious need to consider their future replacement. The initial step towards a smaller type was made in 1925 with studies that led to the cruiser *York*. At the time nothing less than the 8in gun seemed acceptable to the Naval Staff and the primary weight-saving device was to reduce the 'County' design by the omission of one turret and lowering the freeboard by one deck abaft the bridge. It was hoped that this would provide a 2000-ton reduction in displacement but the ship, laid down in 1927 and completed in 1930, was actually of 8425 tons and, apart from an improvement in the protection to the machinery (3in

Britain's last pre-war cruisers with twin mounted 6in guns were the *Arethusa* class constructed during 1933-7. The design was contemporary with that of the *Amphion* class of which they were essentially cut-down versions with 'X' turret omitted in order to reduce the design displacement from 7000 tons to 5000 tons. They were primarily intended to serve as fleet cruisers although the main incentive for a reduction in size was a desire to increase cruiser numbers rather than produce a specialist type. The class were not particularly outstanding in comparison to the *Leander*s, having less protection and endurance as well as a reduced main armament, but nevertheless served with distinction during the Second World War. They did, however, introduce a major technical advance in adopting a high degree of welded structure. Some welding had been included in the *Leander* class, primarily for the bulkheads, but in the *Arethusa* class this was extended to most of the hull and superstructure except for those areas of major structural importance. The latter included the shell plating (except for the foremost 80ft), the upper deck from the forecastle break to abaft 'Y' barbette, and the areas of the upper and forecastle decks immediately surrounding the forward barbettes. The initial work on establishing the welding arrangements was carried out on the lead ship – *Arethusa* – at Chatham Dockyard.

The Southampton class

The initial commitment to small 6in gun cruisers was short-lived. Like Britain, Japan was limited to 6in-gun cruiser construction under the terms of the 1930 Treaty but, unlike Britain, chose to aim for a high qualitative advantage. In 1931 construction began of the *Mogami* and *Mikuma*, two 37kt, 8500-ton cruisers, armed with no

Manchester

Displacement:	As completed – 9400 tons standard, 12330 tons deep
Dimensions:	558ft (pp), 591ft (oa) x 64ft 10in x 17ft 3in (mean)
Armament:	As completed – Twelve 6in MkXXIII (4 x 3); eight 4in MkXVI HA (4 x 2); eight 2pdr (2 x 4); eight 0.5in (2 x 4); six 21in torpedo tubes (2 x 3)
Armour:	Machinery 4.5in belt (+ 1in side),1.5in deck, 2.5in bulkheads; Steering gear 1.5in sides, 1.25in deck; Magazines 4.5in sides, 2in crown, 2.5in bulkheads; Turrets and ammunition trunks 2in and 1in
Machinery:	Four shaft, Parsons geared turbines, 82,500shp = 32kts; four Admiralty 3-drum boilers; 1950 tons oil fuel; range 8900nm at 16kts
Complement:	800

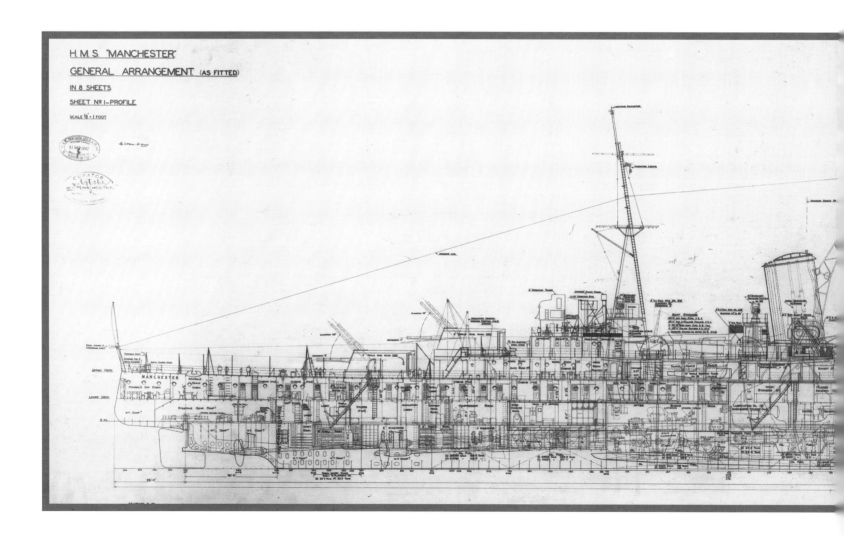

HMS Manchester, *Profile (as fitted), Hawthorn Leslie, 13 March 1942. Despite the date stamp of the ship's builders these drawings show Manchester as she was when completed in August 1938. Why there should be such a large gap between these dates is not clear, although it is possible that these were from a spare set, which was not stamped until passed to the Admiralty in 1942. Coincidentally the* Manchester *was sunk on 13 August 1942, torpedoed by Italian MTBs off Tunisia during Operation Pedestal. Like those of Cammell Laird, the 'as fitted' drawings produced by Hawthorn Leslie are among the best and most detailed available. Note that they described all their 'as fitted' drawings as 'General Arrangements' the actual view description (profile, upper deck,* etc) *appearing as a subtitle. Among the more interesting internal features are the unit machinery arrangement with its alternate boiler and engine rooms and the small auxiliary boiler fitted against the forward boiler room bulkhead between the two main boilers. The after boilers are arranged on the centre line, fore and aft, with auxiliary machinery compartments outboard of them. In the later Fiji class the after boilers were rearranged athwartships which greatly aided the reduction in length and displacement in that class. Immediately forward of the fore bulkhead of the forward boiler room, in the hold, is the ship's main transmitting station and, on the deck above it the forward HA control position. The tanks shown in the hold forward, (rectangles with curved ends) are for aviation spirit (large tank) for the ship's aircraft and petrol (small tank) for the ship's motor boats. This location, common to all surface ships at this time, was chosen to keep these highly inflammable and explosive liquids as remote from the ship's vitals as possible. The broken lines showing the 6in guns at their full elevation of 45° illustrates clearly the fact that the centre gun of each mounting was set back from the other two. This arrangement was adopted when it was found that projectiles fired from these closely-spaced weapons could mutually interfere with each other in flight – setting back the centre gun increased the spread.*
(Plan No NPA4922, Neg No 646383)

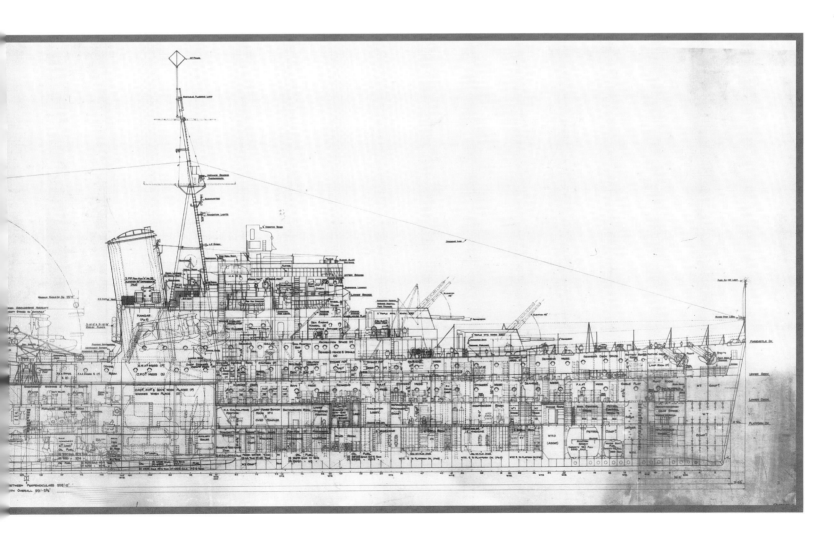

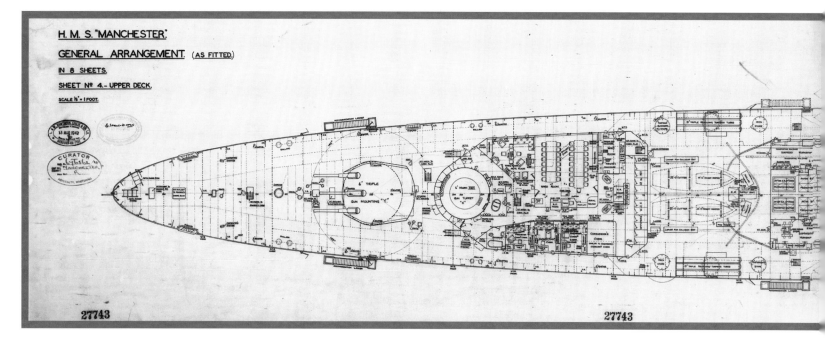

Above: *HMS* Manchester, *Upper deck (as fitted), Hawthorn Leslie, 13 March 1942.* The majority of the enclosed areas on this deck were employed for accommodation, seamen and senior rates forward and senior officers' cabins, and the wardroom, in the after superstructure. The main exceptions to this are the 6in barbettes and the uptakes for the funnels, which, as this is a protective deck, are provided with protective gratings (individually indicated by the crossed rectangles). Externally the deck carries the cross-deck aircraft catapult (just forward of the 27ft whalers), the ship's two triple torpedo tube mountings (one on each beam abaft the second funnel) and, at the extreme after end on the port side, a depth charge rail (with a rack for three spare charges on the centre line). Note the boats (two 32ft cutters each with a 16ft dinghy inside) stowed between the torpedo tube mountings – these were accessed via an opening in the shelter deck above which in turn was fitted with portable skid beams for the stowage of two other boats.

(Plan No NPB6514, Neg No 676362/4)

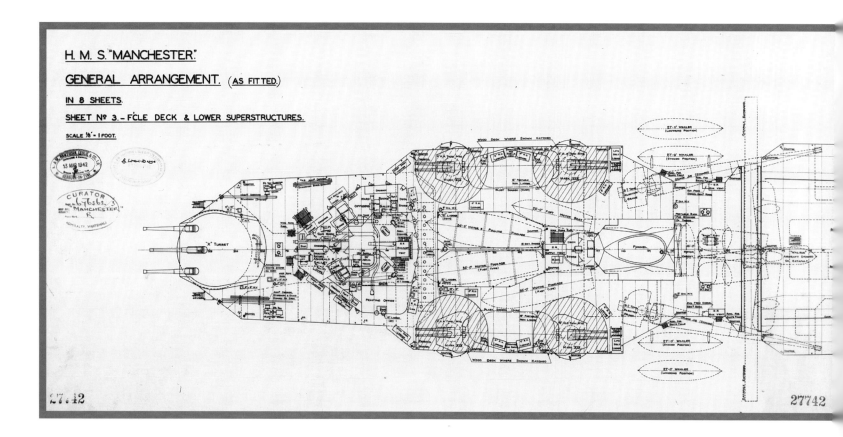

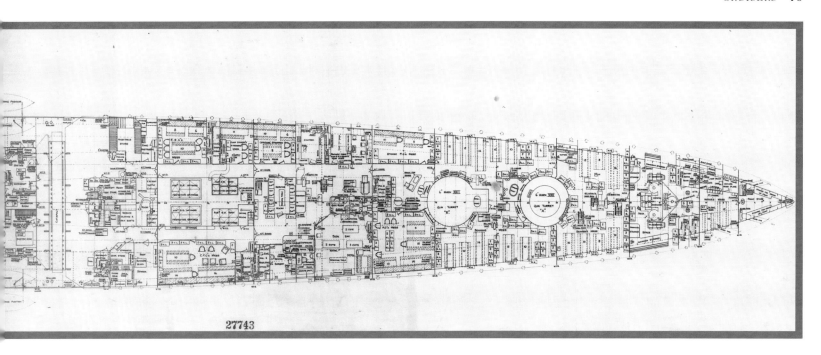

27743

Below: *HMS Manchester, Forecastle deck and lower superstructures (as fitted), Hawthorn Leslie, 13 March 1942.* Again, the enclosed areas on this deck, albeit of limited area, are largely employed for accommodation or recreation, the primary exceptions being the aircraft hangars on each side of the fore funnel. The shaded areas around the twin 4in MkXIX mountings indicate the extent of the wood planking provided around the guns. The boats between the 4in mountings are from port to starboard a 35ft fast motor boat, 36ft auxiliary motor pinnace, 36ft fast motor pinnace and a 35ft fast motor pinnace. The two 36ft boats are stowed over the opening giving access to the boats below. Also worthy of note is the illustration of the aircraft catapult fully extended. (Plan No NPB6518, Neg No 676352/3)

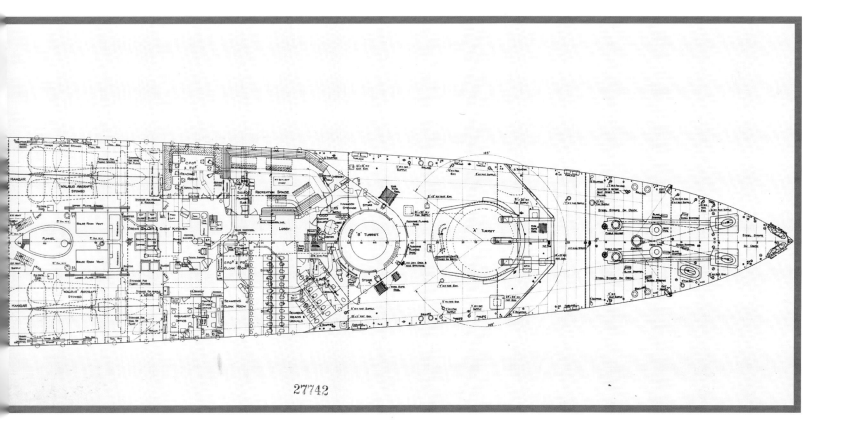

27742

less than fifteen 6.1in guns in five triple turrets, together with eight 5in guns on twin HA/LA mountings and twelve 24in torpedo tubes. They were followed by two sister-ships in 1933-4. This achievement, on a relatively light displacement, looked impressive and led to criticism of British cruisers for being under-gunned and slow by comparison.[25] However, the *Mogami* design was seriously flawed in stability and hull strength and major, and very necessary, reconstruction in the late 1930s, which included upgrading the main armament to ten 8in (5 x 2), increased the displacement by 4000 tons and dropped the speed to 35kts. Not unexpectedly, in 1933 the USA announced their intention to build similar ships armed with fifteen 6in guns but with displacement increased to the Treaty maximum of 10,000 tons, better protection and a standard design speed of 32.5kts. These ships became the *Brooklyn* class, nine of which were laid down during 1934-6 and completed during 1937-9.

The Admiralty considered that a reply to the *Mogami* class was essential even if this compromised the policy on cruiser numbers. Design work began in 1933 for a ship carrying twelve 6in guns in four triple turrets and protected against 6in gun fire. The resulting *Southampton* class were less ambitious than their Japanese rivals but considerably more practical, the design finally approved having a speed of 32kts on a standard displacement of 9100 tons. The ships introduced to cruisers the advanced aircraft installation already adopted for the modernisations of *Repulse* and *Malaya* with hangars, for two aircraft, fitted abreast the fore funnel and a fixed cross-deck catapult amidships. Compared to the *Leander* they were better protected, of higher endurance and gave a 50 per cent increase in main armament firepower. They also had an enhanced AA capability, being fitted with four twin 4in HA/LA mountings in place of the single 4in fitted in earlier ships. However, this latter innovation was subsequently extended to earlier ships and the majority of the 'County' class and later 6in gun cruisers had been similarly fitted by the outbreak of war.

The original 1933-4 Programme had provided for the construction of three cruisers of the *Amphion* type, these being the final allotment of new construction allowed by the 1930 Treaty for completion in 1936. The displacement available – 23,400 tons – was reallocated to two of the new ships and one of the *Arethusa* class. The former pair, *Southampton* and *Newcastle*, were laid down late in 1934 and completed in 1937. They were followed by six sister ships, under the Treaty allocation of replacement tonnage – the *Sheffield*, *Glasgow* and *Birmingham*, laid down in 1935 and completed in 1937, and the *Manchester*, *Liverpool* and *Gloucester*, laid down in 1936 and completed in 1938-9. The design of the last three differed slightly from the earlier ships in having increased deck and main armament protection, requiring an increase in beam to maintain stability and, in turn, an increase in engine power to maintain speed.

Two modified *Southampton* class cruisers, *Belfast* and *Edinburgh*, were included in the 1936-7 programme. These were 10,000-ton ships originally intended to carry sixteen 6in in four quadruple turrets in a desire to match more closely the greater number of guns

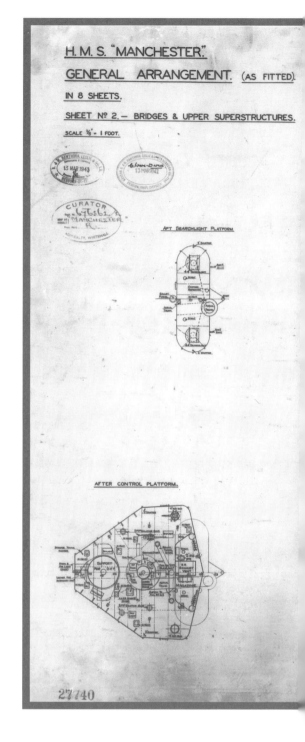

in Japanese and US 6in gun cruisers. Unfortunately, after the initial design was complete, serious problems arose with the design of the quadruple mounting due to the guns being too close together. As there were serious weight and design problems in further separating the barrels it was decided to revert to the standard triple mounting and both ships completed with the same main armament as the original *Southampton* class. The weight saved was utilised to improve the ship's protection and for the first time in a post-war cruiser 'box' protection for the ammunition gave way to the more satisfactory arrangement of extending the main belt and deck protection fore and aft to cover the magazines.

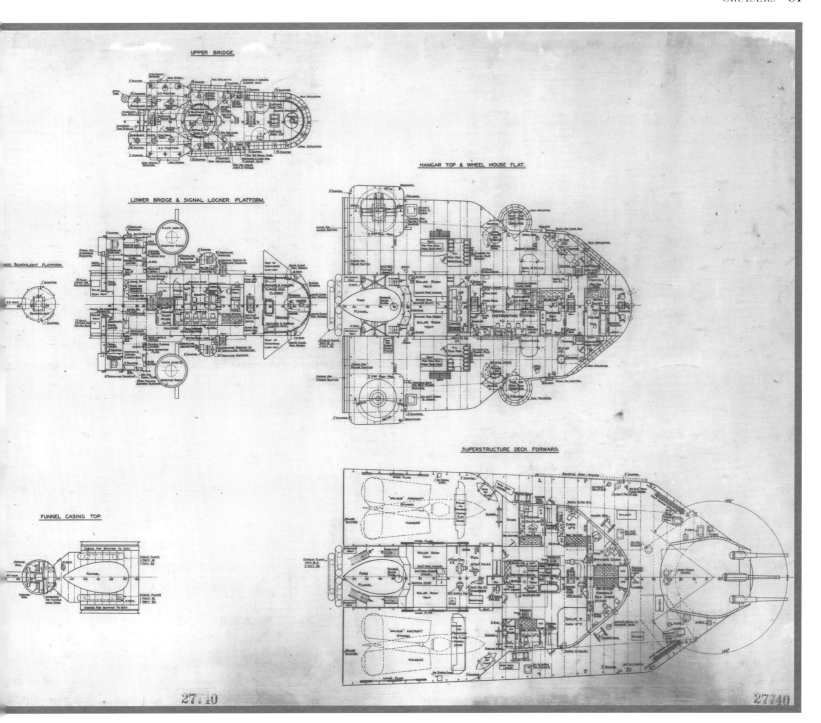

HMS Manchester, *Bridges and upper superstructures (as fitted), Hawthorn Leslie, 13 March 1942.* These drawings illustrate well the extensive bridge structure of the Southampton *class cruisers. Belonging to the second group of the class, the* Manchester *has the semicircular front to the bridge, which replaced the partially* curved fronts of the earlier ships. Note that the hangar roof, which carries the ship's two MkVII quad pom-pom mountings, is integrated with the lower bridge platform. This level carries the wheelhouse at its forward end while, working upward from this position, the signal platform has a closed bridge and the upper bridge an open compass platform. The area carries a large amount of fire control gear, including two pom-pom directors (forward of the pom-poms in circular enclosures projecting outboard), the two HACS MkIV directors abreast the lower bridge and the DCT on the upper bridge. (Plan No NPB6520, Neg No 676362/2)

The Dido class

1936 was the last programme year subject to the Washington and 1930 London Naval Treaties and the Admiralty sought to make up the remaining over-age cruiser tonnage with a mixture of large cruisers to counter the Japanese and small fleet cruisers to replace the 'C' and 'D' classes.[26] The former were covered by the two ships of the *Edinburgh* class, while the latter were generated from an extension of the *Arethusa* design. In essence the new small cruisers were *Arethusa*'s with the armament altered from a mixed 6in LA and 4in HA/LA armament to a uniform dual purpose main battery of ten 5.25in guns in five twin mountings. This choice was prompted by demands for fleet cruisers capable of supporting destroyers and of providing fleet defence against cruisers, destroyers and aircraft. The 5.25in fired an 80lb shell, compared with the 112lb projectile of the 6in gun, which weight was judged to be a reasonable compromise between the requirements to inflict significant damage on medium /small size surface ships and the maximum that could allow a good sustained rate of fire in AA defence. The mounting provided a maximum elevation of 70° and was designed for a rate of fire of around 12rpg/min but in practice this was not much more than 8rpg/min,

equal to the maximum of the 6in gun. In addition, relatively slow rates of training and elevation meant that the mounting could not always perform adequately against a high-speed aircraft attack

The *Dido*'s speed and endurance was the same as in the *Arethusa* but the length was increased from 480ft(pp) to 485ft and the beam reduced from 51ft to 50ft 6in which allowed a reduction in machinery power from 64,000 to 62,000 shp. The belt armour abreast the machinery was increased from 2.25in to 3in but the magazine box protection was abandoned in favour of 2in protective decks and end bulkheads over the full width of the hull. Although this left the magazines more exposed in surface attack it improved the defence against air attack and reduced the weight absorbed by armour. Above the citadel protection was limited to splinter and bullet-proof plating to the turrets, ammunition trunks and control positions and was again primarily aimed at defence against air attack. No aircraft arrangements were fitted but the design provided for an enhanced close-range AA capability with the fitting of two quad pom-pom mountings. The light construction proved something of a problem in heavy weather and the early units which joined the Home Fleet were soon shipped to the Mediterranean where their AA capability was in any case of greater value.

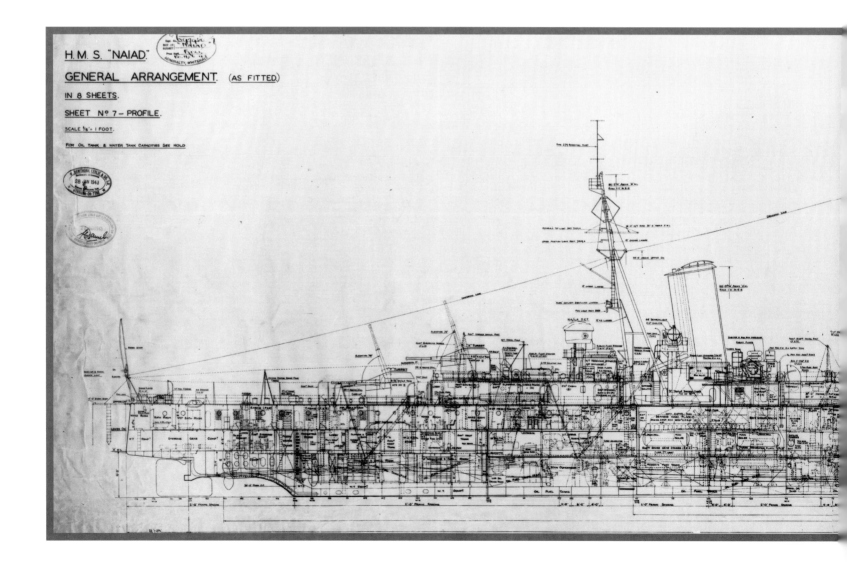

Naiad

Displacement:	5450 tons standard, 7081 tons deep
Dimensions:	485ft (pp), 512ft(oa) x 50ft 6in x 17ft 3in (mean)
Armament:	As completed – Ten 5.25in MkI HA/LA (5 x 2); eight 2pdr (2 x 4); eight 0.5in (2 x 4); six 21in torpedo tubes (2 x 3)
Armour:	Machinery and magazines 3in belt, 1in-2in deck, 1in bulkheads; Turrets 1in
Machinery:	Four shaft, Parsons geared turbines, 62,000shp = 32.25kts; four Admiralty 3-drum boilers; 1100 tons oil fuel; range 5500nm at 16kts
Complement:	490

HMS Naiad, *Profile (as fitted), Hawthorn Leslie, 28 January 1943.* Another superb set from Hawthorn Leslie and not only date stamped well after the ship's completion in July 1940 but also well after her loss to a U-boat's torpedo off Crete in March 1942! Again the drawings are unmodified and show Naiad as completed, the only noticeable deviation from the intended fit in this profile being the addition of Type 279 radar, with its aerials at the heads of the masts. The armament is as designed, with the impressive three tiers of twin 5.25in MkII turrets forward, two 5.25in turrets aft, a quad pom-pom MkVII on each beam abreast the fore side of the after funnel and two quad 0.5in machine gun mountings at the after corners of the forward shelter deck. The layout of the machinery (including the auxiliary boiler) is identical to that in Manchester. (Plan No NPC4368, Neg No 697950/7)

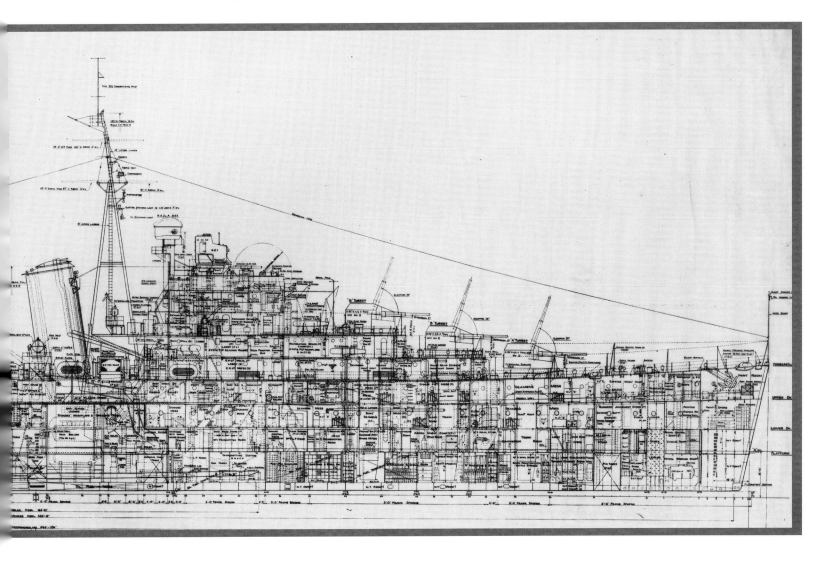

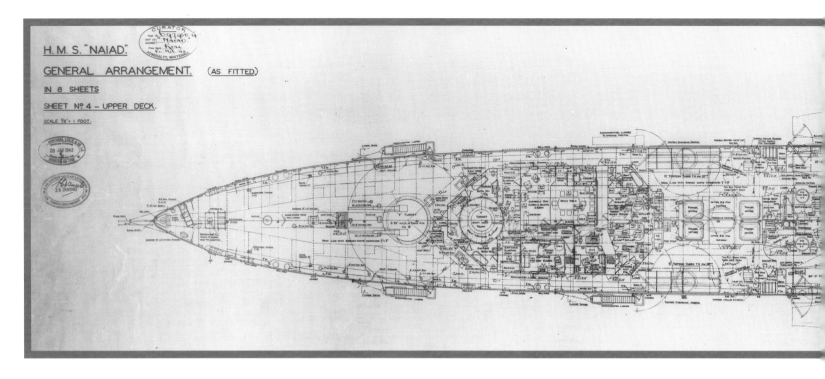

Above: *HMS* Naiad, *Upper deck (as fitted), Hawthorn Leslie, 28 January 1943.* The area under the forecastle is mostly crew accommodation but also includes the sick bay (below the bridge on the starboard side). The after superstructure contains the admiral's and captain's accommodation while the area amidships is occupied with the machinery uptakes and downtakes, various workshops, the bakery and galley – the latter functions accommodated in the relatively open area of the upper deck to improve their ventilation. Noticeable is the comparatively small boat complement, resulting from the limited space available. There is a 27ft whaler to port and starboard, abreast the fore funnel, with a 14ft sailing dinghy to port and a 16ft motor dinghy to starboard stowed underneath them. Slightly further aft is a 32ft motor cutter to port and a 30ft fast motor boat to starboard. Armament details visible include the two triple torpedo tube mountings MkIV** on each side of the after funnel and the depth charge chute at the extreme stern (port side).

(Plan No NPC3469, Neg No 697950/4)

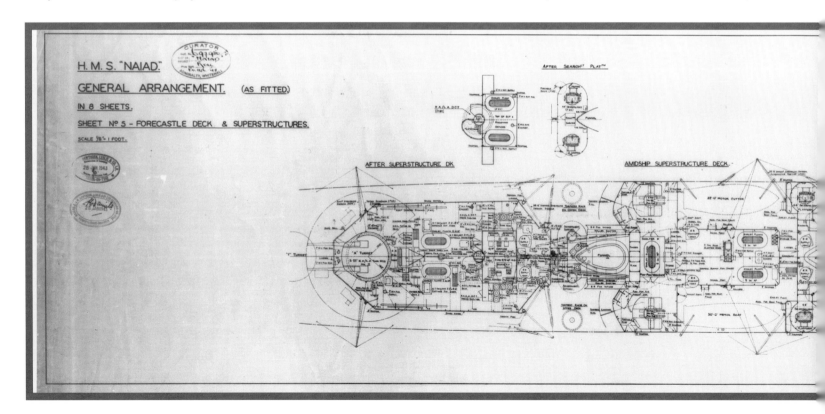

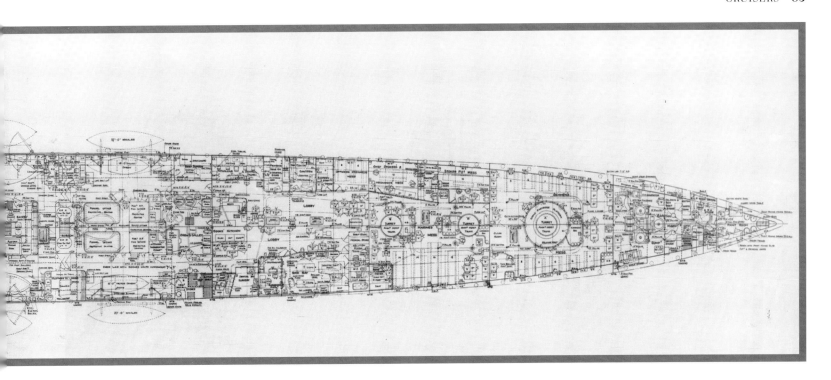

Below: *HMS* Naiad, *Forecastle deck (as fitted), Hawthorn Leslie, 28 January 1943. This view gives a clear indication of the positions of the pom-pom mountings and the ships four 44in searchlights. The latter were mounted on platforms abreast the fore funnel and at the rear of the after funnel – the last being* shown as a sub view above the position of the torpedo tubes as this platform was one deck higher than that forward. The other sub view is the roof of the direction finding office which also accommodated the receiving office of the Type 279 radar. Following standard practice these sub views are shown directly in line with the *positions they would occupy in the main view. Like the area below, the forecastle deckhouse is utilised for crew accommodation except for the area around 'B' mounting and the smith's shop at the extreme after end.*
(Plan No NPC3474, Neg No 697950/5)

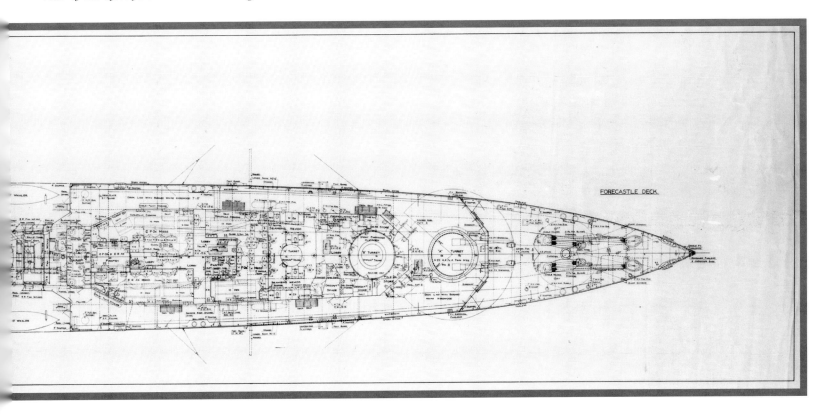

FORECASTLE DECK.

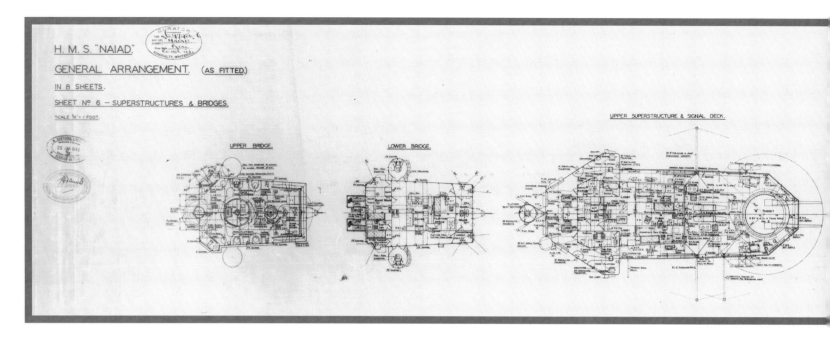

HMS Naiad, *Superstructure and bridges (as fitted), Hawthorn Leslie, 28 January 1943. The bridge platforms reveal the cramped nature of the* Dido *class cruisers, the limited command and control areas being restricted by the ship's small size and the large area occupied by the forward turrets – designated 'A', 'B' and 'Q'. From forward to aft down the centre line of the upper bridge are a 3-metre range finder, the main DCT (for LA control) and the forward HA director (raised on a cylindrical support). The second HA director was mounted on the after superstructure. The lower bridge carries the pompom directors on platforms projecting from the sides and accommodates the wheelhouse at its forward end. The enclosed areas below, on the signal and shelter decks contained cabins and crew recreation space. (Plan No NPC3473, Neg No 697950/6)*

The first four ships of the class, *Bonaventure, Naiad, Dido* and *Phoebe*, were completed in 1940 but production difficulties with the 5.25in mounting resulted in three completing with only four of their intended outfit of five mountings. *Dido* and *Phoebe* were without 'Q' turret and *Bonaventure* was without 'X' – the vacant position being occupied by a 4in starshell gun. The design armament was restored in *Dido* in 1941 but not in the other two. The remaining ships of the original design, *Euryalus, Hermione, Sirius, Cleopatra, Charybdis, Scylla* and *Argonaut*, were completed in 1941-2. Most shipped the designed armament but the bottleneck in armament production was such that two of the 1938 Programme ships, the *Charybdis* and *Scylla*, were modified to carry eight 4.5in in four twin, open shield mountings of the same type as those fitted in the carrier *Ark Royal* and various depot ships. *Charybdis* also mounted a 4in starshell gun.

Construction of the last five units of the class, *Spartan, Royalist, Bellona, Black Prince* and *Diadem*, was suspended as a result of labour and material shortages for four months from June 1940. During this time the opportunity was taken to modify the design by omitting 'Q' turret (presumably to ease the problem of mounting supply). This allowed the reduction of the height of the forward superstructure, bridge and funnels and, in turn, for the bridge to be fitted further forward allowing the adoption of vertical masts and funnels. The weight saved was employed for the addition of a third quad pom-pom mounting, forward of the bridge, and the fitting of $3/4$in splinter protection on the sides abreast the magazines and shell rooms.

The Fiji class

Although subject to several variations in design the *Fiji* group were effectively the last British cruiser group to be constructed. The original design was a variation on the *Southampton* with the displacement reduced to the 8000-ton limit imposed by the Second London Naval Treaty. The ships carried the same armament as the earlier class but weight was saved by a reduction in hull length – achieved primarily by placing the after boilers abreast each other instead of fore and aft. Although the belt armour was reduced from 4.5in to 3.25in, compared with the *Southampton*, it was extended fore and aft, at 3.5in, to cover the magazines and shell rooms and the deck protection was increased to a uniform 2in. The end result, although rather cramped, proved very popular despite wartime additions that strained both accommodation and stability. The first eight, which formed the original *Fiji* class, completed during 1940-2 well after the suspension of treaty restrictions and displacement was actually slightly over 8500 tons. The last three ships, *Newfoundland, Uganda* and *Ceylon*, were completed to a modified design in which the aircraft arrangements and 'X' turret were omit-

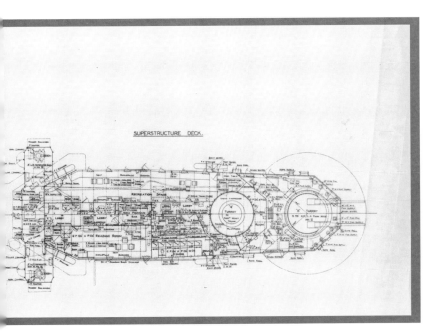

ted to make space and weight available for additional close-range AA weapons, radar and accommodation. Despite these changes displacement was still higher than desirable, stability less than ideal and accommodation extremely cramped. The remaining ships of the class also had their aircraft arrangements and 'X' turret removed during the latter half of the war. The wartime variations on the design, the 9000-ton *Swiftsure* and *Tiger* classes, had these modifications designed-in. They also provided for an increase in beam which improved the level of stability but in those ships completed during 1944-5 – the *Ontario* (ex-*Minotaur*), *Swiftsure* and *Superb* – the accommodation and space problems, albeit slightly reduced, remained.

Modernisations

As the older ships in the fleet neared obsolescence, consideration was given to giving them major refits to extend their useful lives. At the same time work began on improving what was considered the major shortcoming of the 'County' class – namely the weak protection to the machinery – and to updating their AA armament and aircraft arrangements. Progress was slow and, apart from the ships already in dockyard hands, the outbreak of war brought a virtual halt to both projects.

Proposals for the older ships were first put forward in 1934 with a suggestion to rearm the later 'C' class cruisers as AA vessels and this received approval in the following year. The first two ships taken in hand, *Coventry* and *Curlew*, which were refitted during 1935-6, had their entire original armament removed and replaced by ten single 4in HA/LA, two 8-barrel pom-poms (*Curlew* had quad pom-poms) and two HACSs. The 4in were of the type being replaced by the twin 4in in other ships so plenty were available. As the conversion involved additional top weight, permanent ballast

was fitted to maintain stability. The next four ships taken in hand, the *Cairo* and *Calcutta* during 1938-9 and *Carlisle* and *Curaçoa* during 1939-40, were refitted with a more modern but less extensive armament – four twin 4in, one quad pom-pom, two quad 0.5in and two HACSs – and were arranged to minimise the structural alterations required. These conversions were considered very successful and two more ships were converted in the mid-war period before it was decided that the modernisation of old ships was a waste of resources. The *Caledon* and *Colombo* were converted during 1942-3 along similar lines to the *Cairo* except that the main armament was reduced to three twin 4in and the close-range AA armament increased to two twin 40mm and six twin 20mm mountings.

The only other group of older ships to come up for modernisation in the 1930s was the *Hawkins* class. The *Frobisher*, *Vindictive* and *Hawkins* were demilitarised during 1936-7 in accordance with treaty requirements as being in excess of Britain's allowance of ships with guns over 6.1in calibre. However, the fourth ship, *Effingham*, was modified to bring her in line with treaty requirements by reducing the calibre of her main armament from 7.5in to 6in. This was undertaken during 1937-9 when, apart from fitting her with nine single 6in, she was equipped with four twin 4in, two 8-barrel pom-poms, three quad 0.5in, two HACS and an aircraft catapult. In addition the after boilers were removed to provide additional oil fuel stowage and the remainder trunked into a new single, vertical funnel which rather spoilt the appearance of the original but provided a unique and distinctive profile. It was intended to similarly convert the *Hawkins* and *Frobisher* but the war brought these plans to a halt. However, this also removed the treaty restrictions and *Hawkins* had her original 7.5in gun armament restored in 1940. *Frobisher* followed in 1942, having been delayed by lack of dockyard capacity, with only five of her original seven 7.5in mounted but an enhanced AA armament.

As with the AA conversions, work on the improvement of the 'County' class began with the oldest ships of the group – the *Kent* class – and ended on the outbreak of war with only that class and one vessel of the *London* class actually taken in hand. The main features of the reconstruction of the *Kent* class were an increase in the thickness of the armour belt abreast the machinery to 4.5in, the enhancement of the AA armament and the modernisation of the aircraft and fire control equipment. Some of the weight required for these changes was available from the fact that they completed below their design displacement but advantage was also taken of a gentlemen's agreement among the signatories of the limitation treaties that 300 tons could be allowed for natural growth. In addition weights were reduced by removing the torpedo armament, cutting down the quarter-deck and removing obsolete fittings. The refit programme began with *Cumberland* and *Suffolk*, which were reconstructed during 1935-6. They were fitted with an odd mixture of 4in AA mountings – both retained two of their original single 4in but had the other two replaced by new twin mountings in *Cumberland* and singles (of similar design to the twins and easily mistaken for same) in *Suffolk*. The single mountings were replaced by twins in *Cumberland* in 1939 and in *Suffolk* during 1940-1. In addition they mounted two quad pom-poms (actually supplied post-refit), two quad 0.5in, a fixed cross-deck catapult amidships and a double aircraft hangar. The last three ships did not have their quarter-decks cut-down and were fitted with twin 4in mountings and two 8-barrel pom-poms. In other respects they were refitted much the same as the earlier pair except that *Kent* was not equipped with a cross-deck catapult or hangar, although she was fitted with a new catapult arrangement.

Plans for the *London* class were much more extensive and represented a cruiser equivalent of the capital ship reconstructions of the mid-1930s but without the machinery upgrade. The basic changes followed the pattern of those of the *Kent* class but with the belt armour abreast the machinery reduced from 4.5in to 3.5in. The major difference was a complete rebuild of the superstructure to modern standards – only the original shelter decks remaining –with the funnel uptakes re-routed into two vertical funnels. The result was a profile very similar to that of the *Fiji* class except for the lack of a forecastle break. Unfortunately the reconstruction was less than satisfactory – the new superstructure, and changes in the deck openings for the uptakes, overloaded what was, despite its depth, a comparatively lightly-built hull. Structural weaknesses first appeared in the upper hull and, once this was strengthened, re-occurred in the lower hull. After several visits to dockyards, involving a substantial amount of additional structural weight, these problems had been largely corrected by mid-1943, two years after she had returned to service.

One other old cruiser was to see wartime modernisation – in this case by somewhat unusual means. In 1940 the Admiralty instigated a request to the USA for the installation of a complete US 5in/38 dual purpose armament in a British ship. Not only did the US authorities agree to this, they also offered to fit the entire system themselves – an offer enthusiastically accepted given the difficulties of dealing with equipment with which the British were not familiar. As a result the cruiser *Delhi* was refitted and rearmed at New York Navy Yard between May and December 1941 and emerged with five single 5in turrets, a US Mk37 director, two quad pom-poms, six single Oerlikons and a new bridge. The result was highly successful but the increasing pressures on resources resulting from the USA's entry into the war halted future plans for similar conversions. Later, the USA did supply the Mk37 system for the battleship *Vanguard* and the 1943 Programme 'Battle' class destroyers but these were fitted in Britain and employed British radar systems. These ships competed too late to take part in the war so *Delhi* remained the only RN ship to carry this very advanced HA/LA fire control system during the war. The Mk37 equipment seriously outclassed the British HACS and was one of the many signs of the coming ascendancy of the US Navy over that of Britain.

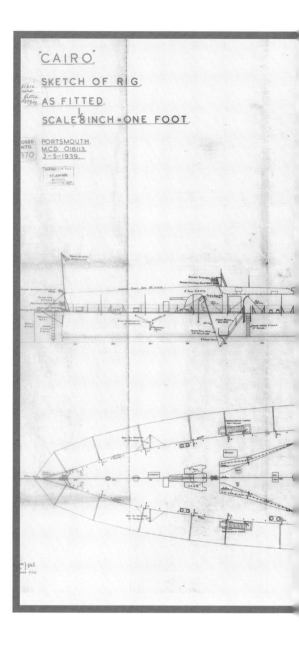

Cairo

Displacement:	4290 tons standard, 5215 tons deep
Dimensions:	425ft (pp), 451ft 6in (oa) x 43ft 6in x 14ft 3in (mean)
Armament:	1939 – Eight 4in MkXVI HA/LA (4 x 2); four 2pdr (1 x 4); eight 0.5in (2 x 4); six 21in torpedo tubes (2 x 3)
Armour:	Machinery and magazines 3in-2.25in side, 1in deck
Machinery:	Two shaft, Parsons geared turbines, 30,000shp = 28kts; six Yarrow boilers; 935 tons oil fuel
Complement:	400

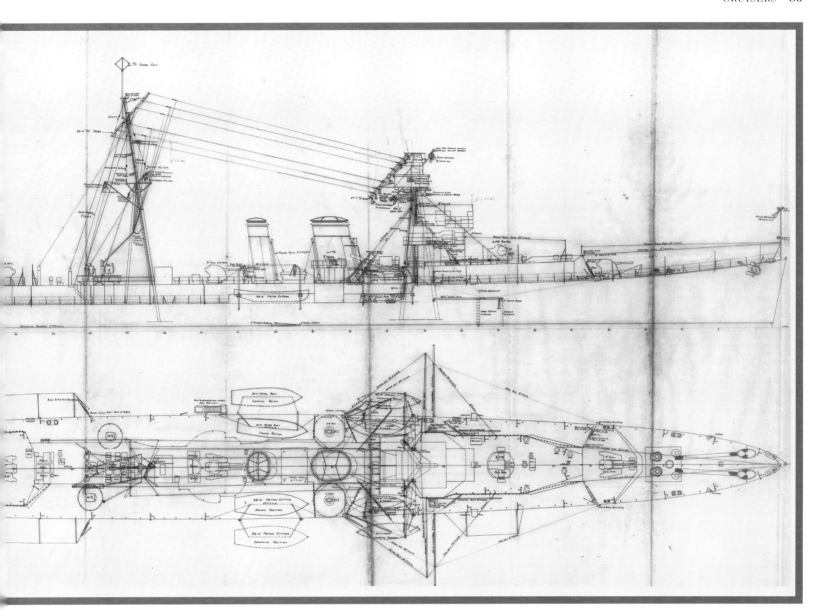

HMS Cairo, *Sketch of rig (as fitted), Portsmouth Dockyard, 3 May 1939.*
Yet another variation on the rig drawing in which, besides the standard rig features, the main W/T aerials have been included. It provides sufficient detail to give a clear idea of the general layout and principal features of Cairo's conversion to an AA cruiser at Chatham during 1938-9. Unlike the earlier 'C' class conversions the main armament is provided by the relatively new twin 4in MkXIX HA/LA mounting rather than the old
single 4in MkV. However, the conversion shows minimal alteration of the original structure to accommodate her new role. The four twin 4in, together with the quad pompom in 'B' position, occupying the same locations and supports as the 6in guns they replaced. Similarly the quad 0.5in MG mountings fitted on raised platforms abreast the fore funnel are immediately above the positions formally occupied by the ship's original 3in AA guns. Other alterations include the removal of the
torpedo tubes and after control and searchlight structure, a new tripod mainmast, two 36in searchlights on platforms abreast the after shelter deck and a new fore top platform for the HACS MkIII director. The conversion of Cairo's *sister ship,* Calcutta, *was almost identical except that the latter ship also had a second HACS director mounted on the after superstructure.*
(Plan No NPA7867, Neg No 621310)

DESTROYERS

Between the end of the First World War and 1924 the Admiralty disposed of all the older destroyers in the Fleet. What remained was just under 200 destroyers and destroyer leaders, the majority of which were of recent design and construction and had proved their utility under war conditions. Of these ships, sixty-four belonged to the 'V' and 'W' class, acknowledged to be one of the finest destroyer designs of their time. This happy situation of having both adequate numbers and first class ships, combined with financial stringency, produced little incentive for new construction and it was not until 1927 that a regular programme of destroyer replacement was initiated. In the meantime the Admiralty decided on the construction of two experimental destroyers, both of which were put out to tender, against a basic set of Staff Requirements, in 1924. The contracts were awarded to the two leading destroyer builders – Thornycroft and Yarrow – and became respectively the *Amazon* and *Ambuscade*, completed in 1926. The Admiralty requirements were

based on the 'W' class destroyer and included the same main armament of four 4.7in guns and two triple 21in torpedo tubes. The main differences were in the adoption of more modern machinery, including superheaters for the boilers, the use of 'D' steel for the hull structure to save weight, and the provision of the latest type of destroyer fire-control gear. The builders took advantage of light construction and improved machinery to give a very high designed speed of 37kts – which both ships exceeded on trial. Thornycroft produced the larger ship at 1350 tons, the extra weight going into machinery power, while Yarrow aimed at reduced weight (partly by adopting an aluminium alloy bridge structure) and higher boiler pressures to keep the displacement down to 1170 tons. With a more conservative speed the *Amazon* provided the basis for the next generation of Admiralty designed destroyers. Unfortunately, the excellence of the 'V' and 'W' design led to complacence and it was some years before any real advance on the basic design was

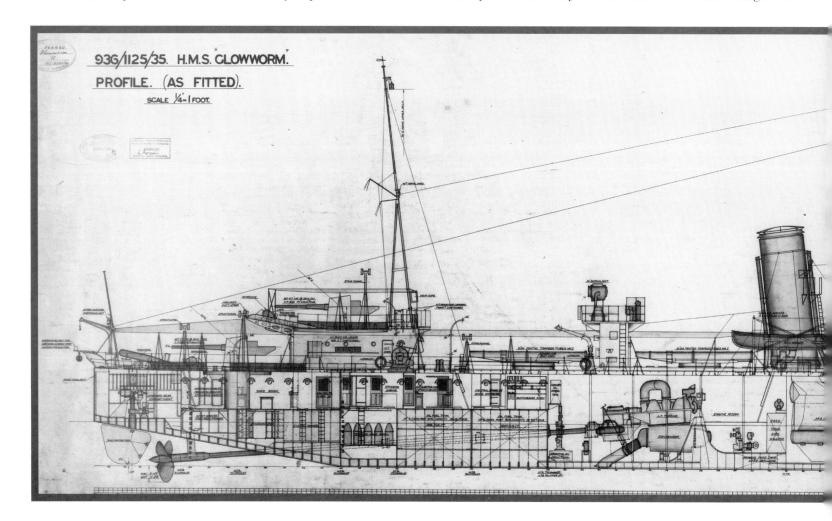

936/1125/35. H.M.S. "GLOWWORM".
PROFILE. (AS FITTED).
SCALE ¼=1 FOOT.

HMS Glowworm, *Profile (as fitted), John I Thornycroft, Southampton, 20 February 1936. The* Glowworm *gained fame for the dramatic nature of her loss in action with the German heavy cruiser* Admiral Hipper *off Norway in April 1940. She has the classic profile of a British destroyer introduced with the 'V' and 'W' classes in the First World War which lasted until the 'I' class of the 1935 Programme. The internal layout is also common to virtually all destroyer types with the machinery taking up the entire centre section of the hull, while moving fore and aft from these spaces the hold is taken up with oil fuel tanks, magazines/shell rooms and then stores with the steering gear compartment at the extreme after end. The*

enclosed decks above are almost entirely turned over to accommodation – crew forward, officers aft. The principle exception to the latter is the area of the upper deck immediately under the bridge which contained the transmitting station and main W/T and fire control office. Some points of interest include the petrol tank (fuel for boats) in the second hold compartment from forward, the Asdic dome (shown in its extended position below the keel and directly under the muzzle of 'A' gun) and the torpedo head magazine between the after fuel tank and after 4.7in shell room. The small rectangle at the top left of the forward oil fuel tanks is the diesel oil tank for the ship's generators; the insulated (thick walled) space between the

Asdic dome and forward 4.7in magazine is the refrigerating compartment; and the ellipses in each of the boiler rooms are the ventilation fans for those compartments with trunking to the intakes on the upper deck (forecastle deck for 'A' boiler room). The engine room is an undivided single compartment (the vertical lines within it are pillars supporting the deck above) while each boiler has its own compartment. Note that, in common with all as-fitted profiles, watertight bulkheads are indicated by the letters WTB (or OTB if oil-tight) immediately below the keel and although these may not be readable in these reproductions their positions should be discernible.

(Plan No NPB2870, Neg No 564460)

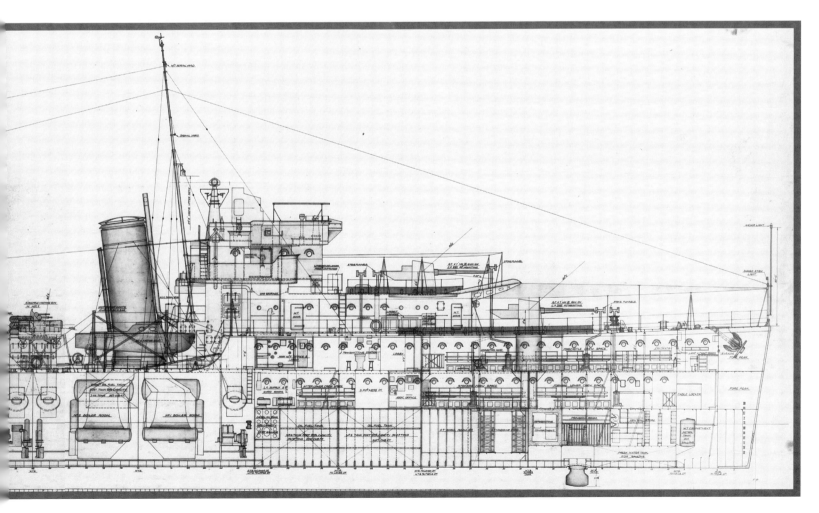

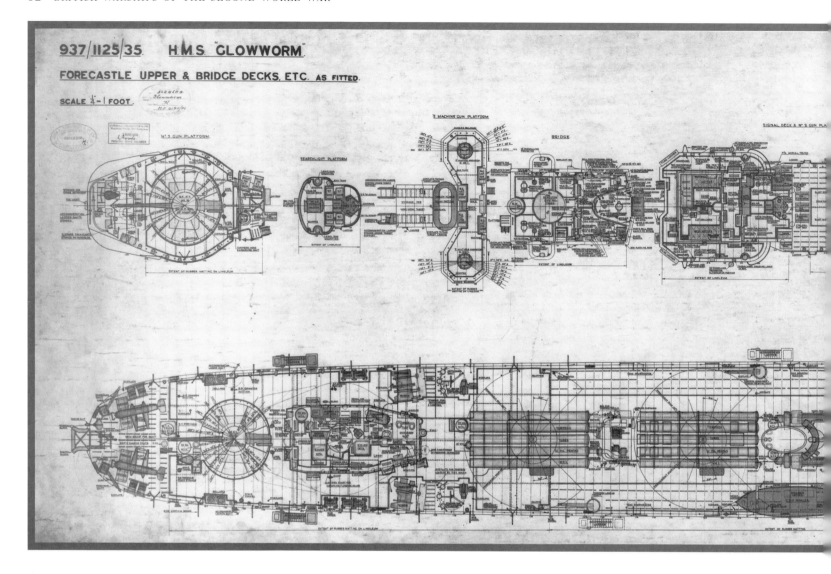

HMS Glowworm, *Forecastle, upper and bridge decks, etc (as fitted), John I Thornycroft, Southampton, 20 February 1936. These plans conveniently cover all the weather decks and platforms on a single sheet – not always the case as such drawings were often divided between two sheets. The most outstanding features in this view are the Glowworm's* two quintuple MkI 21in torpedo tube mountings. These were prototype fittings for the mountings later adopted in the 'H' and 'I' classes and she was the only ship of the 'G' class to carry them. The thick lines on the decks (most noticeable as circles surrounding the 4.7in guns) are the edge strips to the non-slip deck covering (various rubber compositions were employed for this purpose). The areas subject to heavier treatment – mainly those around the anchor gear on the forecastle, the TSDS and depth charge equipment on the quarterdeck and along each side from the forecastle break to the TSDS winches abreast the fore end of the after superstructure – were bare steel with anti-slip provided by short metal strips. The ship's boats are two 27ft whalers, one 25ft motor boat and a 16ft dinghy (the latter stowed under the port whaler) which was the standard outfit for the 'A' to 'I' group destroyers. Note that apart from the 4.7in guns and torpedo tubes the only armament carried is two quad 0.5in mountings on the platform over the boiler room vents between the funnels, a depth charge chute on the centre line at the stern and two depth charge throwers – one on each side just forward of the TSDS winches. The main director tower on the bridge, with a separate 9ft rangefinder abaft it (an arrangement introduced in the 'C' class) were linked to an AFCC MkI in the transmitting station which covered low angle fire for the 4.7in guns but provided no AA function. The guns could, however elevate to 40° where they had a very limited capability in barrage fire.

(Plan No NPB2871, Neg No 564460a)

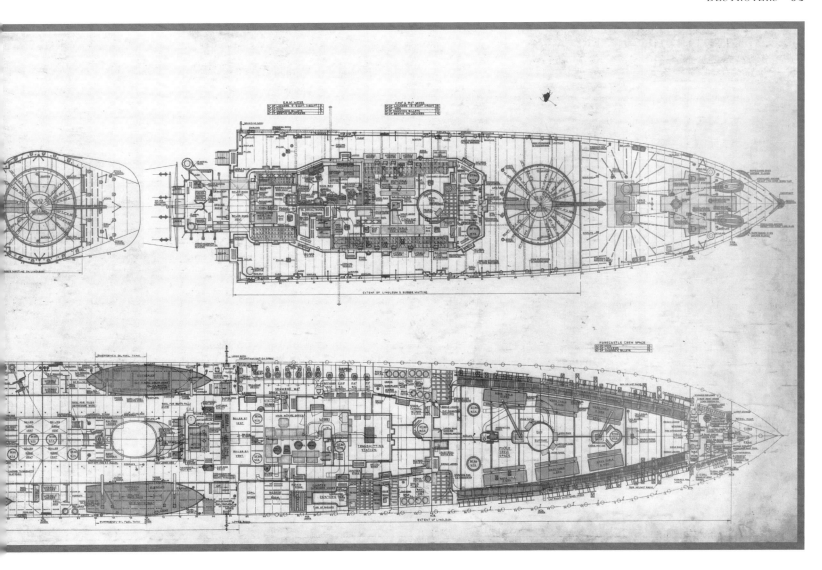

Glowworm

Displacement:	1350 tons standard, 1877 tons deep
Dimensions:	312ft (pp), 323ft (oa) x 33ft x 8ft 6in (mean)
Armament:	Four 4.7in MkIX* (4 x 1); eight 0.5in (2 x 4); ten 21in torpedo tubes (2 x 5); one DC rail, 20 DC, TSDS
Machinery:	Two shaft, Parsons geared turbines, 34,000shp = 35.5kts; three Admiralty 3-drum boilers; 450 tons oil fuel; range 5300nm at 15kts
Complement:	147

actually contemplated. In the meantime, between 1930 and 1937, some sixty-eight ships, of the 'A' to 'I' classes, whose essential design was an evolution of the 'V' and 'W' type, were completed for the Royal Navy.[27]

The 'A' to 'I' classes

A yearly programme of eight destroyers and one leader was maintained from the 1927-8 to the 1935-6 Estimates with the exception of 1929-30 ('C' class) when the number of destroyers was reduced to four as an economy measure. Each year's flotilla was named in alphabetical sequence (except for the leader) starting with the design of the *Acasta* or 'A' class in 1927 and ending with the *Intrepid* or 'I' class in 1935. All the destroyers were of generally similar size and appearance. The principal gun armament remained, as in the earlier ships, four single 4.7in guns but quadruple 21in torpedo tubes were introduced to replace the triple mountings. This was subsequently uprated further with the introduction of the quintuple tube, the prototypes of which were fitted in *Glowworm*, of the 'G'

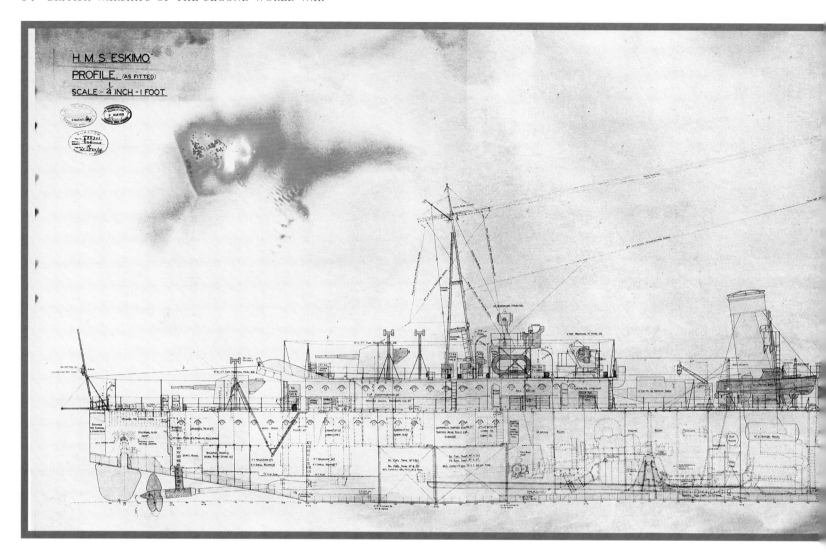

H.M.S. 'ESKIMO'
PROFILE. (AS FITTED)
SCALE - ¼ INCH - I FOOT

class, prior to being fully introduced in the 'I' flotilla. The enhanced torpedo armament emphasised their role as 'fleet' destroyers – designed principally for torpedo attack and fleet screening duties against both destroyer and submarine attack. The leader of the 'A' class, *Codrington*, was larger than her charges (necessitating more powerful machinery) to accommodate Captain (D) and his staff and mounted a fifth 4.7in gun amidships. However, in the next three flotillas the leader was limited to the same dimensions as the destroyers and the fifth mounting was dropped, the only differences being a slight increase in displacement and accommodation. A return was made to the larger leader with the fifth 4.7in gun reinstated from the 'E' class onward.

The 'A', 'C', 'F', 'G' and 'I' classes were fitted for minesweeping, with the primary function of clearing a path at high speed ahead of the main fleet. The equipment for this purpose was known as the 'two speed destroyer sweep' or TSDS and could be used at 20kts (25kts in an emergency) for fleet work or at 12kts for standard mine clearance.[28] All ships were fitted with Asdic and depth charge throwers and racks but the fitting of TSDS required a reduction of the depth charge equipment for reasons of space. In addition the 'E' class were designed to serve as minelayers, although only the *Esk*

and *Express* were so fitted (to compensate for the added topweight when mines were carried it was necessary to land two of the 4.7in guns and the torpedo tubes).

The principal armament shortcoming of these ships was weak AA defence. Although some thought was initially given to providing a 4.7in mounting with 60° elevation, and prototypes were tried, the difficulties of hand-loading what was a relatively simple mounting at this sort of angle brought the project to a premature close. Consequently the mountings provided had only 30° elevation until the 'E' class when 40° was made possible by the somewhat impractical expedient of placing a 'well' around the base of the mounting.[29] The 'H' class introduced another new mounting that provided 40° elevation without the need of a well but since none of these ships were equipped with an AA control system their value for air defence was negligible. The AA armament was, therefore, initially restricted to two single 2pdr pom-poms and four Lewis guns but in the 'C' and 'D' classes this was enhanced with a single 3in AA gun. From the 'E' class onward the 3in and pom-pom were dropped in favour of two quad 0.5in mountings – a poor substitute as, although these guns had a high rate of fire, they employed solid bullets and lacked hitting power and accuracy.

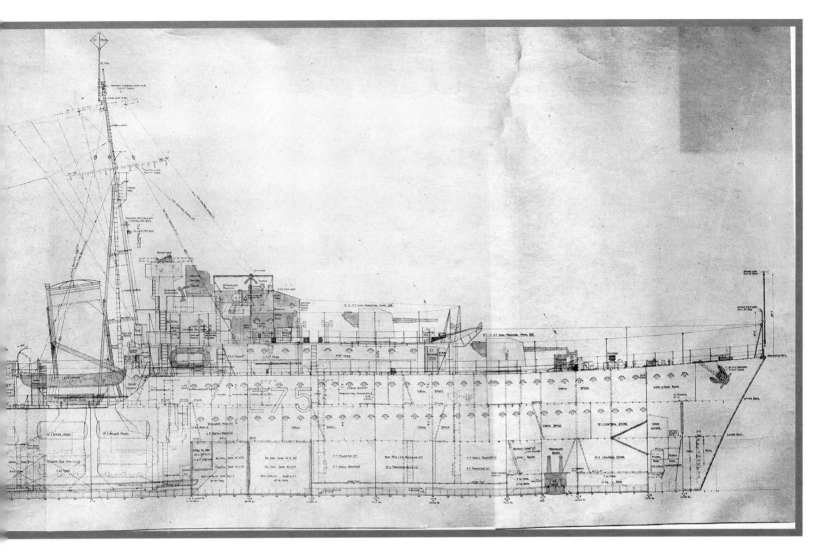

HMS Eskimo, *Profile (as fitted), Vickers Armstrongs, Newcastle, 9 March 1939. The* Eskimo *was one of only four of the original sixteen 'Tribal' class destroyers to survive the Second World War. The steeply raked stem and larger fore funnel gives her a markedly more streamlined profile than that for* Glowworm *but a close examination reveals little major difference in the basic layout of these two ships. In fact the original design which had a stem design of the older type showed a profile similar to an enlarged version of the 'I' class. Noticeable in this drawing is the lack of internal detail but this in turn makes what is present easier to see. The guns in this class were supplied with shells by two dredger hoists per mounting which ran vertically from the shell room to the* deck below the guns except for 'Y' where the hoist terminated on the upper deck. The shells for 'A', 'B' and 'X' mountings were transferred from the tops of the hoists to the gun deck via hand-operated sliding chutes which ran diagonally between the two decks. The shell cartridges were sent up separately by the more traditional method of passing them up by hand. The shell hoists can be seen in the profile as tubes running upward from the shell rooms in the hold. The only other fittings shown internally are the main machinery, steering gear, Asdic dome, the forward petrol tank, the ladders and a few cabin doors. The 'V' shape projecting diagonally sideways from the lower deck to the rear of the foremost (collision) bulkhead is a pair of permanent wooden shores provided to improve the strength of the structure in the event of damage forward. Unusually, this profile gives some detail of the rig and includes the W/T aerials, navigation lights and both standing and running rigging. The 'H' topped funnels projecting above deck are stove pipes from the coal-fired stoves provided for heating on the mess decks and officers' accommodation (they can also be seen, complete with stoves, in the drawings of *Glowworm*). These fittings together with other projections above the deck, including the awning stanchions and some of the guardrails were removed and stowed when the ship was at action stations – partly to clear arcs of fire and partly to avoid them being damaged by gun blast.
(Neg No 622301)

The initial steps toward enhancing machinery power by the adoption of boiler superheaters was taken a stage further with an experimental high pressure (500psi), high temperature (750° F) machinery installation in the 'A' class destroyer *Acheron*. Unfortunately, this advanced arrangement proved troublesome and unreliable in service and tainted the Admiralty's interest to such an extent that the future development of main machinery fell well behind that of other navies. The standard boiler pressure was to remain 300psi until 1942, while boiler temperatures were conservatively raised from 600 to 630° F during the same period. The machinery installed was reliable and did perform satisfactorily but was comparatively heavy. The loss from the failure to invest in advanced machinery technology was thus not so much a reduction in performance as in the overall balance of design, where the weight saved could have been used to enhance other features, especially in the treaty-limited ships of the 1930s.

The designed maximum speed of the 'A' to 'I' group in standard condition was 35.5kts with slight variations in the installed power to accommodate the variations in displacement of the different classes. Although, this speed may seem moderate compared with those achieved in foreign destroyers, it is worth remembering that extreme speeds attained on trial were substantially diminished in actual service and under different conditions of weight (the design speed of the 'A' to 'I' group at deep displacement was 4kts less than in standard condition). The ideal conditions of light displacement, smooth water, clean bottom and ideally running machinery at best only served to provide comparative and design data. The loss in speed under real conditions was, moreover, generally greater for extreme speeds.

In the 'A' to 'D' flotillas the boilers were fitted in two compart-ments, with the single boiler room forward of the double, while the later flotillas had each boiler in its own room in order to improve water-tight subdivision. With the 'G' class the omission of cruising turbines and other machinery modifications allowed for a reduction in the length of machinery spaces and this in turn, combined with other design changes, allowed for a general reduction in the size of the ships.

The 'Tribals'

While Britain was busy building standard fleet destroyers, foreign nations had embarked on much more exotic forms of the type, which seriously outclassed their Royal Navy rivals. Between 1922 and 1932 France laid down twenty-six light and thirty heavy destroyers. The former were roughly equal to the Royal Navy's 'A' to 'I' group but the latter were much larger ships which grew from the 2100-tonne, 35kt *Chacal* class of 1922 (five 5.1in, six torpedo tubes)

Eskimo

Displacement:	1950 tons standard, 2530 tons deep
Dimensions:	355ft 6in (pp), 377ft (oa) x 36ft 6in x 11ft 3in (mean)
Armament:	Eight 4.7in MkXII (4 x 2); four 2pdr (1 x 4); eight 0.5in (2 x 4); four 21in torpedo tubes (1 x 4); four DCT, one DC rail, 30 DC
Machinery:	Two shaft, Parsons geared turbines, 44,000shp = 36kts; three Admiralty 3-drum boilers; 525 tons oil fuel; range 5200nm at 15kts
Complement:	233

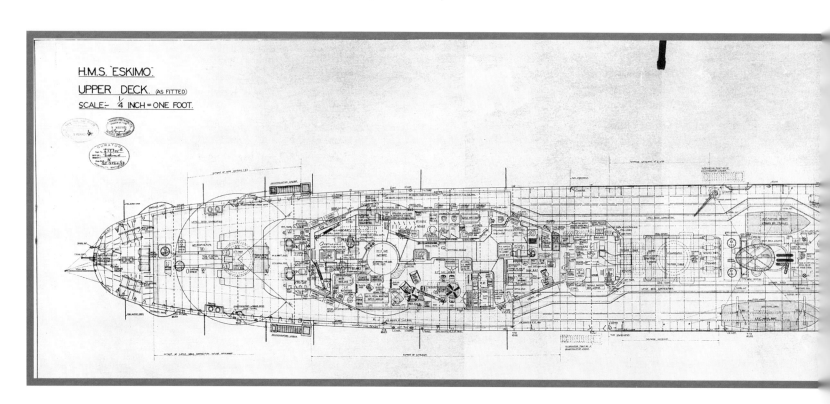

H.M.S. "ESKIMO".
UPPER DECK. (AS FITTED)
SCALE:- ¼ INCH = ONE FOOT.

to the 2610-tonne, 37kt *Le Fantasque* class of 1931 (five 5.5in, nine torpedo tubes). These ships prompted replies from Italy in the shape of the small light cruisers of the 'Condottieri' type and the 1900-ton, 38kt destroyers of the 'Navigatori' class (six 4.7in, six torpedo tubes). In the meantime, on the other side of the world, the Japanese had laid down during 1926-30 twenty-four 1750-ton, 38kt destroyers of the *Fubuki* and *Akutsuki* classes (six 5in, nine torpedo tubes).[30] As there was no longer any serious rivalry with France, her ships did not present a problem, but those of Japan, and to a lesser extent Italy, were seen as a serious threat which could not be ignored. This problem was, moreover, increased when Germany recommenced destroyer construction in 1934 with 38kt ships of over 2000 tons displacement, armed with five 5in guns and eight torpedo tubes.

Discussions on strengthening the British destroyer flotillas began in 1934 with the general aim of providing an increase in the num-bers of ships in the general area of light cruiser/large leader categories. The primary aims were:

1) To increase the number of vessels capable of fleet cruiser functions.
2) To relieve standard destroyers of cruiser duties.
3) To provide gun support to the destroyer flotillas.

Discussions evolved around designs, which ranged from several 6in gun light cruisers varying from 4500 to 5500 tons (which ultimately led to the design of the *Dido* class) to a large destroyer designated 'V' Leader. There was also a 3500-ton, 38kt unprotected small cruiser armed with five single 6in but such a vessel would have eaten into the available cruiser tonnage. It was also considered too large a target for an unprotected ship and there were doubts about whether its 6in gun could be operated efficiently in a

HMS Eskimo, *Upper deck (as fitted), Vickers Armstrongs, Newcastle, 9 March 1939. The larger size of these ships is reflected in a slightly larger boat complement when compared with* Glowworm. *A 25ft motor boat to port of the fore funnel, and a 27ft whaler (with 14ft dinghy under) to starboard, and a 16ft planning dinghy (on a trolley) to port of the after funnel with a second 25ft motor boat to starboard. The reduced torpedo armament is seen in the single quadruple 21in tube mounting MkIX between the after* funnel and after superstructure. At the extreme stern, on the centre line, is a triple depth charge rail and forward of that is a group of three racks for the stowage of three depth charges each. The areas of deck covered by rubber composition are indicated by shaded edges to their boundaries and are most obvious in the two pathways that run down each side amidships. The main fire control centre is located, as in Glowworm, on the middle line immediately below the bridge – the forward compartment being the transmitting station and that abaft it the main W/T and fire control office. These two areas are shown in reasonable detail and in the former the locations of the main fire control gear are indicated, including the AFCC MkI for low angle fire and the FKC MkII for AA fire. The many circular objects scattered about the deck are mostly hatches, this being the standard form in destroyers rather then the rectangular type employed in larger ships.
(Neg No 622301a)

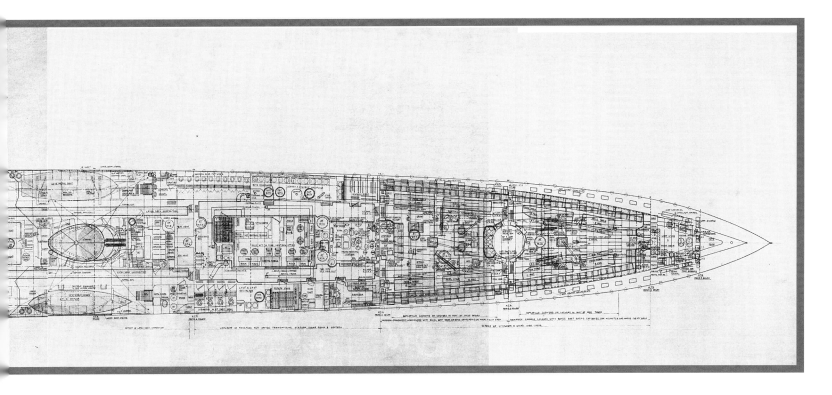

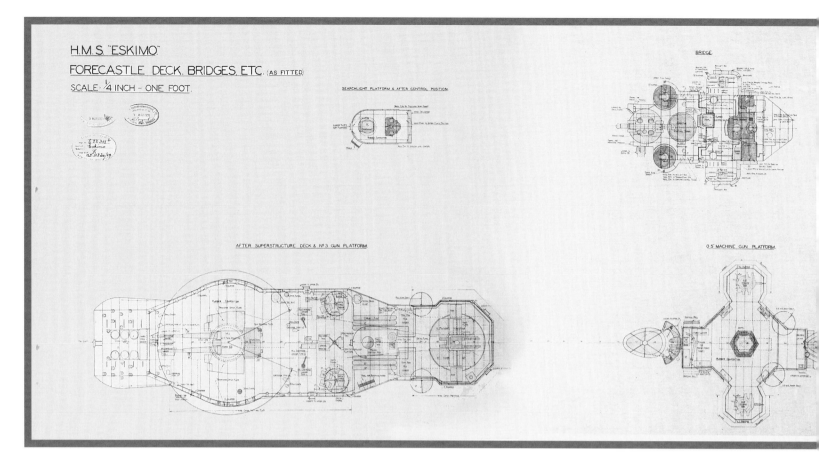

HMS Eskimo, *Forecastle deck, bridges, etc (as fitted), Vickers Armstrongs, Newcastle, 9 March 1939. The 'Tribal' class represented the first British attempt at providing destroyers with a reasonable AA capability which, apart from providing a HA fire control system for the main armament, included the addition of a quad pom-pom mounting located at the fore end of the after superstructure. The original intention was to provide two such mountings, the second being positioned on the platform between the funnels. The latter was replaced by two quad 0.5in machine gun mountings on extensions to the original platform during construction. The base for the pom-pom was, however, retained (covered in the drawing by a hexagonal wooden seat located centrally between the 0.5in mounts) so presumably there was an intention to fit these when sufficient numbers became available – in the event no ship of the class was so fitted. The fire control gear on the bridge included the standard surface fire DCT but the position abaft it accommodated a rangefinder director MkII. This last served simply as a rangefinder for surface action and followed the motions of the main DCT but operated as an independent AA director when the ship engaged aerial targets with her 4.7in guns. No director was provided for the pom-pom which operated under local control. The darker areas on the bridge, around the compass platform and the searchlight controls at the after corners, indicate areas with wood gratings. Note that the ship's two depth charge throwers are located on the after superstructure abreast the mainmast, one deck higher than usual. (Neg No 622301b)*

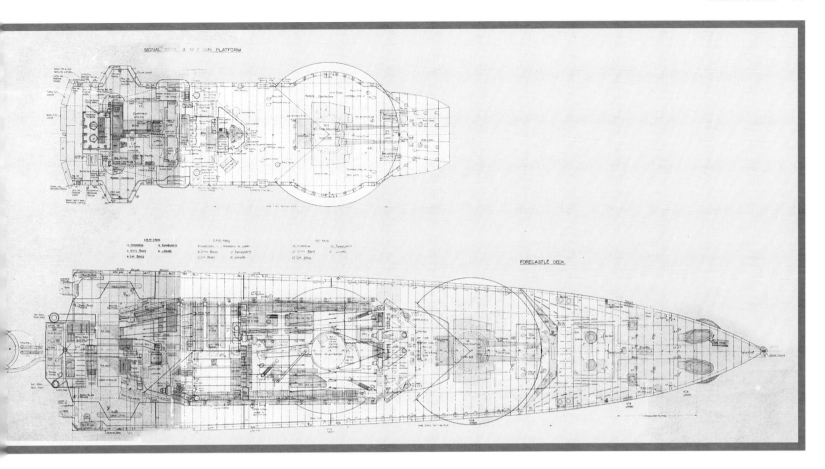

seaway. On the other hand the 'V' Leader with ten 4.7in had the advantage of possessing more faster-firing guns and could be built in greater numbers as it could be included in Britain's total destroyer tonnage. However, although 2000 tons was considered the ideal displacement for this type, to fit into the destroyer category displacement could not exceed the treaty limit of 1850 tons.

Opinion in the Admiralty and in the Fleet was divided on the relative merits of the two types but by the end of 1934 the Board had decided in favour of the 'V' leader. Staff Requirements anticipated a wide range of duties which related more to cruiser than destroyer functions, indicating their special status as cruiser substitutes rather than simple destroyer leaders – patrols, shadowing, reconnaissance, close support of destroyer flotillas, escort duties and AA defence. The last named was added to the ship's functions as a result of demands from sea officers for improvements in fleet AA defence. The new twin 4.7in mounting with which the ships were to be fitted was still only capable of 40° elevation but, unlike the 'A' to 'I' group, it was to be supported by a HA control system. It was optimistically anticipated that this would strengthen the fleet's barrage fire against high level and torpedo bombers. It *was* realised that existing systems of AA defence from a small ship were unlikely to be accurate without some form of stabilisation but there was expectation of a capability in breaking-up attacking formations, even though the time of firing against even slow bombers was very short. Debate on air defence also led to a reduction in the proposed armament from ten to eight 4.7in, the midships twin mounting

being replaced by a second quad 2pdr pom-pom mounting. This enhancement of the close-range AA was primarily for self defence, particularly against dive bombers. In the completed ships the second pom-pom was not fitted – probably due to the ships being above their designed weight but there was also a shortage of mountings. The final design, approved at the end of 1935, also included two quad 0.5in mountings but only one quad torpedo tube – a reflection of their intended role as gun support vessels. Nevertheless, there was some criticism that this would compromise any opportunities the ships might have in torpedo attacks despite the fact that additional tubes could only have been provided at the expense of the gun armament.

The 16 per cent of total destroyer tonnage that could be employed for the 1850-ton type allowed, according to Admiralty calculations, for the construction of fourteen such vessels. Seven were therefore provided for each of the programme years 1935 and 1936. In the event the 1936 group was increased to nine ships to provide a total of sixteen, as a result of the tonnage limitation being dropped from the 1936 Treaty. All were laid down in the space of six months, between June 1936 and January 1937, and completed during 1938-9. The 'V' Leaders became the 'Tribal' class, initially designated as 'Tribals' in recognition of their special status but ultimately classified simply as destroyers. They were fast ships, averaging 36.9kts on trial, of handsome appearance and saw considerable front-line service in the early years of the war. They suffered a very high loss rate like most of the immediate pre-war destroyers – a total of twelve ships, of which half were sunk by aircraft. A further eleven 'Tribals' were constructed during the war, three for the Royal Australian Navy and eight for the Royal Canadian Navy.

The last of the pre-war flotillas

The 'Tribals' were followed by a return to more moderate dimensions with the design of the 'J' class of the 1937 Programme. The design of these ships was, in part, the result of reaction against both the size and limited torpedo armament of the 'Tribals' and almost all the aspects of their design were subject to controversy in one form or another. Nevertheless, the design finally decided upon proved both successful and popular and provided the basis for the majority of Britain's wartime destroyer construction. In essence they were reduced editions of the 'Tribal' class with weight saved by adopting two boilers instead of three (an arrangement that the E-in-C strongly objected to) and omitting the aftermost twin 4.7in mounting. As an added benefit the clear quarterdeck had the advantage of providing additional space for the depth charge armament and TSDS. The torpedo armament was upgraded to two banks of quintuple tubes but despite this obvious emphasis on battlefleet surface actions they were still expected to fulfil the fleet AA defence role required of the 'Tribal' class. In this latter respect the close-range AA was equal to that in the 'Tribals' and they only differed in the 25 per cent reduction in main armament for long-range barrage fire.

A primary innovation in the design of the 'J' class was the employment of longitudinal framing for the hull structure, an arrangement that improved on longitudinal hull strength without added weight. This mode of construction became standard in all subsequent British destroyers despite resistance to the change from commercial shipyards. The 'Js' displaced 1690 tons standard as designed but actually came out heavier by about 70 tons. Nevertheless, they still proved capable of exceeding their designed speed of 36kts at standard displacement. The boilers, arranged in two compartments, fed a single funnel – an arrangement not seen in a British destroyer since the 1890s. The earlier practice of building a separate leader was abandoned in the 'J' class, a few of which were fitted-out with additional accommodation and communication gear to serve as leaders. The design was repeated in the 'K' class of the 1937 Programme and the 'N' class of the 1939 Programme. All the ships of the 'J' and 'K' Flotillas entered service in 1939 but several of the 'N' flotilla were delayed by war production problems and the completion of this flotilla was spread over the period 1940-2.

A design variation on, and contemporary with, the 'J', 'K' and 'N' classes, the 'L' and 'M' classes of the 1937 and 1939 Programmes respectively reverted to larger dimensions to accommodate an HA/LA main armament and an enhancement of design speed to 37kts. The armament change represented the next stage in the attempted development of a satisfactory dual-purpose gun mounting but the result was compromised by a combination of conflicting opinions and production/design difficulties. The elevation desired was 70° but this was impossible without full power-ramming and this, combined with the additional clearance required for recoil, would have made the mounting both complex and heavy. The requirement was therefore reduced to 50°, which allowed for the loading of a new 62lb shell by hand with mechanical assistance.[31] While this was an improvement on the existing 40° elevation, it was hardly sufficient to provide destroyers with a truly capable AA defence. The complex twin mounting was provided with a fully-enclosed weatherproof gunhouse and the guns, unlike those of the 'Tribals' and 'Js', could be elevated independently. They were controlled from a new HA/LA director, which was also heavy and complex, and, while giving acceptable surface fire characteristics, lacked the full stabilisation required for effective AA control. The additional top-weight of the gun armament was partially compensated by a reversion to quadruple torpedo tubes but it was necessary to increase design standard displacement to 1920 tons, 210 tons above that of the 'Js', to accommodate the added weight of guns, ammunition, fire control gear and machinery. The latter was increased in power from 40,000 to 48,000shp which, besides giving the above-mentioned increase in speed, provided the power required for the larger hull.

The 'L' flotilla was laid down in 1938 and completed during 1940-2. As with most pre-war programme vessels under construction at the beginning of the war, they were subject to serious delay by a shortfall in the supply of their armament. Four of the class, *Lance*, *Larne*, *Legion* and *Lively*, were completed with an extemporised armament of eight 4in in four twin mountings which, while reducing their surface action capability, markedly enhanced their value in AA defence. The 'M' flotilla was laid down during 1939-40 and completed during 1941-2 with the original armament in all ships.[32]

The emergency war flotillas

The realisation that war with Germany was fast approaching and that the difficulties of the armament industry would limit the production of destroyers in the numbers required led, during 1938-9, to consideration of simpler designs. These included a type which represented a reversion to the comparatively simple general characteristics of the 'A' to 'I' type. The intention was to mount much the same armament as in the earlier ships except that the single 4.7in mountings were to have 62lb shells and the close-range AA was to be enhanced by the fitting of a quadruple pom-pom mounting. They were intended for general fleet duties, patrol and escort work and as replacements for the ageing 'V' and 'W' class destroyers that remained from the First World War. After the outbreak of war the proposed design was modified to accelerate construction by reverting to the 4.7in gun mountings of the 'I' class with their 50lb shells and utilising the machinery design of the 'J' class. Both these were aimed at employing existing designs for which patterns and production experience were already available but even this proved to be a problem in the first two flotillas to be built. The design of these 36kt, 1570-ton vessels provided the basis of fourteen 'Emergency War Flotillas' – a total of 112 ships – the first of which was laid down in December 1939 and the last of which completed in April 1947. All but twenty-two were completed before the end of the war. Although of generally similar design a fair degree of evolution took place reflecting production needs, war experience and the introduction of new equipment. The general development of the group was as follows:

'O' class: Original 'intermediate' design. Four of class (*Opportune, Orwell, Obdurate* and *Obedient*) were modified while under construction for rapid conversion to minelayers and main gun armament reduced to four 4in (if equipped with mines 'Y' gun and the torpedo tubes were landed). Three of the four units with 4.7in guns (*Oribi, Offa* and *Onslaught*) were completed with a 4in HA gun in place of after torpedo tube mounting.

'P' class: Design modified for four single 4in HA before completion.[35] All except *Petard* and *Pathfinder* completed with a fifth 4in HA gun in place of the after bank of torpedo tubes.

'Q' and 'R' classes: To provide greater hull volume for wartime additions and reduce the amount of work involved in providing new drawings and moulds for hull construction these and later emergency destroyers adopted the hull design of the 'J' class. As the latter ships had four guns forward rather than two, the additional space made available by the reduction in magazine volume was utilised for additional fuel oil giving a 25 per cent increase in endurance. Displacement increased to 1700 tons.

'S' to 'W' classes: The 'S' class introduced a new 55°, 4.7in mounting and the quad pom-pom was replaced by the fully stabilised twin 40mm Hazemeyer mounting. In addition the form of the bow was changed to that of the 'Tribal' class on the basis that this gave better seakeeping qualities than that of the 'J' class.

'Z' and 'Ca' classes: Introduced improved fire control arrangements with a new design of interim 'Type K' HA/LA director based on that fitted earlier in the 'L' and 'M' classes. The calibre of the main armament was reduced to 4.5in in this class in line with an Admiralty policy to standardise on this weapon. In general the new mounting was of the same design as the 55°, 4.7in of the 'S' class.

'Ch', 'Co' and 'Cr' classes: Provided with new production MkVI HA/LA director and remote power control for the 4.5in mountings. The increased topweight of this weapon fit required the omission of the forward set of torpedo tubes and reductions in the anti-submarine armament in compensation. In several ships the Hazemeyer mountings were replaced with the simpler 40mm twin MkV.

The most notable evolution in these wartime 'utility' types is the gradual improvement of their AA weapons. The final group were equipped with a reasonably capable AA system and were only limited by the 55° elevation of the 4.5in mountings. However, most of the ships so equipped did not complete in time to take part in the war. The interim HA/LA 'K' director fitted in the 'Z' and 'Ca' classes was not up to the same standard and suffered from unreliability. The close-range armament, initially directed towards replacement of the 2pdr pom-pom and 0.5in MG with 40mm Bofors and 20mm Oerlikons, was eventually aimed at uniform outfits of 40mm – for most ships not achieved until after the war. In addition the ships saw considerable additions in radar, communications and other electronic equipment which, together with the increase in weapons, caused problems with accommodation and the maintenance of stability. Despite their faults, and the fact that they were an interim measure based on pre-war designs, these ships ended up as the backbone of the British destroyer force and gave exceptional service in all roles from convoy escort to fleet action and in all theatres from the Arctic to the Pacific. The second-generation ships that were to outclass them by a substantial margin were, with few exceptions, too late to join the fight.

'Battles' and 'Weapons'

In 1941, with the War Emergency Programme well under way, consideration was given to the production of a more advanced design with the primary aim of improving AA capability. The design finally developed carried two twin 4.5in MkIV mountings capable of 80° elevation – both of which were mounted forward. These were 'between decks' or BD mountings similar in principle to the twin 4.5in fitted in carriers and reconstructed capital ships. The mounting rested on the deck below the gunhouse, thereby providing the space for clearance of the breech and recoil at high angles of elevation without having to raise the trunnions to an excessive height. Ammunition supply, from the deck below via the trunk, and loading was power operated and the mounting was provided with remote power control (RPC). The main fire control was from the new MkVI HA/LA director, which was also adopted in cruisers, battleships and the later war emergency destroyers. The design also provided for a single 4in starshell gun, mounted abaft the funnel, to relieve the main armament of this function. The intended close range armament, a considerable advance on earlier arrangements, consisted of four twin 40mm Hazemeyer mountings (a fully stabilised mounting with RPC and built-in fire control) and six single 20mm. The ships also had the standard outfit of two quad torpedo tubes. The cost of this great increase in the quality of the armament was a design standard displacement of 2330 tons – a 600-ton increase on the war emergency type – and even then the design was squeezed in order to keep the displacement as low as possible. The turbine installation was based on that of the 'L' class, with power increased from 48,000 to 50,000shp, but the larger size meant accepting a 1.25kt reduction in speed. The boiler installation showed the first signs of the introduction of more advanced steam conditions for British warships – compared with the emergency group, pressure rose from 300 to 400psi and temperature from 630 to 700° F.

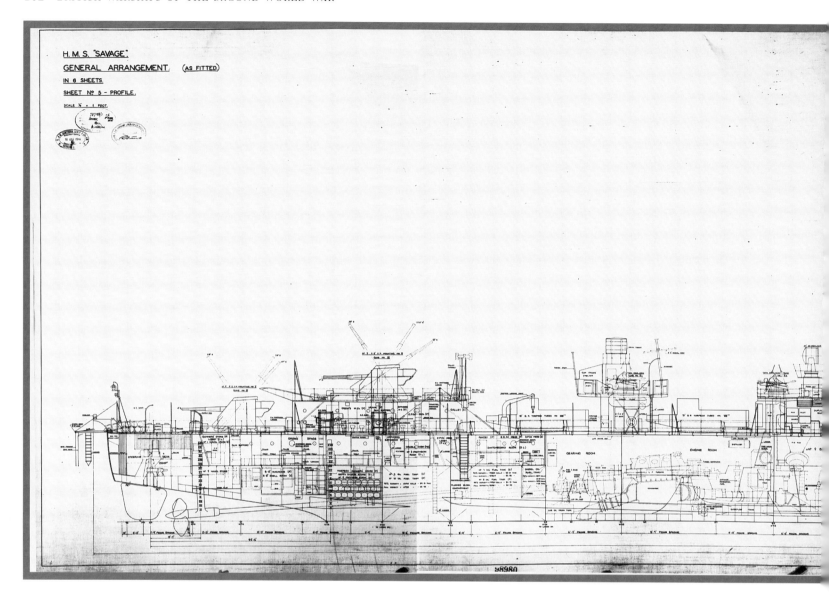

H.M.S. 'SAVAGE'.
GENERAL ARRANGEMENT. (AS FITTED)
IN 6 SHEETS.
SHEET Nº 5 - PROFILE.
SCALE ¼" = 1 FOOT.

HMS Savage, *Profile (as fitted), Hawthorn Leslie, Hebburn on Tyne, 16 October 1944. From the builders of one of the Royal Navy's most famous destroyers – the* Kelly *– this destroyer provides an example of the wartime 'Emergency Construction' which formed the bulk of British war production for the type. The design is something of a mixture with machinery and slightly modified hull form of the 'J' class, the bow form of the 'Tribals' and an updated version of the armament of the 'A' to 'I' group – together with the addition of a wartime outfit of close-range AA weapons and radar. The profile illustrates the major change in the appearance of British destroyers that* occurred with the construction of the 'J' class – the adoption of two boilers in place of three and the consequent provision of a single large funnel. This arrangement lasted until unit machinery distribution was adopted in the design of 'Weapon' and Daring classes towards the end of the war. The Savage *has one feature which sets her apart from her many sisters, in that she carries for trial and test the prototype 'Battle' class twin BD (between decks) 4.5in MkIV in 'A' position rather than two single mountings at 'A' and 'B'. In addition, to keep the gun calibre uniform, the single mountings aft were converted to 4.5in MkV, which were not introduced generally as replacements for the essentially similar* 4.7in single in the 'Emergency Destroyers' until the much later 'Z' class. How the AA fire control problem of having a mounting forward with 80° elevation and two aft with 55° elevation was dealt with is not known. The profile drawing has a simple clarity which is typical of war production 'as fitted' sets. The internal layout, apart from having only two boilers is virtually identical to that of Glowworm – including the specific detail noted in the caption for that ship's profile. The fire control gear is practically the same as that fitted in the 'Tribal' class except that the rangefinder director is a MkIIIW (the 'W' indicating that it has a windshield) and the drawing shows it fitted with the aerials of radar Type 285.

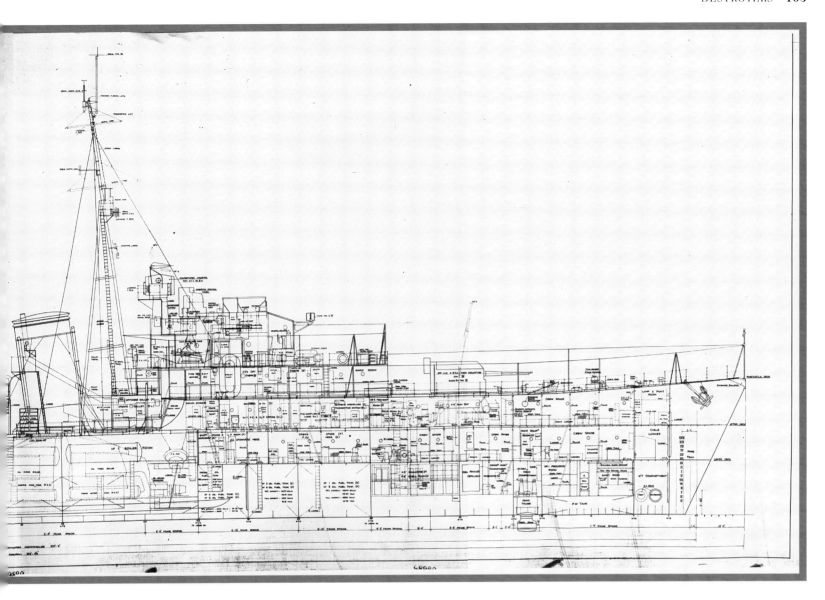

The other radar aerials shown are for Type
291 air warning at the foremast head (on
the aft side, that at the top of the pole on
the fore side is a Type 86 TBS aerial) and
Type 271 surface warning in the lantern on
the raised platform between the torpedo
tubes.

(Plan No NPC1251, Neg No 737158/1)

Savage

Displacement:	1800 tons standard, 2530 tons deep
Dimensions:	339ft 6in (pp), 362ft 9in (oa) x 35ft 8in x 11ft 3in (mean)
Armament:	Two 4.5in MkIV (2 x 1); two 4.5in MkIII (1 x 2); twelve 20mm (6 x 2); eight 21in torpedo tubes (2 x 4); four DCT, one DC rail, 70 DC
Machinery:	Two shaft, Parsons geared turbines, 40,000shp = 36kts; two Admiralty 3-drum boilers; 615 tons oil fuel; range 4680nm at 20kts
Complement:	233

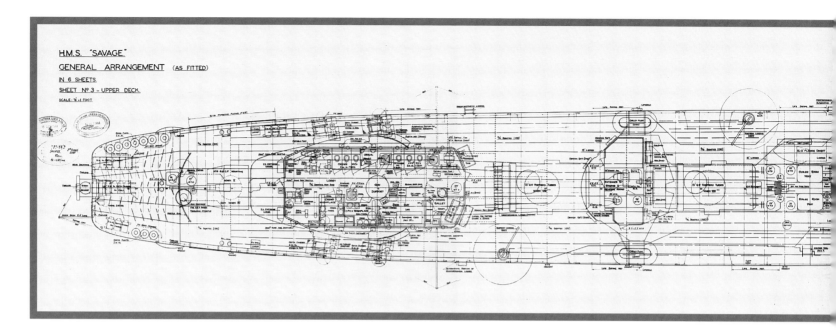

Above: *HMS Savage, Upper deck (as fitted), Hawthorn Leslie, Hebburn on Tyne, 16 October 1944.* Compared to earlier destroyers, there is a noticeable difference in the upper deck profile at the stern resulting from the adoption of a flatter and broader transom. This was introduced with the 'Q' class as it gave a small advantage in speed and endurance but, incidentally, also provided a larger area of upper deck aft. The ship has two sets of depth charge rails, one on the centre line and one offset to port, each holding six charges. In this same area there are three depth charges stowed on the after starboard side and several smoke floats – the circular objects located to port and starboard. There are three more spare depth charges further forward to port and the ship carries the standard outfit of four depth charge throwers mounted abreast the after superstructure. The two sets of quadruple torpedo tubes are MkVIII** mountings. The boat outfit is minimal – a reflection of wartime conditions – with a 27ft whaler and 16ft planing dinghy to port and a 25ft motor cutter to starboard. The area under the forecastle follows the general layout seen in *Eskimo* and the only notable difference is the large space occupied by the lower section of the twin 4.5in gun mounting.
(Plan No NPC1252, Neg No 737158/3)

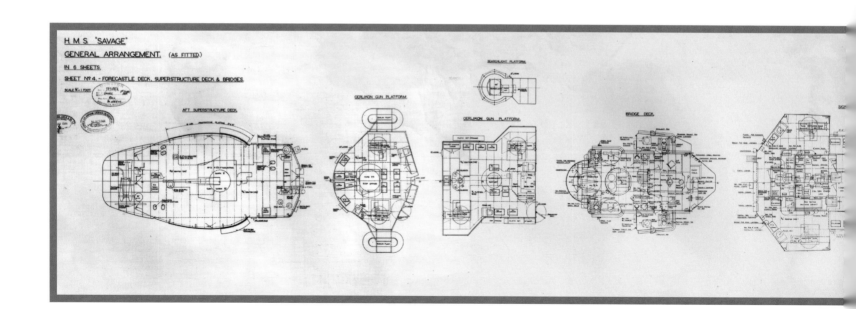

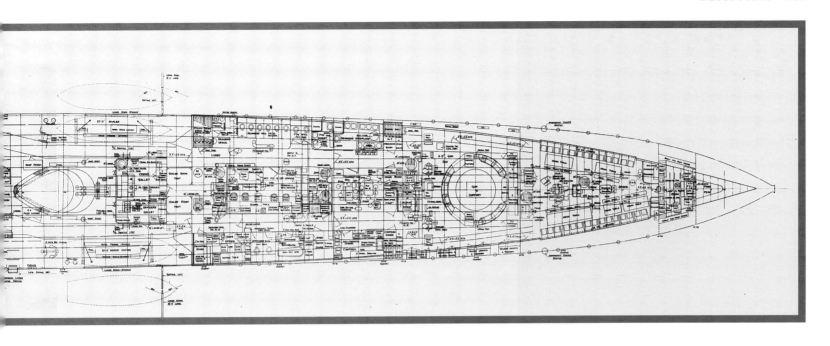

Below: *HMS* Savage, *Forecastle deck, Superstructure deck and bridges (as fitted), Hawthorn Leslie, Hebburn on Tyne, 16 October 1944.* The lines shown on the decks of as fitted drawings indicate the location of the beams, bulkheads and longitudinal girders under the deck. Those shown here on the forecastle deck and on the drawing for the upper deck are worth comparing with those in the Eskimo *and* Glowworm, *those ships being transversely framed while* Savage *is longitudinally framed. Another difference from earlier ships is the accommodation of the wardroom and officers' cabins in the forward superstructure – an arrangement adopted from the 'R' class onward in order to distribute the officers and crew closer to their probable action stations. The mess decks were arranged in the usual forward positions on the upper and lower decks forward but both officers and men were accommodated aft – on the lower deck and in the after superstructure. The ship's entire outfit of close-range AA weapons are located in this plan – six twin 20mm Oerlikon mountings, two mounted in the bridge wings and four on the platforms amidships. (Plan No NPC1256, Neg No 737158/2)*

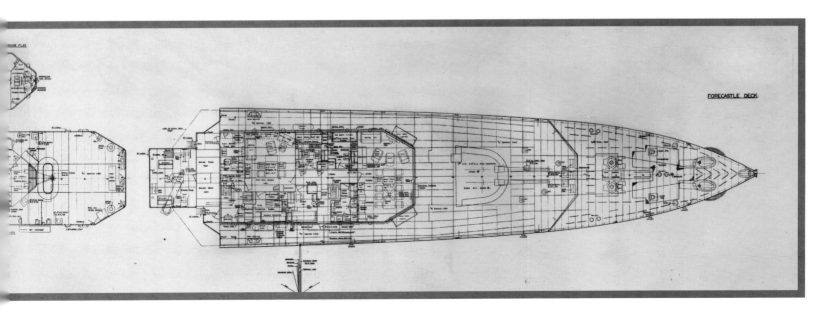

FORECASTLE DECK.

The first ships of the type, the sixteen vessels of the 1942 'Battle' class, were ordered in April 1942 (twelve ships) and March 1943 (four ships) and laid down during 1942-4. There were the usual delays in supply as a result of the relatively sophisticated guns and fire control gear and only five of the ships completed before the end of the war.[34] Thus the struggle to produce a solution to the AA problem which had begun in the mid-1930s came to a moderately satisfactory conclusion too late to have any material effect on the war. The 1943 Programme provided for an additional twenty-four 'Battle' class destroyers but sixteen of these were cancelled after the war. These ships were of slightly modified design with beam increased from 40ft 3in to 40ft 6in to accommodate a further increase in topweight. The torpedo armament was increased from two quad to two quintuple sets of tubes and a fifth 4.5in gun was fitted on a single mounting abaft the funnel. More importantly they were fitted with the US Mk37 fire control system (the British MkVI being subject to serious production problems) – the most advanced dual-purpose fire control system to be produced during the Second World War. The close-range armament was also enhanced in theory with the introduction of the twin 40mm STAAG mounting.

However, this complex equipment proved less than reliable and its great weight limited the number that could be fitted to two. To compensate for the loss a 'war utility' twin 40mm was fitted as well which, because it was simple and reliable, probably had greater value than both STAAG mountings combined. The design was to be further developed in the 1944 Programme, 2600-ton *Daring* class which were enlarged versions of the type, armed with six 4.5in and intended primarily to serve as main fleet escorts.

Also included in the 1943 Programme were the 'Weapon' class of which only four of the nineteen ships ordered were to be completed – during 1945-6. These were the non-utility development of the 'S' to 'C' classes which combined the functions of fleet anti-submarine and anti-aircraft vessels with the torpedo attack role but sacrificed gun power in order to keep dimensions within reasonable limits. The designed armament consisted of three twin 4in HA/LA, two twin 40mm, two twin 20mm, ten 21in torpedo tubes and the standard A/S outfit of the time. They introduced the unit machinery arrangement to British destroyers with alternate boiler and engine rooms – a system also adopted in the *Daring* class.

ESCORTS

The isolation of particular aspects of a war as key events in the progress towards its final outcome create, perhaps, too great an emphasis on subjects which are simply part of the whole. Nevertheless, it is arguable that the Royal Navy's greatest contribution towards the Allied victory in the Second World War was its role in the Battle of the Atlantic. For once the Admiralty, although initially underestimating the area of operations, had a clear idea of what was required from the lessons of the First World War. That conflict had seen the introduction of the convoy system, the development of effective anti-submarine weapons and the employment of a vast fleet of escort vessels of all types from fleet destroyers to requisitioned trawlers. Although the threat from the U-boat fleet of Nazi Germany was perceived rather late, an extensive and broad-based construction programme, initiated just before the war, provided the basis for all war production escorts and gave a sufficient edge to prevent the strangulation of British seaborne trade. As in the First World War, the primary need was for effective anti-submarine vessels that could be constructed quickly and in large numbers. The demands were, however, somewhat more severe in that a reasonable AA capability was also demanded and, because of the increased speed and capability of submarines, vessels such as requisitioned trawlers were no longer as suitable for coastal A/S work. There were also some initial problems with over-confidence in the existing anti-submarine equipment – partially because many were under the false impression that ASDIC had solved the 'submarine problem'.

The war saw the development of vastly improved anti-submarine weapons and tactics – an evolving war of measure and counter-measure as the combatants sought to gain advantage over each other. The critical technical developments for the British were:

1) High-frequency direction finding which allowed the location of U-boats via their wireless transmissions.
2) The introduction of Type 271 centimetric radar in 1941 which could accurately locate U-boats approaching on the surface.
3) The provision of local air defence for convoys.
4) The ahead-throwing AS weapons 'Hedgehog' and 'Squid'.

The primary purpose of the escorts was the protection of their charges and while the sinking of a submarine was of considerable value it was not essential to the main purpose. It is notable that the first three of the above served to force submarines to operate submerged where they were slower and less capable of gaining a good attack position. The location of an approaching submarine allowed escorts to intercept the attacker and force him to submerge, hopefully keeping him occupied for long enough to allow a convoy to pass out of the danger zone unmolested. Such tactics characterised the first reversal for the U-boats which, until the advent of Type 271, had been very successful with night attacks on the surface. Air support and HF/DF extended the range of interception which gave warning of their presence and helped prevent U-boats making a distant run on the surface to get ahead of a convoy. Both sides gained and lost the advantage at various points in the Battle of the Atlantic – a battle that began on the first day of war and ended on its last. In fact in 1945 the German Navy was on the verge of achieving a reversal of its fortunes in the U-boat war with the introduction of advanced submarines of high submerged speed, but fortunately for the Allies this was too late to affect the final outcome.

Escort sloops

As with destroyers, the large building programme of the First World War left the Navy with a substantial surplus of escort vessels and it was not until late in the 1920s that any new construction was considered. Between 1928 and 1933 thirty-six escort sloops of generally similar characteristics were built for the Royal Navy.[35] They displaced around 1000 tons standard, had a speed of a little over 16kts and were armed with two 4in guns (two 4.7in in the last twelve, the *Grimsby* class). All were equipped for minesweeping and were similar to, but larger than, contemporary minesweeping sloops (ships which were also employed extensively for escort duty). They were not originally fitted for anti-submarine work but the majority were converted for this role during the Second World War.

In 1933 work began on a more capable group of ships intended to serve as ocean convoy escorts. The first group of three displaced 1190 tons standard and had a speed of 18.75kts but completed with somewhat varied configurations. The first, *Bittern*, was renamed *Enchantress* and completed as an Admiralty Yacht in 1935. The intended armament was four 4.7in but for her new role she carried only three (reduced to two in 1936). The second ship, *Stork*, completed in 1936 as a survey vessel but was rearmed to the same standard as the third vessel of the class after the outbreak of war. The last ship, a second *Bittern*, was fitted with three twin 4in HA/LA mountings and Denny-Brown stabilisers to serve as an AA/AS escort. This approach was taken a stage further in the next group of three (*Egret*, *Pelican* and *Auckland*) where displacement was increased to 1250 tons to provide for an armament of four twin 4in and an 0.5kt increase in speed. The design was further refined in the *Black Swan* class, which proved to be one of the finest AS escort types of the war. *Black Swan* and *Flamingo* were laid down in 1938, and the *Erne* and *Ibis* in the following year. The first two completed

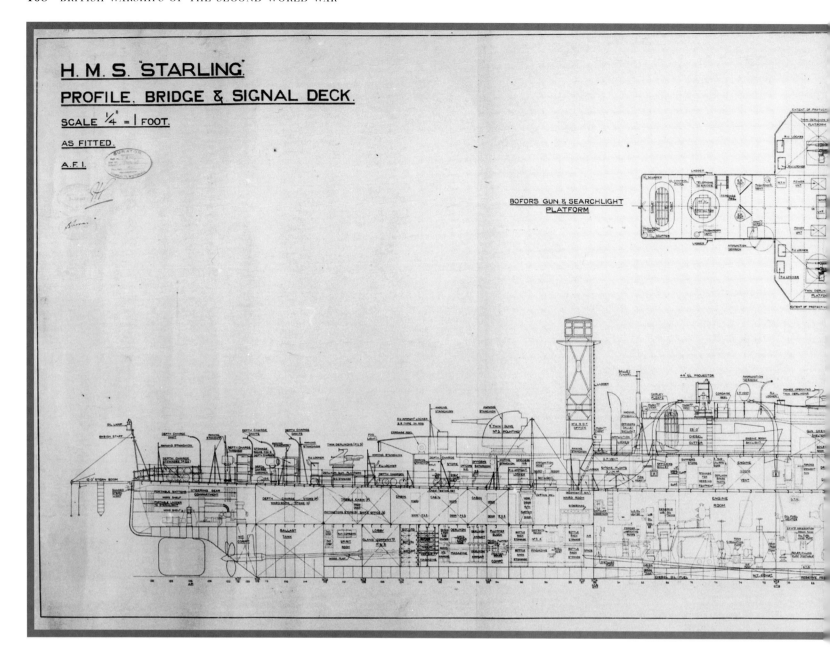

HMS Starling, *Profile, bridge and signal deck (as fitted), Fairfield, Govan, 24 September 1943.* The Starling *became famous as leader of the 2nd Escort Group, under the command of Captain F J Walker, the Royal Navy's most successful U-boat hunter. During the period June 1943 to August 1944 she was responsible for the sinking of three U-boats on her own account and a further ten in co-operation with other ships. She belonged to the 'Modified Black Swan' class, the wartime version of the ultimate development of the pre-war escort sloop. These were powerful ships, displacing* almost as much as a fleet destroyer. With a heavy armament and excellent seakeeping qualities they proved to be one of the best, if somewhat expensive, AS escort types of the war. This drawing shows yet another variation on the theme of layout – the superstructure platforms having been included with the profile. The strength of the AA and AS equipment is marked – particularly the relatively sophisticated fire control outfit with a rangefinder director MkIIIW on the bridge to control the three twin 4in MkXIX mountings in either surface or AA fire. The transmitting station, located in the after starboard side of the forward superstructure, was equipped on par with a fleet destroyer having both an AFCC and a FKC together with auto barrage and gyro-roll units. The close-range armament consists of two single 20mm Oerlikons in the bridge wings and four twin Oerlikons – two on the platform abaft the funnel and two on the quarterdeck. The midships platform was designed to carry two quad 2pdr pom-pom mountings but shortages resulted in the substitution of 20mm guns in many of the class, while others received the more sophisticated twin 40mm Hazemeyer. The 20mm guns aft were fitted on a low platform to give a clear arc of fire over the

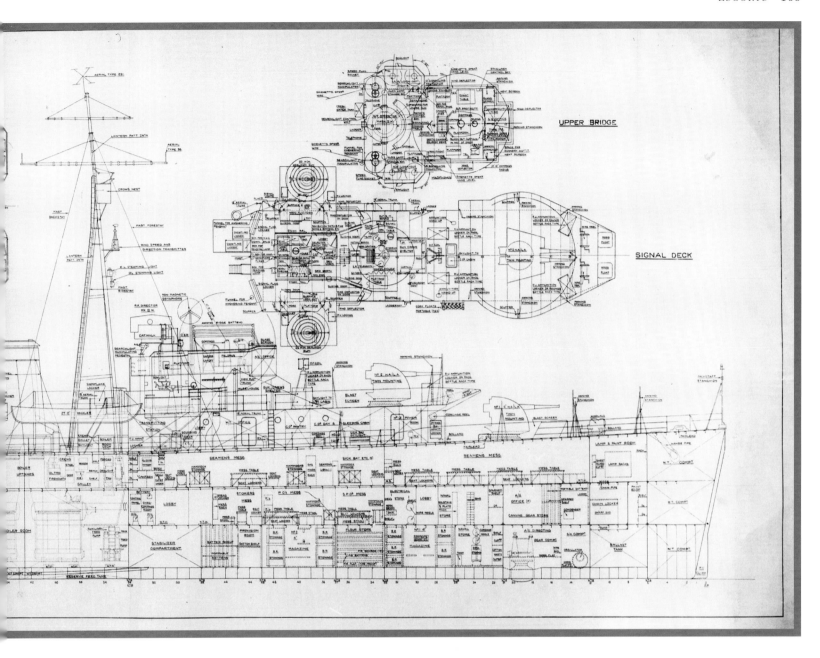

depth charge gear. The radar outfit is Type 291 air warning with its aerial at the head of the foremast and Type 271 surface warning with its aerial in the lantern at the top of the lattice tower (office at base of tower). The ship also carried a Type 285 gunnery radar set but the aerials for this, which were fitted on the rangefinder director, are not shown in the drawing. Note the Denny-Brown stabiliser compartment in the hold, forward of the boilers – equipment adopted to assist in providing a steady gun platform for AA fire. (Plan No NPC2194, Neg No E0722)

Starling

Displacement:	1490 tons standard, 1960 tons deep
Dimensions:	283ft (pp), 299ft 6in (oa) x 38ft 6in x 9ft 6in (mean)
Armament:	Six 4in MkXVI (3 x 2); ten 20mm (4 x 2, 2 x 1); two DC rails, four DCT, 100 DC
Machinery:	Two shaft, Parsons geared turbines, 4300shp = 19.25kts; two Admiralty 3-drum boilers; 420 tons oil fuel; range 6100nm at 15kts
Complement:	192

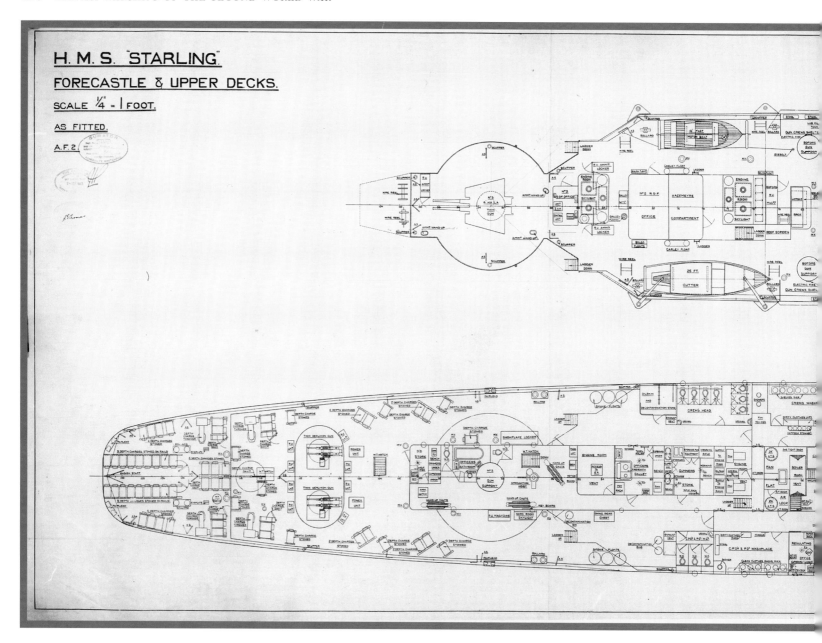

HMS Starling, *Forecastle and upper decks (as fitted), Fairfield, Govan, 24 September 1943.* The Starling's primary wartime role as an AS escort is clearly shown by the amount of depth charge gear on the quarterdeck. The area accommodates 62 charges – nine in each of the stern rails, one in each of the four throwers and the remaining 40 stowed on the deck – more charges were available from a store on the deck below. While the general layout follows that of a destroyer the ship is proportionally broader and the longer forecastle (which provided more space for accommodation) and small funnel present a markedly different external appearance. The transmitting station and wireless office, together with the Type 291 and 285 radar offices, are located in the after part of the forward superstructure on the forecastle deck. The forward section of this area, around 'B' gun support is the commanding officer's accommodation. Note that unlike most 'as fitted' drawings the boats, a 16ft motor dinghy to port and a 27ft whaler and 25ft motor cutter to starboard, are drawn in some detail. (Plan No NPC2195, Neg No E0717)

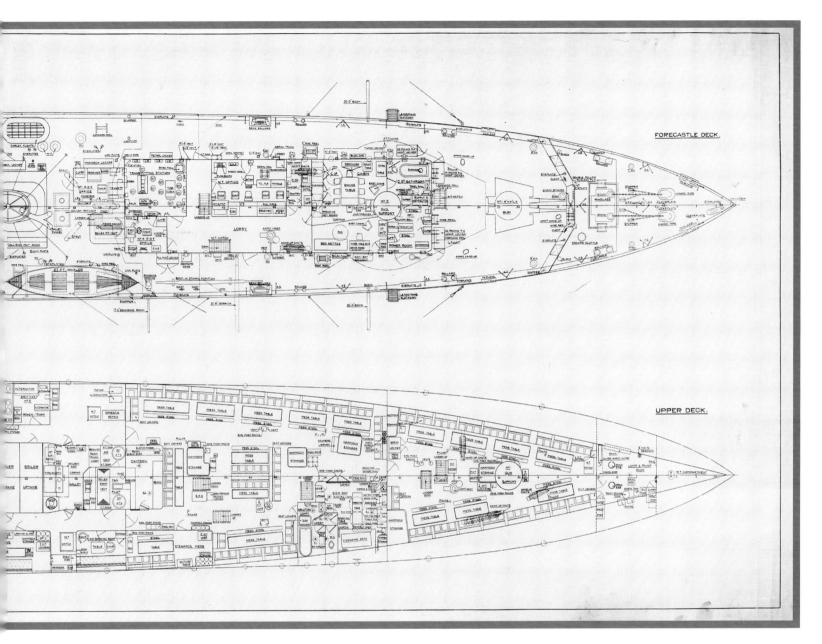

FORECASTLE DECK.

UPPER DECK.

shortly after the outbreak of war but the second pair did not enter service until April 1941. The design was a 1300-ton version of *Egret* with length increased by 10ft, a quad pom-pom fitted in place of one of the twin 4in and speed increased to 19.75kts. Besides the roles of AA/AS convoy escort the first pair were fitted for minesweeping but this gear was removed during the war. Like the *Egret* class they were fitted with stabilisers to aid their effectiveness in the AA role. Unfortunately they were somewhat too sophisticated for mass production and only twenty-nine ships (including two for the Indian Navy) were included in the war construction programmes. These latter vessels were of the 'Modified *Black Swan*' class and differed from the original group in having a 1ft increase in beam to allow for potential war additions, which increased the standard displacement by 50 tons. The initial close-range AA armament was two quad pom-poms but these were fitted in only a few ships, later vessels receiving two twin 40mm Bofors in their place. There were also

variable additions of single and twin 20mm and single 40mm AA, the fitting of Hedgehogs in several ships and, as with most wartime escorts, a substantial increase in the number of depth charges carried.

Escort destroyers

In 1938 the Admiralty decided on the construction of a small destroyer type designed to carry out general patrol duties and serve as AA/AS escorts. This was primarily aimed at increasing numbers with cheap, rapidly-built vessels that would relieve fleet destroyers of their more mundane duties. As these vessels were not, under normal circumstances, expected to work with the main fleet, size could be limited by reducing the specified speed and omitting a torpedo armament. The initial design, approved early in 1939,

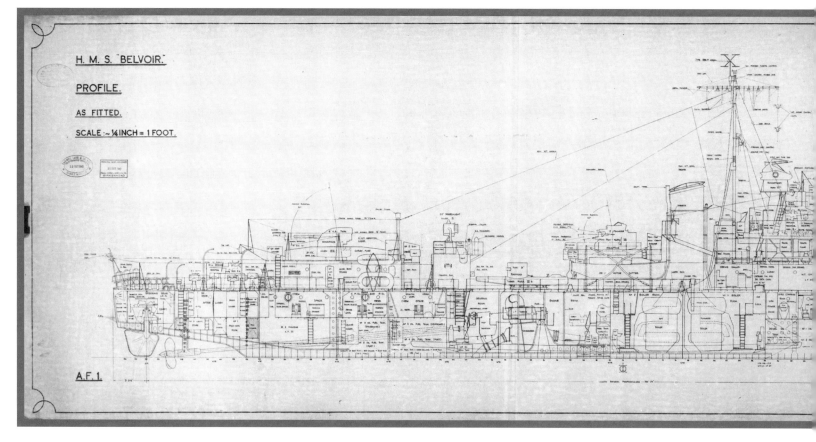

HMS Belvoir, *Profile (as fitted), Cammell Laird, Birkenhead, 12 October 1942. This profile of the Type III 'Hunt' class escort destroyer Belvoir shows clearly that the layout is, with little variation, a cut-down version of a standard destroyer having all the required features on a much reduced scale. In this case complete with a very light torpedo armament consisting of one twin MkVIB torpedo tube mounting – an item which had not been provided in the earlier Type I and II 'Hunts' and which necessitated the surrender of the quarterdeck twin 4in mounting in the Type III. The Type III also differed from the earlier groups in having a vertical funnel and mast. These wartime drawings are less detailed than Cammell Laird's peacetime productions but still contain features rarely found in the 'as fitted' sets of other builders. For example, the stabiliser compartment in the hold immediately below the fore end of the bridge contains the outline of the Denny Brown gear, while on the lower deck the gyro compass can be seen, immediately forward of 'A' boiler room. The fire control gear for the two twin 4in MkXIX includes a rangefinder director MkV**, complete with aerials for Type 285 radar, at the rear of the bridge structure. The transmitting station, unlike that in a full destroyer, is located immediately below the director on the forecastle deck but the main W/T office occupies the usual location on the upper deck. The only radar apart from the gunnery set is a Type 286P air/surface warning set with its aerial (similar to Type 291) at the top of the mast and the office at the base of the mast on the forecastle deck. (Plan No NPA6878, Neg No E0702)*

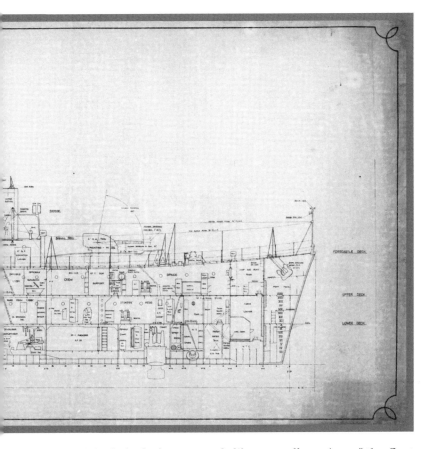

Belvoir

Displacement:	1050 tons standard, 1430 tons deep
Dimensions:	264ft 3in (pp), 280ft (oa) x 31ft 6in x 8ft 3in (mean)
Armament:	Four 4in MkXVI (2 x 2); four 2pdr (1 x 4); three 20mm (3 x 1); two 21in torpedo tubes (1 x 2); two DC rails, four DCT, 34 DC
Machinery:	Two shaft, Parsons geared turbines, 19,000shp = 27kts; two Admiralty 3-drum boilers; 277 tons oil fuel; range 2560nm at 20kts
Complement:	164

unsurprisingly looked very much like a small version of the fleet destroyers of the 'O' class. It specified a vessel of 875 tons standard with a speed of 32kts armed with three twin 4in HA/LA mountings, two quad 0.5in, two depth charge throwers and one depth charge rail. Design modifications in 1939 resulted in a quad pom-pom being substituted for the 0.5in MG mountings and a 9in increase in beam, to 29ft, it having been decided by the DNC that the margin of stability was too low. It was decided to give the new ships 'hunt' names (after fox-hunts), following a pattern set in the First World War with the 'Hunt' class minesweepers. Fifty-six were ordered in 1939, twenty shortly before the outbreak of war and the remainder under the Emergency War Programme. A further thirty were ordered in 1940 but the uniformity of the group was to be disrupted – initially by the discovery of a serious error in the design calculations and later by a reconsideration of the design requirements.

When the first of the class, *Atherstone*, was nearing completion in January 1940 it was realised that her stability was grossly insufficient. This proved to be the result of a mistake in the stability calculations which, in turn, was caused by the pressure on the Constructor's Department to complete the design quickly at a time when there was insufficient personnel to cope with the rearmament programme. The problem required immediate and drastic action which was corrected by the omission of 'X' 4in mounting and the addition of 52 tons of permanent ballast. The only advantage gained was moving the quad pom-pom from abaft the funnel to the position originally occupied by the twin 4in where it had a clearer arc of fire. These changes increased the standard displacement to

1080 tons and reduced the speed to 28.5kts. Twenty-three ships, whose construction was well advanced, were treated in this way to become the 'Hunt Type I'. With the remaining vessels, which became 'Hunt Type II', it was possible to provide an increase in beam from 29ft to 31ft 6in and retain the designed armament. This did, however, result in a further loss of speed, which dropped to 27kts in the standard condition.

The omission of a torpedo armament had been an unpopular decision among some sections of the naval command and after a certain amount of lobbying it was decided to modify the ships ordered in 1940 to carry a twin torpedo tube mounting. This was done on the basis that the ships might on some occasions be required to work with the fleet but the value of such a minimal outfit is questionable when successful torpedo attack was based on the launching of salvos of torpedoes rather than one or two. Compensation for the additional top-weight required the reduction of the main armament and the addition of 40 tons of permanent ballast. In this case 'Y' mounting was omitted which provided a clearer quarterdeck for the AS armament but necessitated the quad pom-pom remaining on the platform abaft the funnel. This group became 'Hunt Type III' – easy to distinguish from their earlier half-sisters as they were fitted with vertical, rather than raked, masts and funnels. For two of the ships ordered in 1940, *Brecon* and *Brissenden*, Thornycroft was allowed to apply their own design expertise to the basic staff requirements for the class and produced the 'Hunt Type IV'. By increasing the beam to 33ft 4in these ships accommodated not only the full designed armament but a triple torpedo tube mounting and an extended forecastle for improved seakeeping. However, as they retained the same machinery, maximum speed dropped to 26kts at standard displacement.

Despite the problems encountered, the 'Hunts' proved highly successful and served with distinction – primarily in the North Sea, English Channel and Mediterranean. They operated in their intended roles as local convoy escorts and on patrols but also served in more aggressive operations against enemy convoys, patrol vessels and E-boats. Although their low endurance prevented their use as deep ocean escorts, a few were employed in defending convoys to Russia and, in the latter part of the war several were

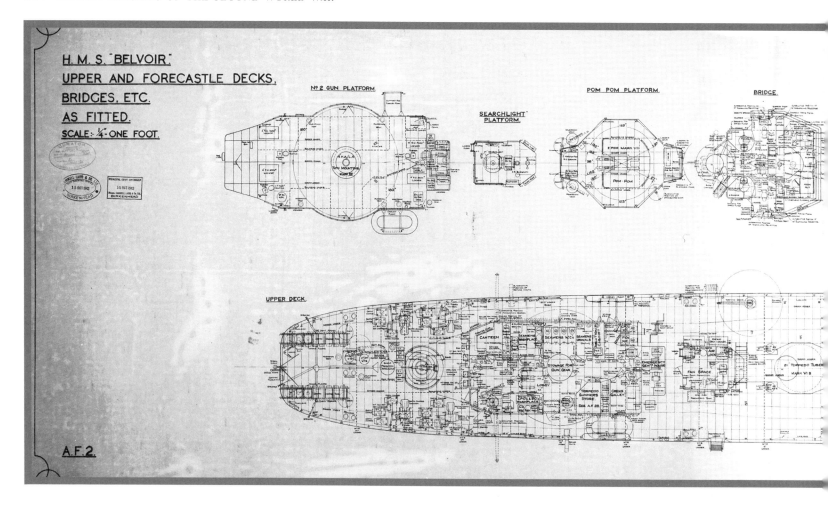

HMS Belvoir, *Upper and Forecastle decks, bridges, etc (as fitted), Cammell Laird, Birkenhead, 12 October 1942. The quarterdeck displays the same outfit of depth charge rails and throwers as found in the* Starling *but fewer spare charges stowed on deck (only three for each thrower) and no spares stored elsewhere. The close-range AA armament consists of one quad pom-pom mounted on the platform abaft the funnel, a single 20mm Oerlikon in each bridge wing and a single 20mm Oerlikon on the centre line of the quarterdeck aft.* Belvoir *later had the 20mm guns replaced by two single 40mm Bofors – one in the after 20mm position and one immediately in front of the bridge.* (Plan No NPA6879, Neg No E0716)

sent out to the Far East to operate with the East Indies Fleet.

The general concept of the 'Hunt' class inspired the production of similar vessels by the United States. However, these 'destroyer escorts' were directed more at deep ocean AS work than the 'Hunt' class and, crudely speaking, accepted a lower speed and a lighter gun armament for greater endurance. Unlike their British counterparts these vessels were aimed at mass production, being of all-welded, pre-fabricated construction. Over 500 were built, of which seventy-eight were transferred to the RN under the Lend-Lease programme. The destroyer escorts represented virtually the entire output of the USA for escort types with the exception of forty-eight patrol frigates – the latter being an adaptation of the British 'River' class, which were adopted to take advantage of their mercantile type construction and machinery. This concentration on a singular type, with its attendant advantages of uniformity of production, contrasts markedly with the great variety of escorts constructed in British yards.

Corvettes

Between 1933 and 1938 nine 'coastal convoy escorts' of the *Kingfisher* and *Shearwater* classes were laid down. These were small, relatively cheap ships designed for off-shore AS duties but

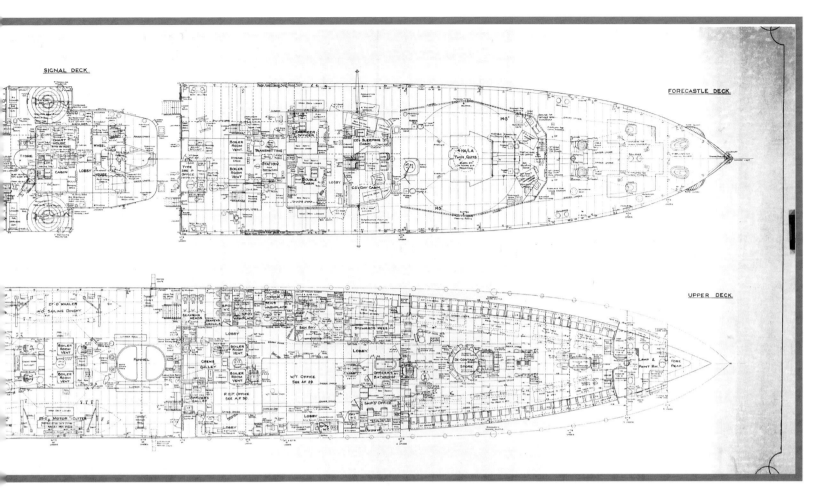

SIGNAL DECK.

FORECASTLE DECK.

UPPER DECK.

were soon recognised as unsuitable as a high volume 'war production' design primarily because they employed 'warship' construction methods and turbine machinery. This problem was addressed in 1938 with the design of the 'Flower' class corvettes in which a mercantile-type hull, based on the design of a whale-catcher, was employed to provide a platform for much the same armament as that carried by the *Kingfisher* type. They were fitted with a single steam piston engine driving a single propeller for a maximum speed of 16.5kts. Being short and broad with a single balanced rudder they were highly manoeuvrable – a distinct asset in AS work – but this hull form also gave them a very lively motion in a seaway. Although intended for coastal work the shortage of escorts resulted in them being employed in the Atlantic where, despite their low endurance, they proved an invaluable stop-gap until more sophisticated escorts became available. To cope with this change of purpose they were subjected to various improvements to enhance their seakeeping qualities, primarily the extension of the forecastle from forward of the bridge to abaft the funnel, deeper bilge keels and a modification of the bow shape. However, although seaworthy they had a reputation for being able to 'roll on wet grass' and were seldom popular with their crews who suffered great discomfort due to stress of weather, overcrowding and insanitary conditions. Although habitability was subject to some improvement, this situation worsened as the war progressed, crew size increasing by

almost 50 per cent to provide surplus to cope with fatigue and the wartime additions of close-range AA guns, additional AS equipment and radar. Construction began in 1939 and continued until 1944 during which time 145 were built in British and 93 in Canadian shipyards.

In 1943 approval was given to an advanced version of the 'Flower' class intended to address the limitations of the original design and make them more suitable for deep ocean work. The new vessels – the 'Castle' class – were larger, with improved accommodation and seakeeping qualities, and greater endurance. The machinery arrangements and speed remained as in the 'Flower' class and apart from the ability to accommodate the latest types of AS equipment, including the 'Squid' three-barrel ahead-throwing mortar, their armament was also much the same. Twelve were ordered under the 1942 Programme and a further eighty-four under the 1943 programme but of the latter fifty-seven were cancelled at the end of the war.

Frigates

In March 1941 approval was given to a new AS escort design which, like the 'Flower' class, was intended for construction on mercantile lines and to employ simple machinery and armament. However, in

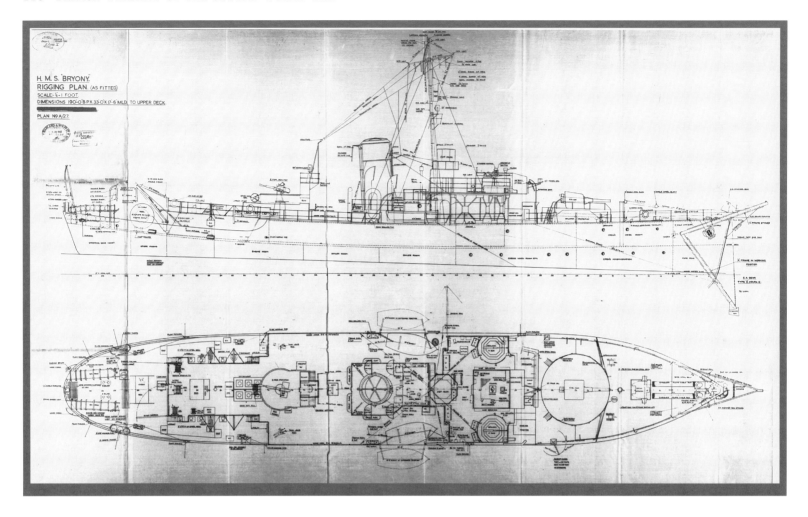

HMS Bryony, *Rigging plan (as fitted), Harland and Wolff, Belfast, 1 July 1942. This drawing of the long forecastle 'Flower' class corvette Bryony is an excellent example of the more detailed rig drawings that some builders produced. Only minor detail and internal features have been omitted and all the ship's primary weather deck equipment and fittings, complete with annotation, are clearly shown. The ship is fitted for minesweeping as well as AS work and carries the 'A' frame for an acoustic hammer forward (shown in the profile in both the lowered operating position and the raised stowed position) and the large cable reel for an 'L-L' magnetic mine sweep on the quarterdeck. The gun armament, from forward, consists of a single 4in on the bandstand forward of the bridge, two single 20mm in the bridge wings, a single 2pdr on the platform abaft the funnel and two twin Lewis 0.303in MG mountings on the forecastle deck abreast the 2pdr platform. The depth charge armament, somewhat reduced because of the minesweeping outfit, consists of two nine-charge rails at the stern, with stowage for ten spare charges underneath each, and two throwers fitted against the bulkheads of the after deck house. The only radar carried is the standard surface search Type 271 with the office at the rear of the bridge and the lantern for its aerial on the office roof. (Plan No NPN1505, Neg No 684834)*

Bryony

Displacement:	1000 tons standard, 1240 tons deep
Dimensions:	190ft (pp), 205ft (oa) x 33ft x 14ft 6in (mean)
Armament:	One 4in; one 2pdr; two 20mm (2 x 1); two DC rails.
Machinery:	One shaft, 4cyl triple expansion engine, 2750shp = 16.65kts; two Scotch cylindrical boilers; 200 tons oil fuel; range 4000nm at 12kts
Complement:	50+

Swale

Displacement:	1350 tons standard, 1855 tons deep
Dimensions:	283ft (pp), 301ft 4in (oa) x 36ft 6in x 8ft 3in (mean)
Armament:	Two 4in MkXIX (2 x 1); four 20mm (4 x 1); two DC rails, eight DCT, 100 DC
Machinery:	Two shaft, 4cyl triple expansion engines, 5500shp = 20 kts; two Admiralty 3-drum boilers; 440 tons oil fuel; range 5000nm at 15kts
Complement:	114

HMS Swale, *General arrangement (as fitted), Smiths Dock, Middlesborough, 23 March 1943. An example of wartime expediency is provided by this general arrangement of the 'River' class frigate* Swale. *All the ship's decks and the profile have been fitted onto one sheet and the detail is minimal in comparison to peacetime 'as fitted' drawings. Despite its relative simplicity it is still date stamped some nine months after the ship's completion! The profile makes an interesting comparison with* Starling *in that the 'River' class are very similar in general layout but much simpler in their gun and radar fit. They also, with a few exceptions, had steam piston engines rather than turbines, which necessitated the large opening in the upper deck to clear the cylinder heads. Being one of the early units of the class she is fitted for minesweeping and carries both a minesweeping winch and the large cable reel for the 'L-L' sweep on the quarterdeck; the sweep floats and kites being located at the after outboard corners of the deck (this gear was later removed). The depth charge outfit includes two long stern rails for fifteen charges each and no less than eight throwers – located four on each side of the quarterdeck. The gun armament consists of two single 4in, which have local control only, and four single 20mm (two in the bridge wings and two on the platform forward of the pole mast aft). The only radar is a Type 271 with office and lantern tower at the rear of the bridge. Noteworthy is the provision of a crow's nest on the foremast – a standard item in escorts where it served as a high position for submarine lookout.*
(Plan No NPN8312, Neg No E0710)

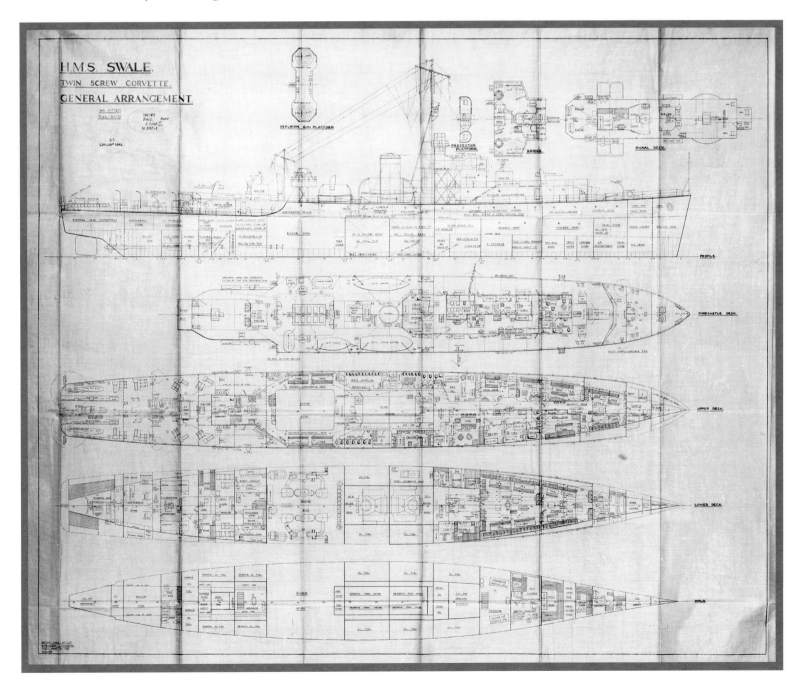

this case a larger and faster vessel was required with greater endurance and improved armament. The result was the 'River' class frigate of which over 110 were constructed in British, Canadian and Australian yards during 1941-5. Two sets of engines of the same type as those in the 'Flower' class provided continuity in machinery production and gave a speed of 20kts – a substantial advantage for submarine-hunting as it was not unusual for a U-boat on the surface to outrun a corvette. The provision of turbine engines was considered for these ships but this would have limited the numbers that could be built. However, six ships of the class were actually fitted with turbine machinery. The early units were armed with two single 4in, six 20mm, eight DCT, two DC rails, 100 depth-charges and minesweeping gear. In 1942 it was decided that endurance should be increased and modification of the oil fuel stowage provided for an increase from 440 to 650 tons which gave a range of 7500nm compared with 5000nm. This alteration was made in all ships except the first twenty-three, the construction of which was too far advanced for the modifications to be easily incorporated, the two groups being referred to as 'short' and 'long' endurance ships. Other alterations included the fitting of Type 271

radar, HF/DF and 'Hedgehog', increases in the depth charge and close-range AA armament and the omission of the minesweeping gear.

As with the 'Flower' class, the 'River' design was followed by a more advanced version on the same principles. The 'Loch' class frigates, the design of which was approved in May 1943, were essentially 'Rivers' with the design adapted for true 'mass production'. Earlier escorts had fallen short of this ideal, particularly as they were mostly of riveted construction – although some welding was introduced during the war. The 'Loch' class were designed

Winchester

Displacement:	1100 tons standard, 1460 tons deep
Dimensions:	300ft (pp), 312ft (oa) x 29ft 6in x 8ft 6in (mean)
Armament:	Four 4in MkXVI (2 x 2); eight 0.5in (2 x 4); two DC rails, two DCT, 40 DC
Machinery:	Two shaft, Brown-Curtis geared turbines, 27,000shp = 34kts; three White-Forster boilers; 325 tons oil fuel; range 2150nm at 12kts
Complement:	134

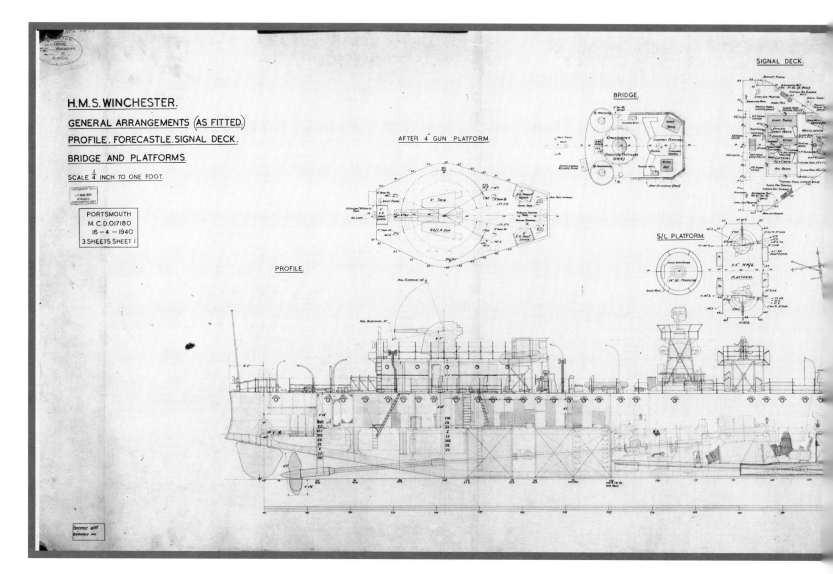

HMS Winchester, *Profile, forecastle, signal deck and platforms (as fitted), Portsmouth Dockyard, 16 April 1940. The 'W' class destroyer* Winchester *is here shown as converted to an AA escort by Portsmouth Dockyard during 1938-9. Modification was almost entirely restricted to replacing the original gun and torpedo armament with a purely AA outfit and the only major* structural change was the removal of the superstructure forward of the bridge. The latter allowed the forward twin 4in to be mounted on a slightly raised platform, while the after twin 4in was fitted as a direct replacement for the gun that had originally occupied the position on the after superstructure. The original searchlight tower is retained but the platform forward of it, carrying two quad 0.5in mountings, is *new. The bridge, slightly modified from the original, accommodates the new control gear for the 4in guns – a rangefinder director at the rear of the compass platform and the transmitting station at forecastle deck level. The wings of the signal deck were later fitted with single 20mm Oerlikons and these weapons subsequently replaced the 0.5in guns as well.*
(Plan No NPC5453, Neg No E0721)

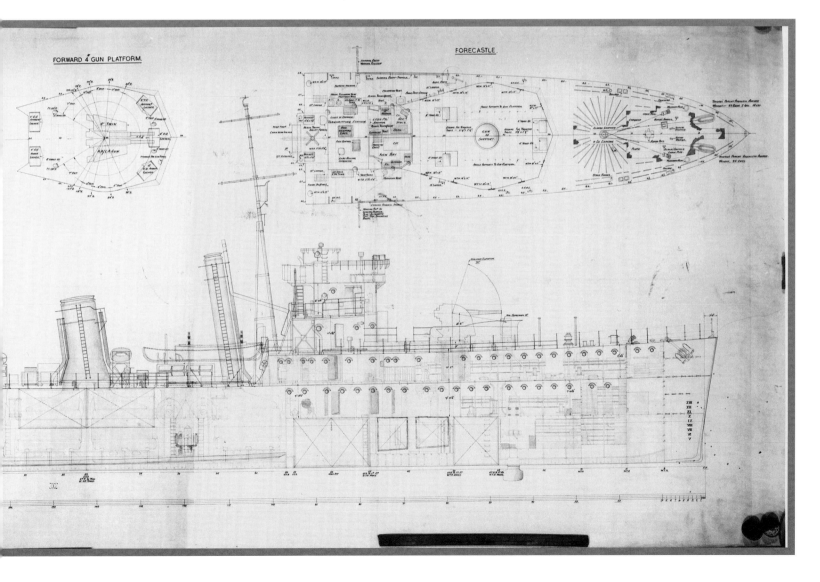

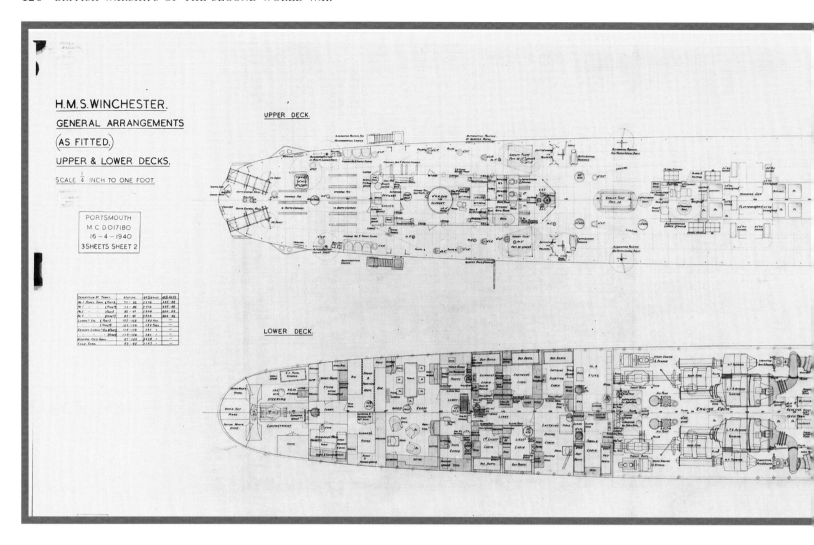

HMS Winchester, *Upper and lower decks (as fitted), Portsmouth Dockyard, 16 April 1940. From forward the lower decks shows a standard destroyer layout – crew accommodation, double and single boiler rooms, the engine room, officer accommodation and the steering gear. The only variations on this are the chain locker and store room at the extreme forward end, the low power (electricity) room complete with gyro compass, on the port side forward of the* boiler rooms and the bread and provision room on the port side aft. The engine room shows the low pressure ahead and astern turbines on the inboard side and high pressure ahead turbines on the outboard side driving into a single gearcase for each shaft. Also visible are the steam-driven dynamos – one in each after corner – and the large intakes for the condensers fitted immediately under the turbines. The upper deck – looking very bare without its torpedo tubes, has two depth charge rails at its after* end, while the depth charge throwers are much further forward than usual being a few feet forward of the after superstructure. The after steering position, at the fore side of the after superstructure, is protected by the overhang of the gun deck above but is otherwise in the open. On the centre line, forward of the fore funnel are the galley and then the W/T office while the remainder of the forecastle area is mainly crew accommodation.*
(Plan No NPC5454, Neg No E0715)

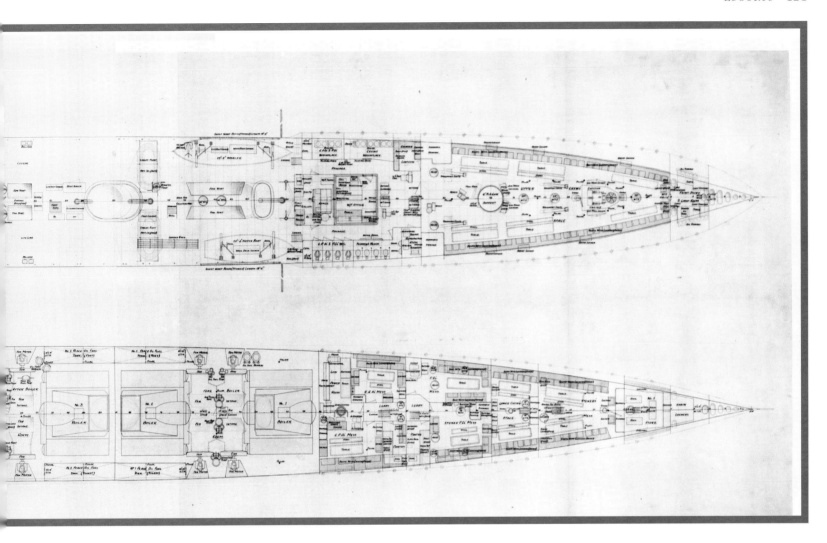

around welded pre-fabrication and standardised fittings and equipment, the pre-fabricated sections being either welded or riveted together depending on the facilities of the shipbuilder. In size, general layout, machinery and speed they differed little from the 'River' class but adopted a modified armament. Two 'Squid' AS mortars were fitted on the forward shelter deck, where they had a high and relatively dry command, displacing the forward 4in gun which was repositioned on a bandstand on the forecastle. The after 4in gun was replaced by a quad pom-pom mounting and, having been supplanted to a large extent by the 'Squid', the standard depth charge armament was reduced. Over 110 'Loch' class ships were ordered but half of this number were cancelled at the end of the war. Twenty eight were completed to the original design but the remaining nineteen (excluding six completed post-war as survey and despatch vessels) were converted to AA frigates for service in the Far East and Pacific where the primary threat was from Japanese aircraft rather than submarines. In these ships, which were renamed after Bays to distinguish their new role, the AS armament was reduced to the more standard 'Hedgehog' and depth charge outfit and the gun armament was increased to two twin 4in and two twin and four single 40mm. The layout forward reversed the arrangement in the *Loch* class, with the twin 4in in the raised position and the 'Hedgehog' fitted on the forecastle. The second 4in mounting was fitted aft and the twin 40mm on either beam abaft the funnel. There were also changes to the fire control gear and radar outfit to reflect their new role.

Conversions

At the outbreak of the Second World War one 'R' class, eleven 'S' class and fifty-eight 'V' and 'W' class destroyers, together with ten leaders of the *Shakespeare* and *Scott* classes, remained in service or in reserve. While some of these vessels were still seen as valuable reinforcements to the more modern fleet destroyers, a large number were converted to serve as convoy escorts giving ships which were effectively obsolete a new and very valuable role. The first of these conversions were carried out during 1938-41 with the modification of nineteen 'V' and 'W' class ships and the leader *Wallace* to fast AA escort vessels – generally referred to as WAIRs. This involved replacing the existing armament, including the torpedo tubes, with two twin 4in HA/LA mountings, fitting a new bridge and a HA control system. Because of their limited range they were primarily employed in escorting East Coast convoys where their guns

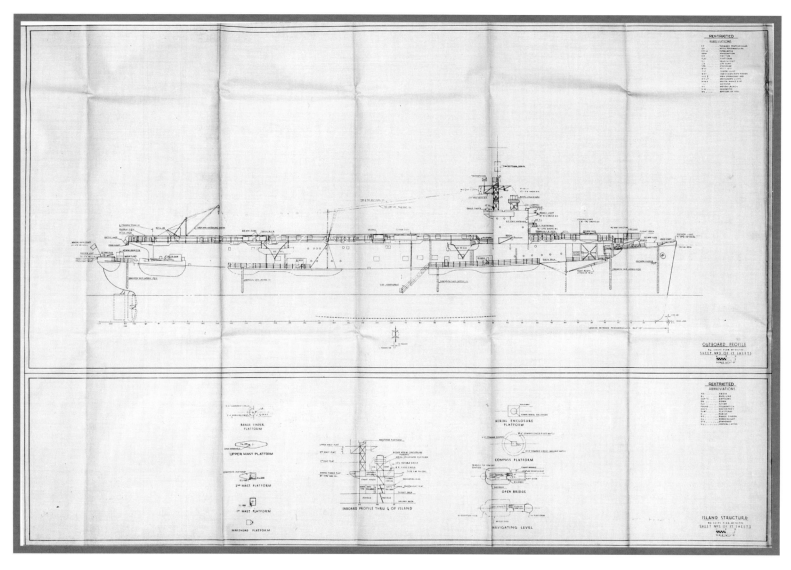

Above, and opposite and following pages. *HMS* Attacker, *Profile and decks, The Western Pipe and Steel Co, San Francisco, Undated. This set of the* Tracker *class escort carrier* Attacker *are from a booklet of general plans produced by the ship's US builders. Similar booklets of plans were produced for Royal Navy ships, as simpler and cheaper alternatives to the 'as fitted' drawings, for general use – particularly by the ship itself. The title sheet, besides the internal profile has an extensive listing of the ship's dimensions, together with a list of fire hose connections and the ship's boats (two 26ft motor whalers and two 30ft motor launches). Although the ship is US-built and equipped with US fittings and gun mountings, the radar outfit is British. This includes the radar lantern for Type 272 surface warning on the island and Type 79M (a single aerial version of Type 79, later redesignated Type 79B) air warning radar fitted at the mast head. The gun armament consists of a single 4in/50 mounting on each side of the main deck aft, four twin 40mm Bofors two at the after end of the main deck and one on each side of the flight deck forward, and ten 20mm Oerlikons, two on the forecastle and the remainder around the periphery of the flight deck. Note that the two aircraft lifts are the same size at 42ft x 34ft but are orientated in different directions. Other flight deck features include the expansion joints (shown as two dark lines bridging the deck) and a single aircraft catapult faintly visible on the port side, forward. The projections extending outboard on each side amidships are the machinery uptakes. (Plan No NPN0397 & 0898, Neg No E0707a & b, E708a & b)*

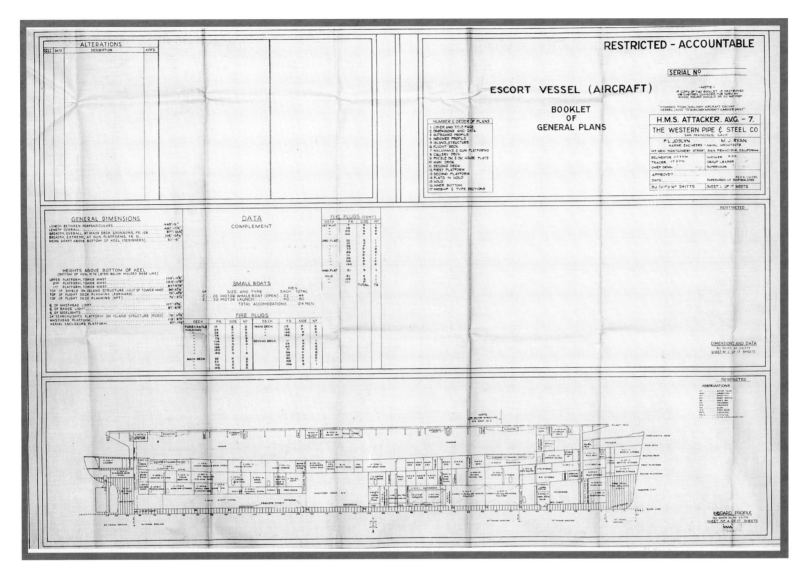

proved invaluable in defending their charges against German aircraft and E-boats.

The WAIRs were followed in 1941 by a more extensive programme of converting twenty-one 'V' and 'Ws' and the leaders *Broke* and *Keppel* into Long Range Escorts. This was in answer to the need to escort Atlantic convoys over greater distances as a result of the stationing of U-boats on the west coast of France. The primary requirement was met by removing the forward boiler and utilising the space gained for additional oil fuel tanks and accommodation. This dropped the maximum speed to 25kts but increased endurance from 3500 to 4500nm at 15kts. Other alterations were aimed at improved AS capability, 'A' gun was replaced with a 'Hedgehog', 'Y' gun was removed to clear the quarterdeck for increased depth charge equipment and Type 271 radar and HF/DF were fitted. In addition the torpedo tubes were removed and four 20mm AA fitted.

Most of the unmodified 'V' and 'W's, together with the surviving 'R' and 'S' class were eventually altered for escort work with various modifications including the replacement of the after set of torpedo tubes with a 12pdr AA gun and, in several cases, the substitu-

tion of a 'Hedgehog' for 'A' gun. Other alterations followed the usual pattern of fitting HF/DF, radar, additional close range AA and depth charge equipment. A large number of the 'A' to 'I' class destroyers received similar alterations as the war progressed being increasingly turned over to escort work as they were superseded by more modern fleet destroyers. Detailed configuration of these ships in the arrangement of fittings and armament varied considerably. Like the long range escorts they were employed primarily on Atlantic escort duty.

Escort carriers

One of the most critical aspects of the Battle of the Atlantic was the vital role played by aircraft. More U-boats were sunk by aircraft than by surface ships and many surface ship successes were the result of initial aircraft locations. Some aircraft cover was provided from shore bases but this was limited in both coverage and range and left a substantial gap in the central Atlantic where no such protection was possible. Another problem was German long-range

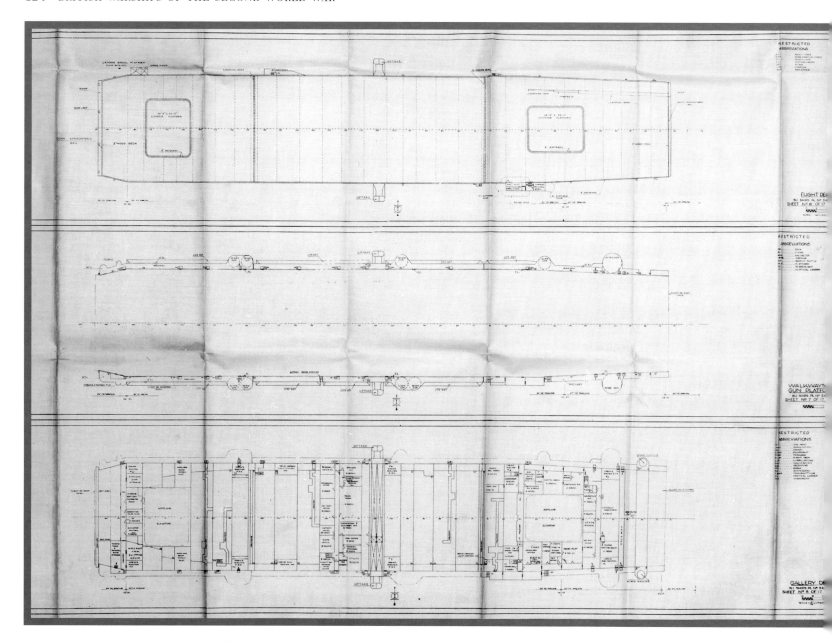

Attacker

Displacement:	10,200 tons standard, 14,400 tons deep
Dimensions:	465ft (pp), 491ft 7.5in (oa) x 69ft 6in (105ft max) x 23ft 3in
Armament:	Two 4in, eight 40mm (4 x 2), ten 20mm (10 x 1)
Aircraft:	20
Machinery:	Single shaft, General Electric geared turbines, 8500shp = 18.5kts; two Foster-Wheeler boilers; 3110 tons oil
Complement:	646

reconnaissance aircraft, which served the U-boats by locating, tracking and reporting on convoys. This last produced the first attempt to produce a sea-based air counter-measure by fitting merchant vessels with aircraft catapults for fighters intended to shoot down or, at the least, chase off the German aircraft. These vessels included thirty-five merchantmen, known as Catapult Merchant (CAM) ships, and five (four ex-mercantile) naval ships known as fighter catapult ships. Both types carried specially adapted Hurricane fighters which, unless within range of shore, had to be abandoned after flight as there was no means of recovering them – the pilot either ditching his plane or parachuting to safety and being picked up by the escort. Needless to say this was expensive in aircraft and occasionally in pilots and was very much a stop-gap measure.

The more sophisticated approach – the provision of local convoy defence with an auxiliary aircraft carrier converted from a merchant ship hull – was an ideal which had first been discussed in the

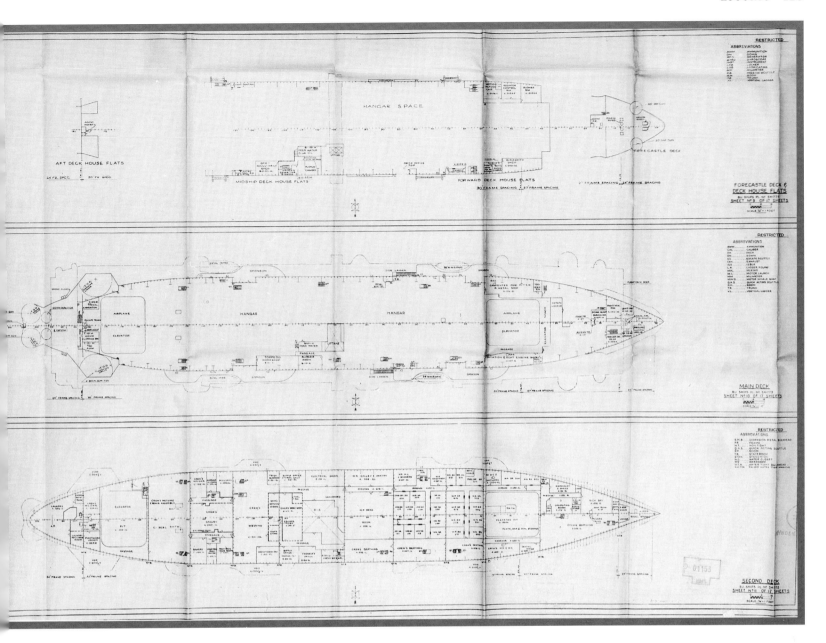

mid-1930s but not revived until 1940. The first such ship was the *Audacity*, converted from a captured German motor ship named *Hannover*. Her superstructure was cut down and she was fitted with a full-length flight deck but no hangar, her six aircraft being parked on the flight deck. Unfortunately, *Audacity* was torpedoed and sunk by a U-boat very shortly after completion in 1941 but her short career served to prove the value of the type. The second escort carrier was *Activity*. Converted on the stocks from a cargo liner, she had two innovations over her predecessor – a hangar for six aircraft and a small island superstructure. *Activity* did not enter service until October 1942 and similar conversions were carried out on only five further ships as the British, wishing to preserve the merchant ship construction programme, had found an easier source of supply in America. In 1941 an order for six escort carriers, which became the *Avenger* class, was negotiated with the United States. In the event only four were delivered (all ahead of *Activity*) as two

were retained – one for training of RN personnel and one for the USN – but by early 1944 a further thirty-four of improved design had been supplied to the RN under the lend-lease programme. The escort carriers found wide employment and, apart from the originally intended roll of convoy air cover, were used for air strikes and in support of amphibious landings and saw service in all the major theatres of war.

A somewhat less sophisticated group of ships was produced in British yards during 1943-4. These were the merchant aircraft carriers or MAC ships which, while being fitted with a flight deck, retained their cargo-carrying capacity. The ships chosen were grain ships and tankers as the flight deck caused little inconvenience with the handling of this type of cargo. They were specifically intended to provide Atlantic convoys with AS air patrols and carried four Swordfish aircraft which, as no hangar was fitted, were parked on the flight deck.

SUBMARINES

A standard type of saddle-tank submarine had been developed during the First World War which formed the basis of the majority of future new construction for the Royal Navy. Progress up to 1945 was directed toward the continued evolution of this standard type and concentrated on detail improvement rather than major change. The most marked change to the basic configuration was in the introduction of welding for the hull structure – adopted on a fairly minor scale prior to 1939 but gradually increasing in use thereafter until the final submarine design of the war (the 'A' class) were of all-welded, pre-fabricated construction. Progress was, however, marked at a detail level and a great deal of development work was carried through on auxiliary machinery and internal systems generally to improve efficiency and operational effectiveness.

The only submarine design markedly outside the normal was *X1* – a large cruiser submarine of 2759 tons surface displacement constructed during 1921-5 which followed a general trend toward vessels of this type that occurred in the years following the First World War. She carried four 5.2in guns and was intended to be capable of engaging minor warships on the surface as well as operating submerged. While she was successful in the general sense, her experimental machinery proved very troublesome and, the type having fallen into disfavour, she was sold for scrap in 1937. Other submarine designs followed a more conventional route but two classes were outside the mainstream production of patrol submarines. The

first of these were the three boats of the *Thames* class which were designed as 'fleet' submarines inspired by the earlier 'K' class – one was provided under each of the Estimates from 1929 to 1931. They differed from the standard type in having a very high surface speed of 21kts to allow them to keep pace with the battlefleet. However, the advent of the fast battleship rendered this employment redundant and they were eventually treated as standard patrol submarines. The second deviation from standard was the *Porpoise* class minelaying submarines, six of which were built during 1931-9. These boats carried fifty mines within a relatively large casing external to the pressure hull. They were successful vessels but the type was superseded by the development of mines that could be laid from the torpedo tubes of conventional submarines. One of the class, *Seal*, was the only British submarine to be captured, being surrendered to the Germans after being damaged by a mine in the Kattegat in May 1940. She was scuttled by her captors at the end of the war. Three others were lost in 1940-1, one off Norway and two in the Mediterranean, while *Porpoise* was sunk by Japanese aircraft in January 1945 leaving only *Rorqual* to survive the war.

Britain's first post-war submarine of the conventional type was *Oberon*, constructed by Chatham Dockyard during 1924-7. Intended primarily for extended patrols in the Far East she was considerably larger than the earlier 'L' class, having a surface displacement of 1310 tons. Designated as an 'Oversea Patrol' subma-

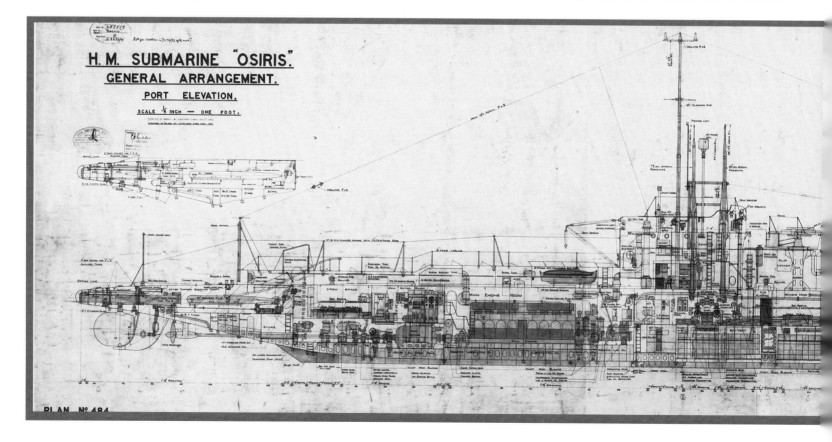

rine she had an extensive surface endurance of 12,000nm at 8kts and mounted eight torpedo tubes, six forward and two aft, with a reload torpedo for each (the standard for all later British submarines). Maximum speed was 14kts on the surface and 9kts submerged and the maximum operational diving depth was 300ft (the hull was designed to withstand a maximum of 500ft). The design was repeated with some detail variations in the *Otway* and *Oxley*, constructed for the Australian Navy during 1925-7, and in the Royal Navy's 'O', 'P' and 'R' classes, six of each were constructed during 1927-31. In all these boats internal space was maximised by storing the majority of the diesel fuel in tanks external to the pressure hull (in *Oberon* 179 tons were held in the saddle tanks and only 7 tons internally). These tanks were of riveted construction and trouble was experienced with leaks, which not only contaminated the fuel but also carried the danger of leaving a trail on the surface. In the *Thames* class this problem was cured to a large extent by welding the tanks and this modification was extended to the earlier boats as

they came in for refit. However, in later boats the problem was avoided altogether by abandoning external tanks and accepting the restrictions on fuel stowage/size by adopting tanks within the pressure hull.

In 1928 work began on producing a smaller submarine for short-range operations in narrow seas. The first two, *Swordfish* and *Sturgeon*, entered service in 1932-3. The reduced requirements of their employment were reflected in their smaller size and lower endurance. They displaced 735 tons on the surface and for a surface range of 5750nm at 8kts they required only 44.5 tons of fuel of which 39.5 tons was stowed inside the pressure hull (the external tanks were removed after completion and later boats were not fitted with them). They also had a reduced armament compared with the 'overseas' type with only six torpedo tubes (all forward) and a 3in gun in place of a 4in. Diving depth was reduced to 200ft (300ft maximum designed depth) reflecting the shallower waters in which they were likely to operate and saving weight on the pres-

HMS/M Osiris, *Port elevation (as fitted), Vickers Armstrongs, Barrow, 1 August 1929. It is very clear from this profile of* Osiris *that the compact complexity of the interior of a submarine contrasts markedly with its streamlined and simple exterior. It is difficult to pick out details but some items can be more clearly seen than others, including the forward and after torpedo tubes, the large area occupied by the batteries and the main diesel engines. The extensions above the conning tower, from forward to aft, are the 9.5in search periscope, the D/F frame coil mast, the 7.5in attack periscope, the steaming light mast and the telescopic main W/T mast. Note that the commanding officer's cabin is in the base of the conning tower immediately above the control room. The sub drawing of the stern just below the title is a Chatham Dockyard alteration to the drawing added in May 1941 to show changes to the position of the firing reservoirs of the after 21in torpedo tubes. The gun is a 4in MkXII on a SI submarine mounting, a standard weapon for inter-war submarines.* (Plan No NPB8389, Neg No 487519)

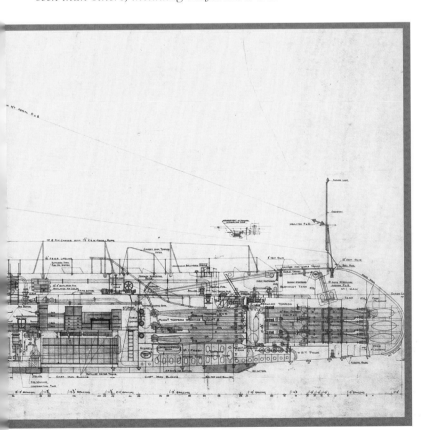

Osiris

Displacement:	1781 tons surface, 2038 tons submerged
Dimensions:	273ft (pp), 283ft 6in (oa) x 29ft 11in x 16ft 1.25in (mean)
Armament:	Eight 21in torpedo tubes (16 torpedoes); one 4in gun
Machinery:	Two shaft, diesel engines, 4400bhp = 17kts (surface); two electric motors, 1320bhp = 8kts (submerged); 174 tons oil fuel; range 11,400nm at 8kts (surface), 52nm at 4kts (submerged)
Complement:	53

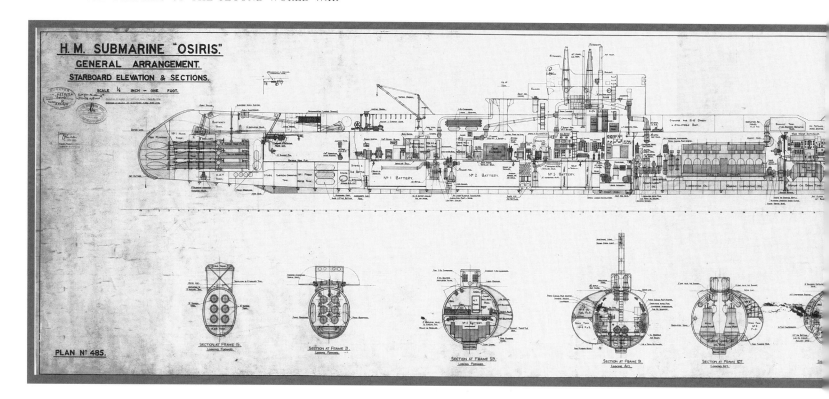

H. M. SUBMARINE "OSIRIS."
GENERAL ARRANGEMENT.
STARBOARD ELEVATION & SECTIONS.
SCALE ¼ INCH = ONE FOOT.

PLAN Nº 485.

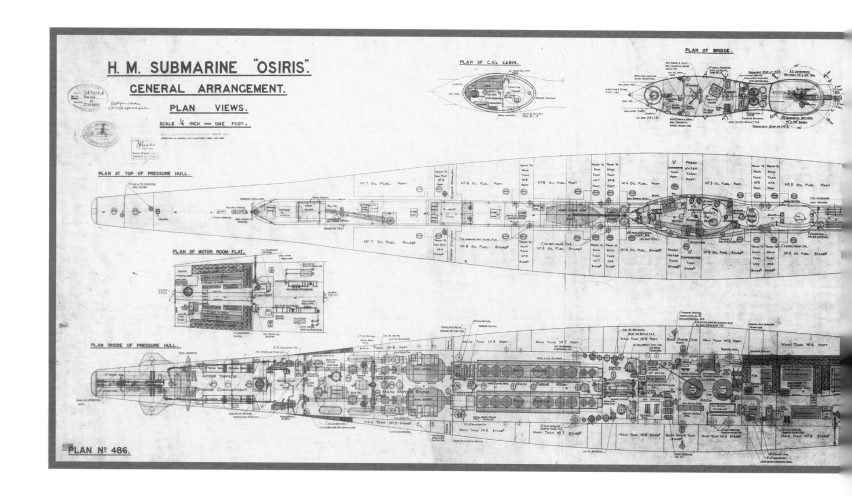

H. M. SUBMARINE "OSIRIS."
GENERAL ARRANGEMENT.
PLAN VIEWS.
SCALE ¼ INCH = ONE FOOT.

PLAN Nº 486.

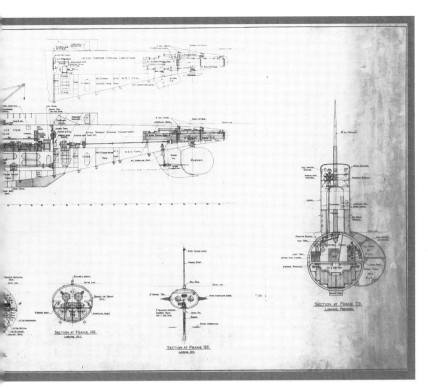

HMS/M Osiris, *Starboard elevation and sections (as fitted), Vickers Armstrongs, Barrow, 1 August 1929.* Submarines are about the only vessels that have both port and starboard profiles – a reflection of the complexity of their equipment. Although these are viewed from the opposite side – in this case from port – the view is of the far side of the submarine because it is cut down the centre line. The profile is cleaner than that for the port side because fitting common to both sides, such as the batteries, spare torpedoes, periscopes and the 4in gun have been omitted. The sections give a clear indication of the circular pressure hull, external saddle tanks (the latter drawn on one side only) and casing. Note that the saddle tanks are divided horizontally with the upper halves serving as oil fuel tanks.
(Plan No NPB8390, Neg No487519a)

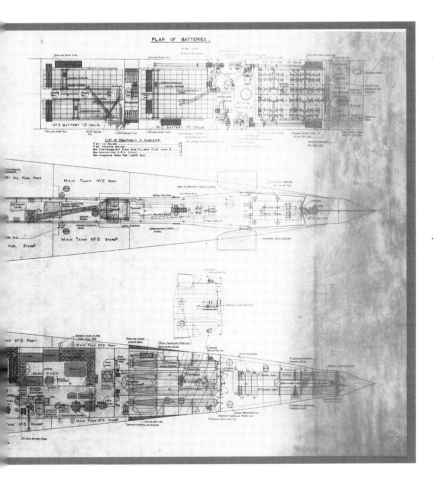

HMS/M Osiris, *Plan views (as fitted), Vickers Armstrongs, Barrow, 1 August 1929.* This drawing provides a main plan view of the interior of the submarine and sub-views for the battery compartments, at top right, and for the upper motor room flat at centre left. The upper views show the exterior of the hull and casing, with notations for the upper sections of the saddle tanks, and plans for the upper and lower levels of the conning tower. The sub-view at lower right is an alteration made at Chatham in May 1941 showing the arrangement of new gear for operating the forward hydroplanes. The internal plan shows clearly the arrangement of the machinery with a diesel engine forward and electric motor aft on each shaft – the clutches for disconnecting the diesels being located on the fore side of the after bulkhead of the main engine room. There are three spaces allocated to the W/T set – one in each after corner of the control room and a third (which is not shown in the plan views) under the control room floor at the after end and accessed via a ladder in the port W/T space.
(Plan No NPB8391, Neg No 487519b)

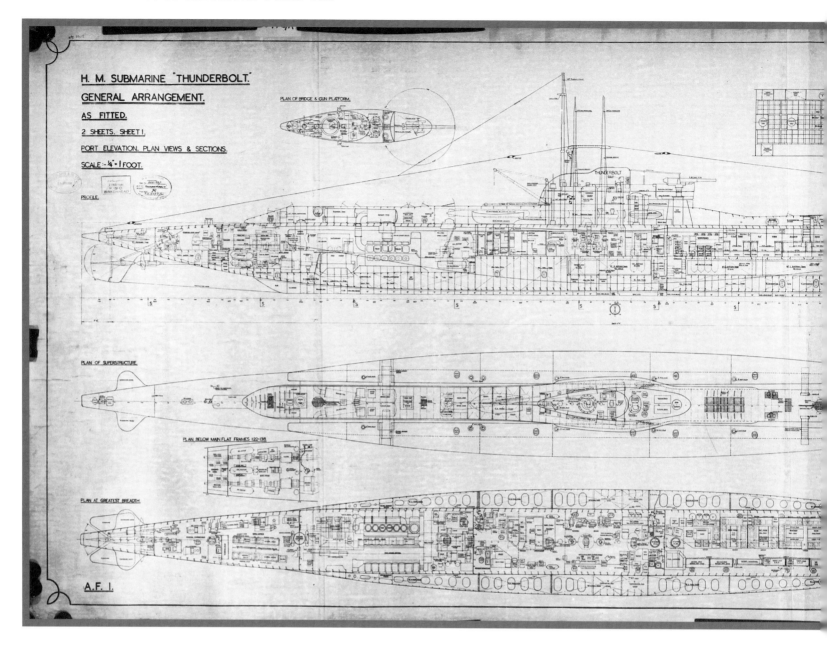

Thunderbolt

Displacement: 1300 tons surface, 1595 tons submerged

Dimensions: 265ft 6in (pp), 277ft (oa) x 26ft x 15ft 10in (mean)

Armament: Eight 21in torpedo tubes (15 torpedoes); one 4in gun

Machinery: Two shaft, diesel engines, 2500bhp = 15.25kts (surface); two electric motors, 1450bhp = 8kts (submerged); 134 tons oil fuel; range 4500nm at 11kts (surface), 80nm at 4kts (submerged)

Complement: 62

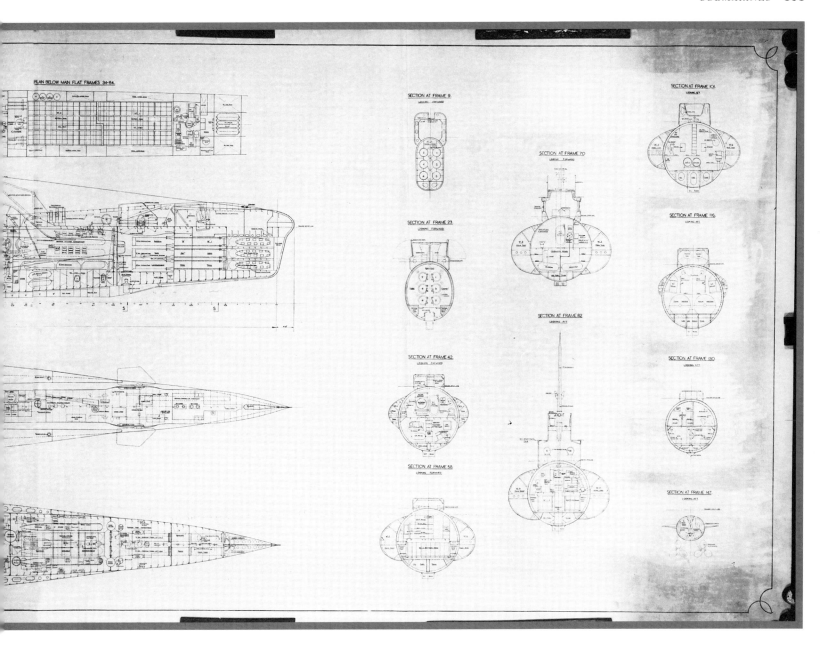

HMS/M Thunderbolt, *Port elevation, plan views and sections (as fitted), Cammell Laird, Birkenhead, 5 April 1941. The* Thunderbolt *was originally launched as the* Thetis *which sank on trial in Liverpool Bay on 1 June 1939. The boat was salvaged, reconditioned by her builders, Cammell Laird, and entered service as* Thunderbolt *late in 1940. These drawings are a new set produced to reflect the change in name. As* Thetis *the boat was equipped with ten 21in torpedo tubes, all firing forward, eight in the bows including two external in the* casing, and two external in the casing abreast the conning tower. When refurbished the two foremost external tubes were removed. The lower plan shows the internal arrangements at the main flat with the hull cut at its widest point. The view above is an external plan and the two sub-views show the areas below the main flat – the battery compartments at top right and the area below the after crew space at lower left. The equipment on the conning tower, from forward, is the standard outfit of 4in MkXII gun, search periscope, attack periscope and telescopic W/T mast. Note *that there is only one spare torpedo for the midships tubes – shown in plan in line with the port tube – whereas the standard in British boats was to provide a reload for each tube. Unlike the* Osiris, *she carries her fuel within the pressure hull, the tanks being located below the main flat from the after end of the control room to part way along the main engine room. Consequently the saddle tanks are not divided into separate compartments horizontally – the lightening holes in the horizontal frames being visible in the lower plan view.*
(Plan No NPC3302, Neg No E0718)

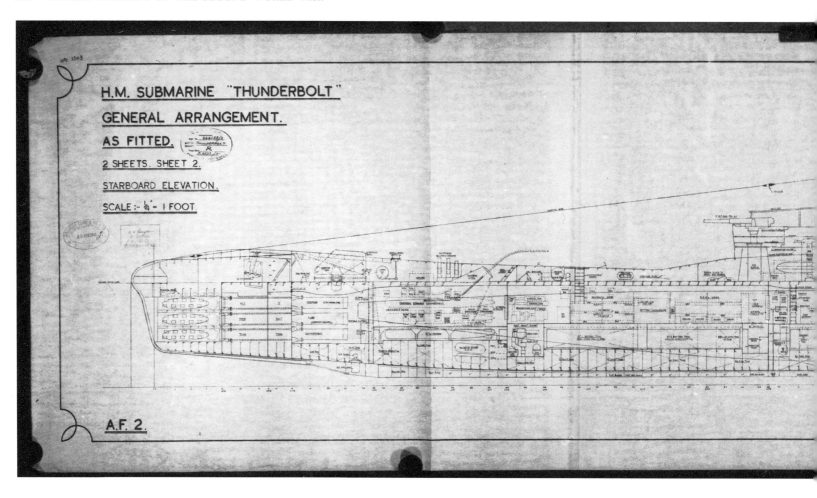

HMS/M Thunderbolt, *Starboard elevation (as fitted),*
Cammell Laird, Birkenhead, 5 April 1941.
(Plan No NPB3303, Neg No E0714)

sure hull as thinner plating could be employed for its construction.
A further ten of the 'S' class were ordered in the 1930s of which the
last eight had two electric motors driving their single propeller
when submerged rather than one – power and speed remaining the
same although displacement increased from 735 to 760 tons.
Construction of an improved version of the class began in 1940
under the Emergency War Programme and a further fifty were
eventually ordered of which four were later cancelled. The initial
boats had welded frames and riveted pressure hulls but later vessels had an all-welded pressure hull which increased the diving
depth to 250ft (350ft design maximum). The weight saved by adopting all welded construction was utilised to enhance the armament
by fitting a single stern torpedo tube and replacing the 3in gun with
a 4in.

Another small submarine, the 'U' class, was developed in the
mid-1930s to serve as both anti-submarine and submariner training
vessels as replacements for the ageing 'H' class. They were also
designed for secondary employment in coastal operations in
wartime and were to prove of value in the shallow, clear waters of
the Mediterranean where their small size made them less vulnerable than larger boats. They differed from all other British submarines of the period in being of single hull design with internal
ballast tanks. They had a surface displacement of 600 tons, a surface speed of 11kts and an endurance of 3600nm at 10kts.

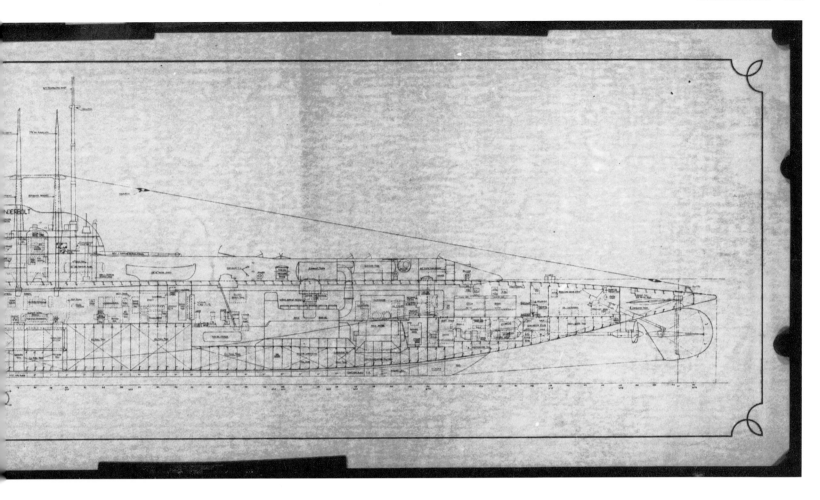

Armament was six torpedo tubes (four internal and two external – all mounted forward) and one 3in gun. Three were ordered in 1936 and completed in 1938, while over seventy boats of the same design were constructed under the 1939 and War Construction Programmes. The later 'V' class is usually listed as a different class but were of the same basic design with welded pressure hulls and thicker plating to increase their diving depth from 200ft to 300ft. The external torpedo tubes were omitted in the later vessels of the class.

In the meantime the development of the 'oversea patrol' type was continued with the 'T' class, the first of which was ordered under the 1935 Estimates. In order to construct the number required within the overall treaty limits for submarines the size was reduced when compared to the 'R' class; lower surface speed and reduced diving depth and endurance being the primary penalties. However, the torpedo armament was increased to ten tubes – six internal and four external all forward firing. Fifteen were ordered pre-war of which four entered service prior to September 1939 and a further thirty-eight were constructed under the 1939 and War Programmes. The use of welding in the construction of these boats gradually increased as the war progressed and the last few had all-welded

pressure hulls and thicker plating which increased the maximum design diving depth from 300ft to 350ft. In the war construction boats a single astern firing external torpedo tube was added and the two amidships torpedo tubes were re-arranged to fire aft – modifications that were also applied to the survivors of the earlier group during the war. Other war modifications followed the general standard with the addition of a 20mm AA gun, air and surface warning radar, air-conditioning equipment and, in some boats, the re-establishment of external fuel tanks for greater range.

The final British submarine design of the war was the all-welded, pre-fabricated construction 'A' class, forty-six of which were ordered but only sixteen of which were completed – all post-war. These were improved versions of the 'T' class and were aimed at employment in the Far East and Pacific for the final stages of the war against Japan. They were of similar size to the 'T' class but had a higher surface speed and endurance and much improved habitability arrangements for service in tropical waters.

MINELAYERS

Minelaying was not given a high priority between the wars and only one specific offensive minelayer was produced prior to 1939 – the cruiser minelayer *Adventure* constructed during 1922-6. Offensive minelaying was planned to be available from destroyers and the 'E' to 'I' classes, and later the 'O' and 'P' classes, were arranged for rapid conversion to minelayers. In the event they were too valuable as destroyers to be spared and very few were so employed, and then only for limited periods. One of the reasons for selecting destroyers was the need for high speed to enable independent fast approach and rapid retirement when mining enemy waters. In the late 1930s it was decided to produce a specific vessel for this purpose which resulted in the six fast minelayers of the *Abdiel* class. Three, *Abdiel*, *Latona* and *Manxman*, were ordered under the 1938 Programme, one, *Welshman*, under the 1939 Programme and two more, *Ariadne* and *Apollo*, under the 1941 Programme. The first four completed in 1940 and the last two in 1943-4. They were relatively large vessels of 2640 tons standard in which the majority of features were subordinated to the mine capacity of 150 and a high designed speed of 40kts standard (37-38kts deep). In service they proved incapable of achieving this ambitious speed being approximately 2kts short of the design intent but they were still very fast ships for their size. Armament was concentrated on AA defence as, in their intended role, they were expected to avoid engagement with enemy surface ships by utilising their high speed. Apart from minelaying they found extensive employment during the war for the rapid supply of stores and troops to hard-pressed locations – in particular Malta.

On a lesser scale vessels of varying origins were employed for defensive minelaying off harbours and estuaries, in coastal waters and shallow seas. Most were converted from mercantile vessels or from minor warship types such as trawlers and motor launches. However, one coastal minelayer, the *Plover*, was constructed just before the war and achieved the remarkable record of laying over 15,000 mines during the war and surviving until the late 1960s.

Latona

Displacement:	2640 tons standard, 3643 tons deep (as designed)
Dimensions:	400ft 6in (pp), 417ft 11in (oa) x 40ft x 11ft (mean)
Armament:	Six 4in MkXVI (3 x 2); four 2pdr (1 x 4), eight 0.5in (2 x 4); one DC rail; 150 mines
Machinery:	Two shaft, Parsons geared turbines, 72,000shp = 38kts; Four Admiralty 3-drum boilers; 750 tons oil fuel; range 5000nm at 15kts
Complement:	236

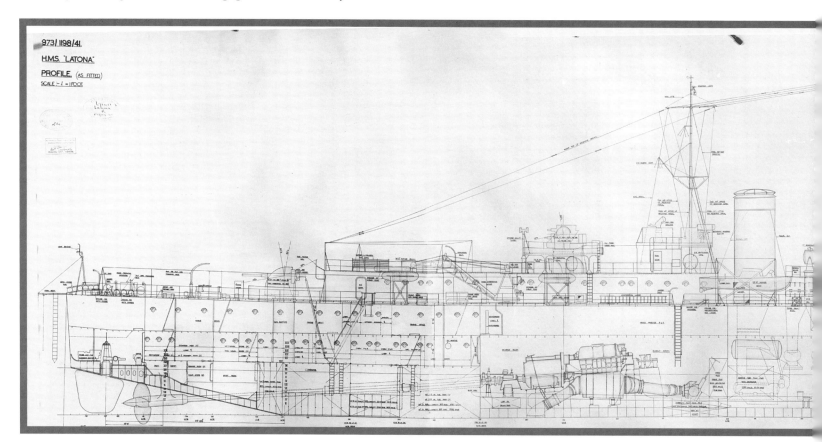

973/1198/41.

H.M.S. 'LATONA'

PROFILE. (AS FITTED)

SCALE :- ⅛ = 1 FOOT

HMS Latona, *Profile (as fitted), J Thornycroft, Southampton, 26 September 1941.* The fast minelayers were designed with two primary features in mind – high speed and a large mine capacity. The weight required for the former and the top weight involved with the latter resulted in these relatively large ships having a gun armament little different from that in the 'Hunt' class escort destroyers of half their size. Three twin 4in MkXIX mountings controlled from a rangefinder director (with Type 285 radar), a quad pompom on the after superstructure and two quad 0.5in mountings in the bridge wings. They did, however, have the advantage of a pom-pom director fitted abaft the mainmast. The mine deck extended from the stern to the after bulkhead of the gearing room and then down passages on each side of the ship as far as the fore end of the bridge. The cranes fitted abreast the after superstructure were for embarking the mines, which were lowered through hatches near the deck edge just under the rear end of the crane's jib. The drawing shows little internal detail apart from the main machinery. The choice is otherwise a little odd – the petrol tank at the fore end, an outline for the Asdic dome below the keel, a profile of the main switchboard (above the after end of the gearing room), the steering gear and the ladders! On the other hand the rig is shown in some detail and includes the main and auxiliary wireless aerials. The pole at the top of the foremast is for the aerial of radar Type 286, its office located abaft the funnel on top of the forward boiler room vents. (Plan No NPB5514, Neg No 671451/5)

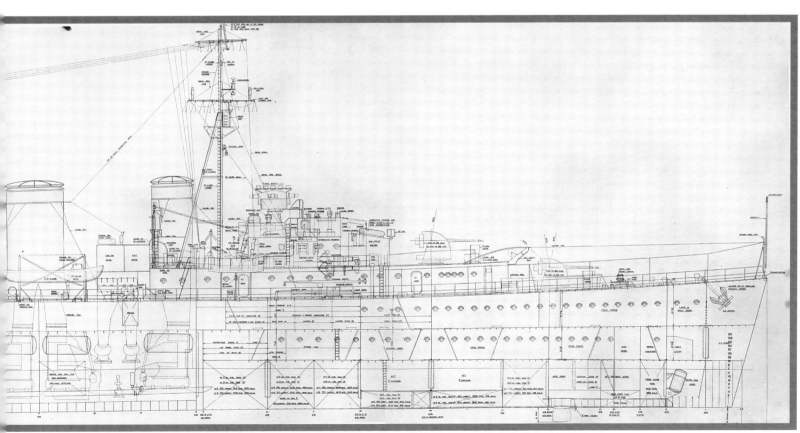

FLEET MINESWEEPERS

During 1933-9 eighteen *Halcyon* class minesweeping sloops were constructed and these vessels, together with some 'Hunt' class ships surviving from the First World War, were the only specific vessels of the type available in 1939. However, the *Halcyon*s were a sub-group of the escort-sloop types previously covered under 'escorts' and were simply biased towards sweeping rather than escort duties. In practice all these early sloops were used for both minesweeping and escort duties but shortage of escorts ensured that they were primarily employed in the escort role. Many had their minesweeping equipment removed to provide for an improved A/S fit. Nevertheless, this combination of duties was continued in the initial units of the 'River' class frigates and several corvettes were fitted with minesweeping gear.

Shortly before the war, work began on the *Bangor* class minesweepers, the design of which was uncompromised by other requirements and was intended to fulfil the usual needs of cheap

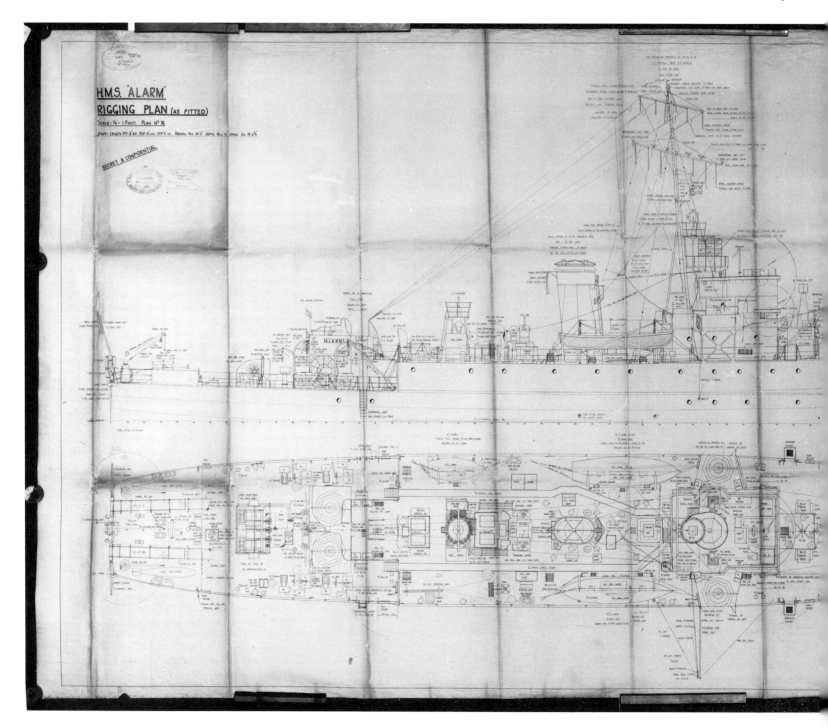

mass production in war. Over 160 were built in the UK, Canada, India and Australia (the latter, to a slightly different and larger design, as the *Bathurst* class). The specialist nature of these vessels was eventually perceived as a limitation rather than an advantage and in the next design, the *Algerine* class, displacement was increased from the 600 tons of the *Bangor*s to 850 tons. This increase provided for a secondary function as A/S escorts and the accommodation of more extensive minesweeping gear. The latter included sweeps to deal with both magnetic and acoustic as well as standard moored mines. The first group of the class, ordered under the 1940 Programme, were fitted with turbine machinery but all later ships were propelled by reciprocating engines. They proved very successful and were employed in all theatres of war for both minesweeping and general escort work. Over 100 were constructed in UK and Canadian shipyards.

Alarm

Displacement:	860 tons standard, 1122 tons deep (as designed)
Dimensions:	212ft 6in (pp), 225ft (oa) x 35ft 6in x 8ft 3in (mean)
Armament:	One 4in MkV; four 20mm (4 x 1); two DC rails, four DCT 80 DC
Machinery:	Two shaft, geared turbines, 2000shp = 16.5kts; two Admiralty 3-drum boilers; 255 tons oil fuel; range 6000nm at 12kts.
Complement:	85

HMS Alarm, *Rigging plan (as fitted), Harland and Wolff, Belfast, 2 July 1942.* This rig drawing for one of the thirty-one turbine-engined Algerine class minesweepers is actually dated only a few weeks after the vessel's completion on 16 May 1942. For a rig it is very detailed, showing all but very minor fittings, but lacks the internal detail and the visibility allowed by separate drawings of the deck and platform levels to be found in the general arrangement as-fitted drawings. Besides the standard rig items it includes the main W/T aerials running from the upper yard to a frame at the after end of the forecastle. The minesweeping gear includes the winch on the quarterdeck, the main cable reel (hidden under the after overhang of the forecastle deck in the plan view) and the davits, floats and kites in the after corners of the quarterdeck. The same area also accommodates a substantial A/S armament consisting of two depth charge rails (for twelve charges each) and four throwers – each with three spare charges. She carries a 4in MkV gun on a MkII** mounting forward, to deal with aircraft and surfaced submarines, and a self-defence close-range AA armament of four single 20mm Oerlikons – one in each bridge wing and two at the after end of the forecastle. There is also a 9ft rangefinder mounted on a raised platform abaft the funnel and a 20in searchlight on the foremast. The lantern at the aft side of the bridge encloses the aerial for her only radar – a Type 271 surface warning set. Only a few months after entering service, the Alarm was beached after being badly damaged by Ju87 dive bombers in Bone harbour in January 1943 and became a constructive total loss. (Plan No NPN0259, Neg No E0705)

MONITORS

Several heavily-armed shore bombardment ships, which were somewhat inaccurately designated as monitors, were constructed during the First World War. The prime function of these ships was artillery support on the left flank of the Western Front – a duty that was carried out with some success. By 1939 only three of these ships, *Erebus*, *Terror* and *Marshall Soult*, remained armed for service in their original role and the last named was not in operational condition. The *Terror* was stationed at Singapore to support the defences of the naval base and only *Erebus* was available in home waters. Envisaging a repeat of the operations of the First World War, work began on a new monitor design shortly after the outbreak

Roberts

Displacement:	7973 tons standard, 9150 tons deep
Dimensions:	354ft(pp), 373ft (oa) x 89ft 8in x 11ft 9in (mean)
Armament:	Two 15in MkI (1 x 2); eight 4in MkXVI (4 x 2); sixteen 2pdr (1 x 8, 2 x 4); eight 20mm (8 x 1)
Armour:	Belt – 5in abreast magazines, 4in abreast machinery; deck 4in over magazines (with sloping 6in glacis), 3in over machinery and steering gear, 2in forward; barbette 8in; turret 13in face, 11in sides and rear, 5in roof; 3in-2in CT
Machinery:	Two shaft, Parsons geared turbines, 4800shp = 12kts; Two Admiralty 3-drum boilers; 550 tons oil fuel
Complement:	442

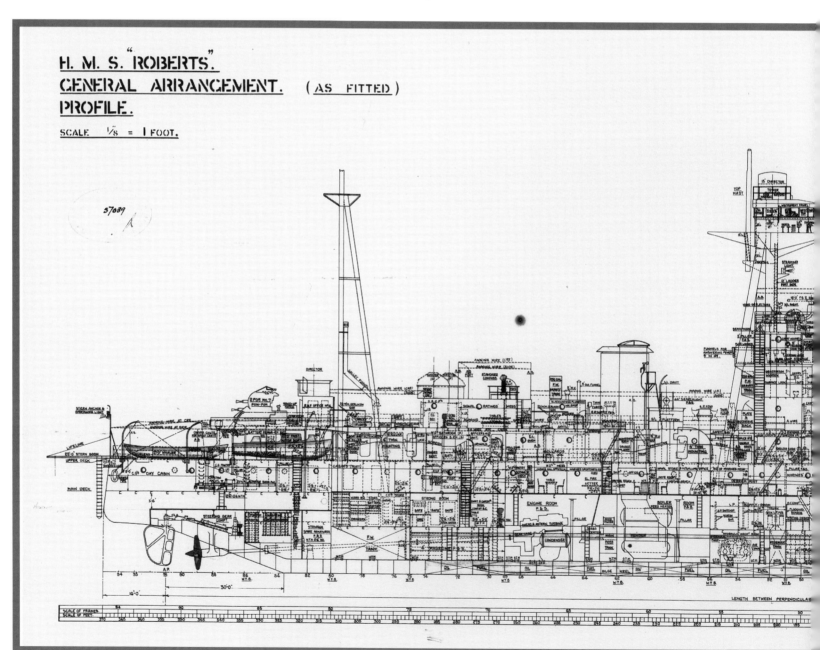

H. M. S. "ROBERTS".
GENERAL ARRANGEMENT. (AS FITTED)
PROFILE.

SCALE ⅛ = 1 FOOT.

HMS Roberts, *Profile (as fitted), John Brown, Clydebank, c.1942. The* Roberts *and her sister ship* Abercrombie *varied little in design from the monitors of the First World War. Moreover, they not only employed a main armament that dated from that period but were also equipped with the associated fire control gear including the original director tower, with its tripod-type director, and a Dreyer fire control table. The tower was fitted on the* roof of the spotting top while the table was located in the transmitting station on the lower deck immediately abaft the 15in magazine. They were also the only ships of post-1918 design to be fitted with an old style spotting top. Notable in this profile is the shallow depth of hull with only three decks above the hold – upper, main and lower – and the small area occupied by the machinery. The raised armoured glacis on the main deck under the barbette had 6in sloping sides – the thickest armour in the ship – and a 4in flat top (outside the area of the barbette). The armour deck can just be discerned as a slightly thicker line extending fore and aft from the glacis which steps down at the base of the main mast before extending aft over the steering gear. The funnel was raised by 12ft in 1943 to reduce smoke interference on the bridge. (Plan No NPC0352, Neg No 673471/1)

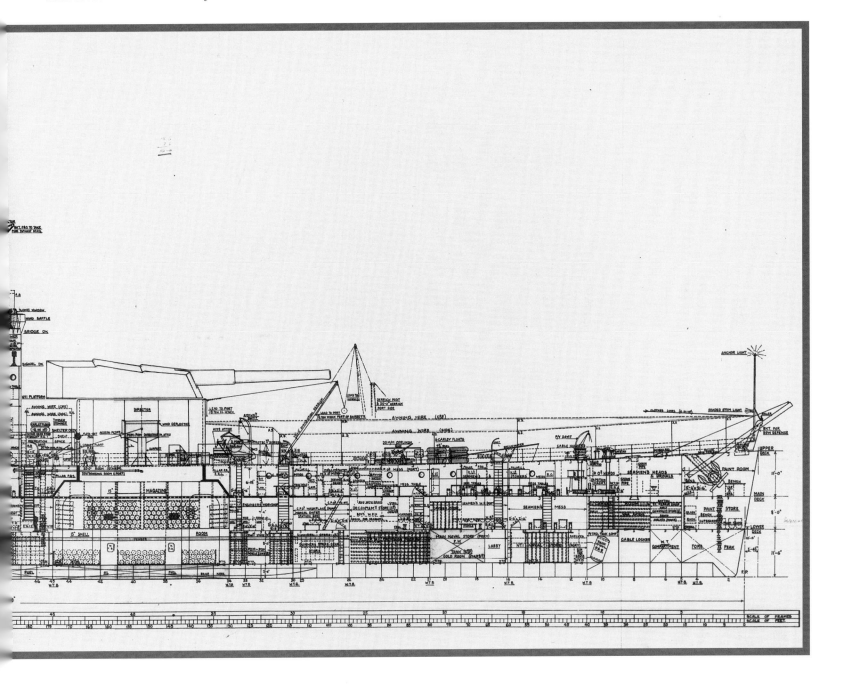

of war. As it was assumed the ship would be required at an early date, the design was worked out rapidly, using the *Erebus* as a model. Several expedients were adopted with a view to rapid construction including the employment of the machinery design of the *Black Swan* class sloops and removing the twin 15in mounting from *Marshall Soult* for the main armament. The latter was, however, subject to modernisation, the elevation being increased from 20° to 30°, the loading gear adapted to modern 15in ammunition and the general standard of equipment updated. Protection was on a similar scale to the earlier vessels with side armour provided against medium-calibre artillery – either shore- or ship-based – but more substantial deck armour was provided as defence against air attack and plunging fire from shore-based howitzers. Another reflection of

HMS Roberts, *Upper deck, shelter deck and bridges (as fitted), John Brown, Clydebank, c1942. The plan of the upper deck is somewhat misleading in the impression it gives of the ship's proportions because the bulges, which are not shown, projected to a maximum of 17ft on each side. These differed from those of First World War monitors in adopting a modern air/water/air sandwich structure complete with inboard torpedo bulkhead of 1.5in thickness. Being potentially a relatively large, slow and often stationary target a good deal of attention was paid to self-*

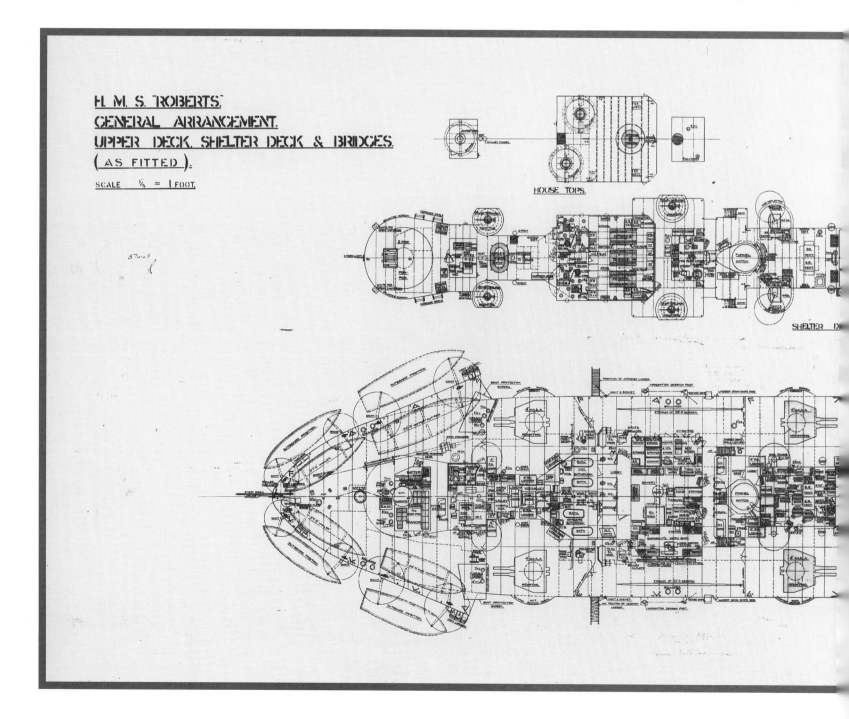

defence and this included a substantial AA outfit. Long-range defence was provided by four twin 4in MkXIX mountings controlled by two HACS directors, complete with radar Type 285, mounted atop the superstructure forward of the mainmast. The HA control positions are located in the deck house immediately below the directors they controlled and were each equipped with a FKC and FCB (fire control box). The close-range AA armament consists of two quad pom-pom mountings fitted abreast the fore side of the barbette, an 8 barrel pom-

pom at the after end of the shelter deck and eight single 20mm Oerlikons – four on the upper deck and four on the shelter deck. Each pom-pom had its own director – one on each side of the barbette and one just abaft the mainmast. In 1943 all but the two single 20mm guns abaft the breakwater were replaced with twin 20mm MkV mountings and in 1945 she was fitted with eight 40mm Bofors. The latter were located one on the roof of the 15in turret and in place of the after pom-pom, the two single 20mm, the 44in searchlights abreast the

funnel and the aftermost pair of twin 20mm guns. The Abercrombie had a circular barbette, unlike the polygonal version seen here, and had her 4in guns mounted one deck higher on extensions to the shelter deck. The 'A' frame extending over the bows was for the paravane towing gear (it can been seen in the raised position in the profile).
(Plan No NPC0353, Neg No 673471/2)

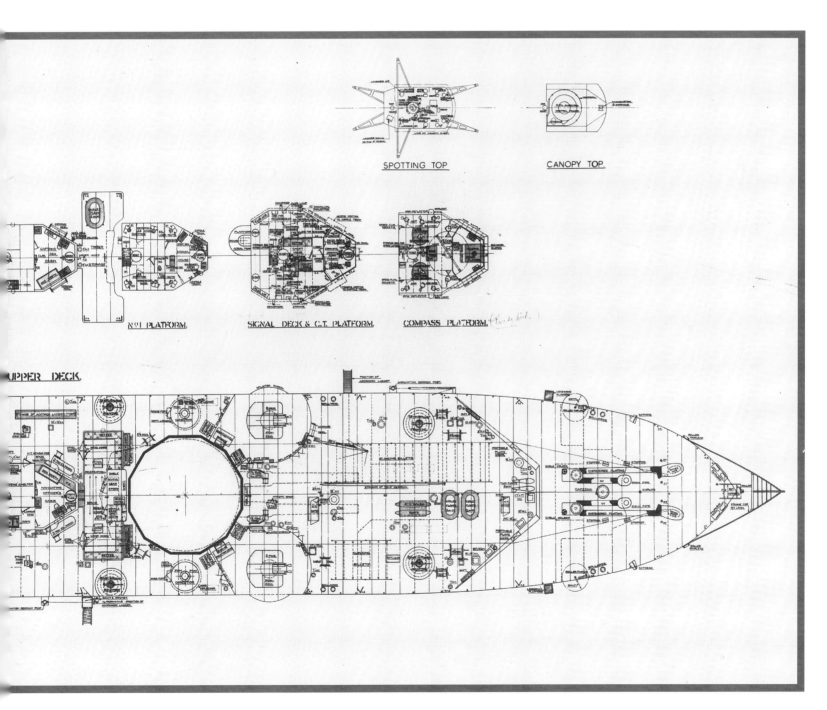

SPOTTING TOP.   CANOPY TOP.

No1 PLATFORM.   SIGNAL DECK & C.T. PLATFORM.   COMPASS PLATFORM.

UPPER DECK.

the changed conditions from the First World War was the provision of an extensive AA armament and control system.

The new ship, named *Roberts*, was laid down in April 1940 and completed in October 1941, taking 6 months longer to construct than was originally intended but probably regarded as less urgent after the fall of France. A sister ship, the *Abercrombie*, provided with a reserve twin 15in mounting and with some small design improvements, was laid down in 1941 and completed in 1943. The new ships, together with *Erebus*, gave their most valuable service in providing support for the amphibious landings of 1942-4. *Roberts* provided shore support for the landings in North Africa in late 1942 and was joined in the following year by *Abercrombie* for the assaults on Sicily and mainland Italy, before returning home for the D-Day landings. Her last major operation, in company with the *Erebus* and the old battleship *Warspite*, was fire support for the assault on the Island of Walcheren in the Scheldt Estuary in November 1944.

HMS Bruiser, *Rigging plan (as fitted), Harland and Wolff, Belfast, 1 May 1943. This vessel was one of only three ships of the LST(1) type all of which were constructed by Harland and Wolff and, while proving too complex for general production, served to establish the basic requirements of the mass-produced LST(2) which followed. The lower deck served as the main tank deck from which vehicles could exit via an extending ramp to the beach through the double doors in the bow. The tank deck also had alternative side doors, seen in the profile just forward of the bridge, that allowed tanks and lorries to be off loaded into LCTs alongside for transport ashore. The upper deck, which was provided with a clear run through the lower bridge structure, carried 3-ton lorries which are illustrated in the plan view as rectangles. A lift, fitted under the bridge, allowed these vehicles to be transferred from the upper to lower decks and the 40-ton crane abaft the funnel could be used to embark or disembark lorries and tanks via the large hatchway immediately under its jib. Note that the funnel is slightly offset to starboard, an arrangement adopted to give a clear passage down the centre of the tank deck. The ship carried twelve single 20mm Oerlikons – four on the raised platforms forward, four in the bridge wings and four on the roof of the after deckhouse. The ship's only other armament, two 4in smoke mortars, are located one on each side of the upper deck just forward of the forward Oerlikon platforms. The ship's name is often spelt as Bruizer but it is assumed here that the builders knew the correct form. All three vessels of the class were converted into fighter direction ships in 1944.*

(Plan No NPN1493, Neg No E0706)

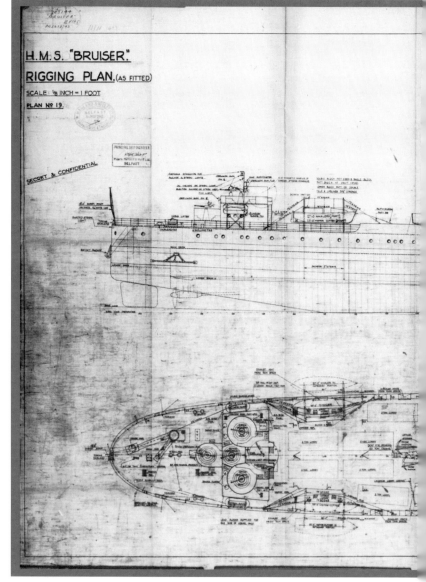

AMPHIBIOUS WARFARE VESSELS

Some thought was given to seaborne assault prior to the Second World War but the only concrete development was the production of a few small landing craft that served as prototypes for the war production LCA (landing craft, assault). These, together with the US-produced LCP (landing craft, personnel) provided the majority of those craft, which were generally carried to the assault areas in larger ships. In 1940 with the introduction of the Combined Operations Command, the prime function of which was raids on enemy-held territory, the need arose for more substantial landing vessels capable of transporting larger numbers of troops, together with tanks and vehicles directly to the assault area. Three types developed from this requirement the LCP(M) (landing craft personnel – medium), the LCT (landing craft, tank) and LST (landing ship, tank) the designs of which were initiated in late 1940.[36] Within

Bruiser

Displacement:	6007 tons deep
Dimensions:	390ft (pp), 400ft (oa) x 49ft x 5ft 6in (fore), 14ft (aft)
Armament:	Twelve 20mm (12 x 1); two 4in smoke mortars
Capacity:	Twenty tanks, twenty-seven lorries, 193 troops
Machinery:	Two shaft, geared turbines, 7000shp = 16.25kts; two Foster Wheeler boilers; 1728 tons oil fuel
Complement:	169

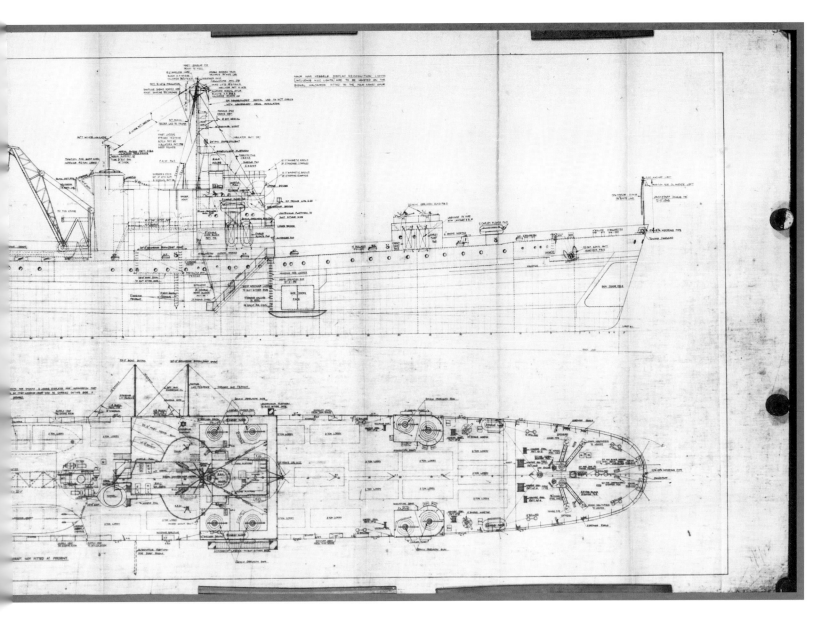

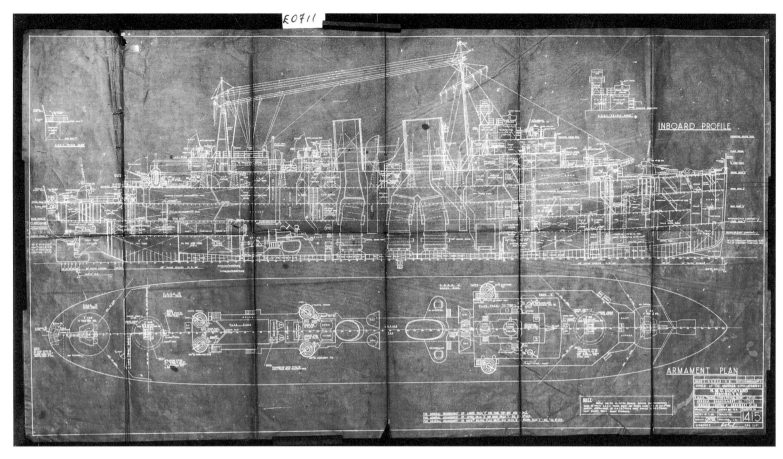

HMCS Prince David *and* Prince Henry, *Armament Plan (as fitted) Esquimalt Dockyard, 18 January 1944. The dark background and white lines of this internal profile and plan view result from it being a blueprint copy of the original. The drawing was prepared to show the armament arrangement of these ex-AMCs after conversion into LSI(M) – landing ship infantry (medium) – in 1943 but also shows details of the rig, radar fit and, in the profile only, the general compartment layout. The main armament consists of two twin 4in MkXIX, one forward and one aft, controlled from a rangefinder director mounted at the top of the bridge structure immediately over its associated transmitting station. There is also a single 40mm Bofors mounting in 'B' and 'X' positions and eight single 20mm Oerlikon mountings – six of the latter are fairly obvious in the plan view as they are surrounded by concentric circles (representing the circular steps around the gun pedestals); the remaining pair, which had variable height cradles and did not therefore require the surrounding steps, are located on the compass platform. The ship also carries two depth charge chutes (for two charges each), located within the hull structure at the top of the stern, and an Asdic set, the dome for which can be seen just above the keel line immediately below the forward 40mm gun. The radar outfit includes Type 291 air warning (cheese aerial at head of fore mast), Type 272 surface warning (aerial in lantern at rear of bridge) and Type 285 gun control (aerials on 4in gun director), together with Type 242 and 253 IFF sets. The main drawing represents* Prince David, *while the sub-views at top right and left show differences for the* Prince Henry *(the fitting of the depth charges on instead of under the deck at the stern and the Type 271Q radar lantern – with office in the support – in place of Type 272). A note on the drawings indicates that the transmitting station and adjacent radar office were fitted with plastic armour. Each ship carried eight landing craft of which the after three on the port side are just discernable in the profile drawing.*
(Plan No NPN7707, Neg No E0711)

a year it was realised that the defeat of Germany would require major amphibious operations and the emphasis shifted to the production of much larger numbers of invasion vessels and to a much broader range of types. In late 1941, difficulties of producing sufficient numbers in home yards led Britain to seek American assistance. Initially, US design expertise was applied to British requirements and ideas, the Admiralty specifying the basic requirements and form for LSTs and LCTs, and later LCI(L) (landing craft infantry – large) but the design process was taken over more or less completely once America entered the war. American-constructed vessels were generally all-welded, mass production types and vast numbers were built. However, while a good percentage of these were transferred to the RN, there were never enough available to fulfil the combined requirements of the European invasions of

Prince David and Prince Henry (LSI(M))

Gross tonnage:	6890
Dimensions:	366ft 3in(pp), 385ft (oa) x 57ft x 18ft 6in (mean)
Armament:	Four 4in MkXVI (2 x 2); Two 40mm (2 x 1); eight 20mm (8 x 1)
Capacity:	Eight LCA, 538 army personnel
Machinery:	Two shaft, geared turbines, 19500shp = 21kts; six boilers; 1470 tons oil fuel
Complement:	227

1942-4 and the extensive island-hopping campaign in the Pacific. LSTs in particular, which absorbed more construction resources than smaller craft, were regarded as key vessels and were in great demand, often being constructed at the expense of other major warship types.

Apart from numbers, the types of vessel required also expanded into a variety of types, which represented practically every conceivable requirement of supporting an invasion and its bridgehead. Merchant vessels were converted to carry large numbers of troops or to serve as HQ or fighter direction ships; purpose-built LSDs (Landing Ship Dock – effectively mobile floating docks) were developed in the USA to launch large landing craft directly off the beaches. Additional to these were vast numbers of support craft, mostly adapted from standard landing craft, which included shore support/bombardment by both gun and rocket, navigational guides, smoke screen generators, repair and recovery vessels and even barges to provide cooking facilities (LBK – landing barge, kitchen).

The LST serves as a good example of the changing pattern of the design and production of assault craft. The requirement for an ocean-going tank transporter capable of landing its cargo directly onto an enemy beach was met initially by the conversion of three merchantmen. This approach was adopted to get vessels into service as rapidly as possible and to some extent was a compromise between time into service and suitability for function. The vessels chosen were small oil tankers whose peacetime trade to Lake Maracaibo, Venezuela, required limited draught in order to cross the bar at the sea entrance to the lake. The three ships, *Bachaquero*, *Misoa* and *Tasjera* were converted to their new role early in 1941. Twenty tanks were accommodated on the upper deck (which was plated-in) and a door, hinged at the base provided in the bow through which they could be landed. However, as they were not purpose-built they beached some distance from the shore and an extending double ramp was required to bridge the gap. Although not ideal, these vessels were valuable in establishing basic requirements for the type and in highlighting solutions to detail problems

for future designs. This initial class, known as the *Maracaibo* class, were followed by three purpose-built vessels of the *Boxer* class, *Boxer*, *Bruiser* and *Thruster*, which were later designated as LST(1). The new ships followed the general pattern of the conversions but were faster, 16kts rather than 12kts, and slightly larger. To allow for the higher speed and improve on seakeeping qualities the form of bow was altered from the flat outer door of the conversions to double, vertically hinged, non watertight bow doors. Behind these a watertight bulkhead was sealed with a second set of doors, again hinged vertically but in this case flat and watertight. An articulated, extending ramp of improved design was fitted to bridge the gap between ship and shore. Like the *Maracaibo* class they could carry twenty tanks but could also accommodate up to twenty-seven 3-ton lorries as deck cargo.

The major disadvantages of the LST(1) design were that it was over-complex and therefore unsuitable for production in numbers and that the draught forward was greater than desirable. These problems were addressed in the design of LST(2), which, unlike the earlier vessels, were primarily intended for large-scale invasions of, rather than raids on, enemy-held territory. The design was primarily American with some British assistance but was based on the Admiralty's outline requirements for a 10kt, 300ft vessel capable of carrying twenty tanks or a complete LCT across the Atlantic under its own power. In the new design the tank deck was moved to a lower level and the draught forward reduced which made possible the provision of a comparatively short draw-bridge type ramp which also served as the forward watertight door. This arrangement saved a great deal of internal space as the large extending ramp of LST(1) was no longer required. In other respects the primary difference between these ships and the LST(1) was a much simplified all-welded construction, the use of diesel main propulsion in place of turbines, greatly increased endurance and a reduction in speed to 10kts.

Over 1000 of these craft were constructed for the USN while a further 115 were delivered to the RN from late 1942 onward. However, towards the end of 1943 it became clear that the British would not receive the numbers they desired from America alone and began the design of their own variation on the type. The new vessels, which became LST(3) were generally similar to LST(2) but were larger because they were mainly of riveted construction rather than welded and employed steam machinery in place of diesels. They were, however, faster having a maximum speed of 13.5kts. Construction began in UK and Canadian Yards in 1944 but only 61 of the 112 ordered were to be completed and most of these entered service too late to take part in the war.

ADMIRALTY TRAWLERS

Britain's fishing fleet provided a rich source of naval auxiliaries during both world wars. The trawler in particular was of considerable value both in numbers and quality, combining good seakeeping qualities with the ability to accept a reasonable level of additional equipment which allowed their use in more aggressive roles than were usual for such craft. They were principally employed in minesweeping, anti-submarine duties and general patrol work but also served in many minor support roles as fleet auxiliaries, tenders, general harbour duties and on the examination service. So many of these vessels were requisitioned in the First World War that the Admiralty had a considerable number built on their own account. While it might be assumed that a true patrol warship

A/S Trawlers, General Arrangement, Smiths Dock, Middlesborough, 28 April 1939.
Smiths Dock was contracted by the Admiralty in 1938 to produce a design, specification and drawings to meet Admiralty requirements for a trawler suitable for either A/S or minesweeping functions. This drawing is part of the result of that work and shows the initial design of the A/S version of what were to become the war production 'Tree', 'Dance',
'Shakespeare' and 'Isles' classes all of which were basically similar. The armament provided is strictly A/S with a single low angle 4in QF gun of First World War origin on the bandstand forward for use against a surfaced U-boat, a Lewis gun mounting on each side of the compass platform, two depth charge rails and two depth charge throwers on the quarterdeck and a Type 123 Asdic set. The Asdic dome, not shown in this drawing, was located in the hold compartment forward designated as 'W.T.
Trunk Space'. Wartime modifications resulted in the addition of three or four 20mm AA guns and surface warning radar and the majority were fitted for both A/S and minesweeping work. The original intention was that the minesweeping type would carry a 12pdr gun and in the event most of the 'Naval' trawlers were so fitted and only a few carried the 4in.
(Plan No NPN4749, Neg No E0709)

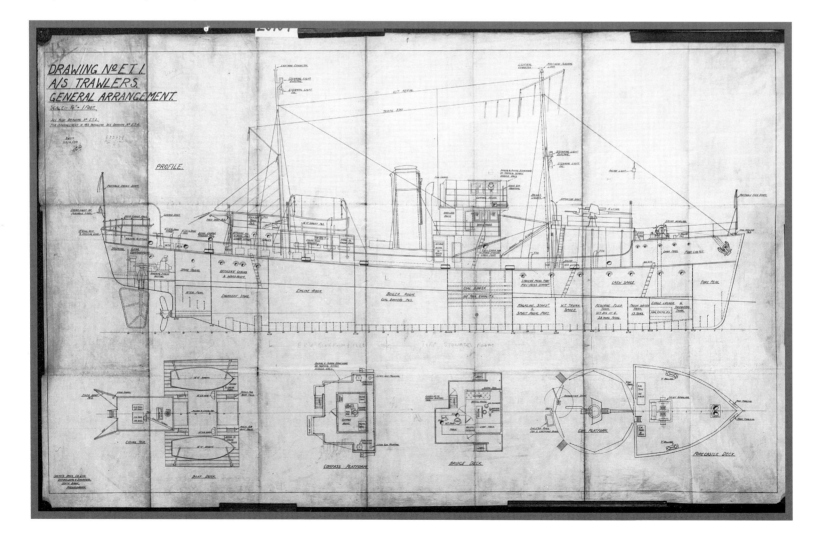

might have been more valuable, the actual purpose was to employ the experience and facilities of existing trawler builders and to construct vessels that could be transferred to commercial service post war. The Admiralty employed nearly 2000 trawlers during 1914-18 of which all but about 20, retained as tenders, harbour service vessels and as fishery protection vessels, were sold or returned to their owners.

Early in the 1930s consideration was given to the probable requirements for auxiliary ships in a future war and it was again envisaged that requisitioned trawlers would require supplementing by specific Admiralty construction. In order to establish a design for such a craft, a trawler was included in the 1934 Estimates and constructed during the following year by Henry Robb at Leith. This was the 550-ton *Basset*, again designed to utilise the experience of the trawler builders but in this case without the requirement of being suitable for the commercial fishing fleet. Consequently the hull was of naval form and the superstructure was moved from the traditional trawler arrangement of aft of amidships to a position slightly forward of amidships, giving an appearance not unlike that of the later 'Flower' class corvettes. She was arranged to serve as either a minesweeper or A/S vessel and could be rapidly converted for either role. However, she completed as an A/S trawler – one of the prime purposes of her construction being to establish if ASDIC would operate satisfactorily in a small shallow-draught hull. She

had a maximum speed of 13kts and an endurance of 3000nm at 9kts and, apart from her depth charge outfit, she carried a single 4in gun forward. She was followed by the *Mastiff*, a generally similar but slightly smaller vessel constructed during 1937-8 for fishery protection service. In addition to these two ships, thirty-five trawlers were purchased for service as minesweepers (twenty 'Tree' class) and A/S trawlers (fifteen 'Gem' class) during 1935-9.

War construction vessels were initially of the *Basset* type of which over 200 were built, primarily in UK yards but with a few constructed in Canada and India. These vessels were of the 'Tree', 'Dance', 'Shakespeare' and 'Isle' classes of which the majority belonged to the last-named group. Despite the division by class name they were all basically similar and were generally equipped for both minesweeping and A/S work although a few (with 'Bird' names) were employed as controlled minelayers. In addition to these vessels the Admiralty began ordering a few trawlers of standard commercial type, as it had done in the First World War. These were of large (830-ton 'Military' class and 750-ton 'Hill' class), medium (590-ton 'Fish' class) and small (430-ton 'Round Table' class) types, the latter being fitted for minesweeping and the remainder for A/S work. The nine vessels of the 'Military' class were particularly well armed with a single 4in and four 20mm guns, two twin machine guns, four depth charge throwers and two depth charge rails.

'Isle' class A/S Trawler

Displacement:	545 tons standard, 760 tons deep
Dimensions:	150ft (pp), 164ft (oa) x 27ft 6in x 8ft 6in (fore), 13ft 7in(aft)
Armament:	One 4in; two DCT; one DC rail; 30DC
Machinery:	Single shaft, triple expansion engine, 850ihp = 12.5kts; one cylindrical boiler; 183 tons coal, 4000nm at 9kts
Complement:	40

DEPOT SHIPS

Depot ships provided the Navy with mobile support vessels for submarines and destroyers with facilities for repair, maintenance, training, accommodation and HQ functions.[37] The two types were essentially similar apart from the obvious variations in engineering support and stores required for their differing charges and in the fact that submarine depot ships provided fuller accommodation for crews needing rest and relaxation after patrols in boats of very limited habitability. In general they could provide everything required except major repairs and were equipped with extensive workshop facilities covering most engineering and shipwright functions. They also acted as storeships providing torpedoes, ammunition, depth charges, fuel, food and general stores. They were not built for speed as they spent most of their time in harbour and rarely moved except when relocating to a new area of operations. In either case they were vulnerable – to submarine attack when moving and to air attack when static, particularly as they carried large amounts of ammunition, and they were generally provided with a much greater level of self defence than was usual for auxiliary support vessels.

The first purpose-built ship of the type was the 14,650-ton submarine depot ship *Medway* constructed during 1927-9 and intended to support eighteen overseas patrol submarines (twenty-one in war). Unlike most RN surface ships and unlike all later depot ships she was diesel-powered with a top speed of 15.5kts and carried 2410 tons of diesel fuel of which 75 per cent was intended for her charges. She carried four 4in AA guns and the hull was provided with a scaled-down version of the torpedo protection system of the *Nelson* class battleships with an inner water space interposed between an outer air space and a 1.5in thick torpedo bulkhead. The next vessel was the destroyer depot ship *Woolwich*, constructed during 1933-5 under the 1932 Programme. At 8750 tons standard she was too small to accommodate the torpedo protection system in *Medway* but did have longitudinal torpedo bulkheads and was slightly faster than her predecessor at 17kts. Self defence was again provided by four 4in single AA guns and 2in protection was fitted over her magazines. She was followed by two submarine depot ships, the *Maidstone* and *Forth*, sister ships of the 1935 and 1937 Programmes, completed in 1938 and 1939 respectively. These were 8900-ton ships generally similar to the *Woolwich* apart from the necessary adaptations for the support of nine (twelve in wartime) submarines of the 'T' class. They also had a much improved AA armament consisting of four twin 4.5in HA/LA mountings – one for-

Adamant

Displacement:	12,700 tons standard, 16,500 tons deep
Dimensions:	620ft (pp), 658ft (oa) x 70ft 6in x 16ft 3in (mean)
Armament:	Eight 4.5in MkIII (4 x 2); sixteen 2pdr (4 x 4); six 20mm (6 x 1); eight 0.5in (2 x 4)
Armour:	2in deck over magazines, torpedo stowage and machinery, 1.5in deck over steering gear, 1.375in torpedo bulkhead
Machinery:	Two shaft, geared turbines, 8000shp = 17kts; four Admiralty 3-drum boilers; 1310 tons oil fuel; 4000nm at 13.5kts
Complement:	1210

ward, one aft and one on each beam, supported by two HA directors, and two quad pom-pom and two quad 0.5in mountings.

In 1937 the Naval Staff decided that improvements were required in the passive defence system of future depot ships and the last three to be constructed showed a substantial increase in displacement. This was primarily necessary in order to accommodate a torpedo defence system based on that then being adopted in new battleships and carriers and consisting of an air/liquid/air sandwich bounded in the inboard side by a protective bulkhead. However, the size of the depot ships was insufficient to give the same depth to the system as that provided in the larger ships and extended inboard only 10ft at the maximum – a depth considered sufficient against air-launched 18in torpedoes. In addition the deck protection over

magazines was extended to cover the machinery spaces. The first two of this group were the destroyer depot ships *Tyne* and *Hecla* of 11,000 tons standard displacement constructed during 1938-41. Apart from the increased size they were generally similar to *Maidstone* and *Forth* except that the 4.5in mountings were rearranged with two forward and two aft, 'B' and 'X' mountings superfiring over 'A' and 'Y'. In the third vessel, the submarine depot ship *Adamant* of the 1938 Programme, displacement was further increased to 12,700 tons standard to accommodate the additional requirements necessary for submarines. She was designed to service twelve 'T' class boats and had accommodation for eleven crews including two in reserve. Two of these depot ships were lost during the war, the *Medway* and *Hecla*, both sunk by submarines in 1942.

HMS Adamant, *Profile (as fitted), Harland Wolff, Belfast, c1942.*

Adamant *was the last purpose-built depot ship constructed for the Royal Navy. Like her predecessors she was a combination of high-capacity storeship, workshop and accommodation vessel and had to provide for both her own fuel, ammunition and provisions and that of her submarine charges. Being of a type that spent most of the time as a static base, she was relatively well equipped for self-defence. The principle AA defence was her four twin 4.5in MkIII UD (upper deck) mountings, a type also found in other depot ships, the carrier* Ark Royal *and the cruisers* Scylla *and* Charybdis. *The BD (between deck) mountings fitted in the* Illustrious *class carriers, modernised capital ships and later the 'Battle' class destroyers were of the same family and together with the twin 4in Mk XIX represented the Royal Navy's most successful long-range AA mountings. Control was from two rangefinder directors, one on the bridge and one abaft the mainmast, via fuse keeping locks accommodated in transmitting stations immediately below the directors. The close-range AA armament is mainly concentrated amidships, two quad pom-pom mountings abreast each funnel, and three single 20mm Oerlikons along each side of the* superstructure. *In addition a quad 0.5in mounting is located on each side of the bridge structure. The drawing is heavily shaded – hence the dark colour of the boats and the broad ink stripe indicating the area below the water line. The darker shaded hold compartments fore and aft are water tanks, that under 'A' mounting being for fresh water and the remainder for trimming. Note that the after funnel serves all four of the ship's boilers (two double boiler rooms arranged athwartships), that forward being a dummy apart from serving minor auxiliaries.*
(Plan No NPA4668, Neg No 17693)

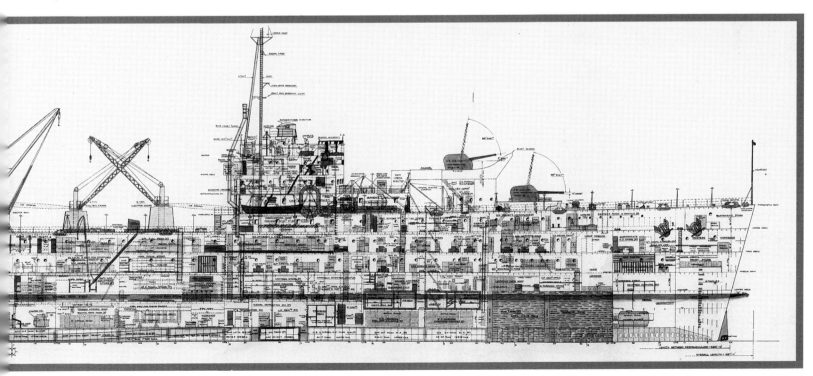

MOTOR TORPEDO BOATS

Until the mid-1930s the Admiralty showed little interest in the development of coastal forces craft despite the extensive use of coastal motor boats and motor launches during the First World War. There were practical reasons for this apparent lack of enthusiasm. Until the early 1930s there was little obvious employment for such craft and finance was short. Moreover, they were of a type that could be built quickly and in large numbers in the event of an emergency utilising the country's boat and yacht builders. In any case the construction and maintenance of what were relatively

Vosper MTB 31-34

Displacement:	35 tons standard, 41.2 tons deep
Dimensions:	71ft (oa) x 17ft 1in x 4ft 6in (max)
Armament:	Two 21in torpedo tubes; two 0.5in machine guns
Machinery:	Three shaft Isotta-Franschini petrol engines, 3450bhp = 39kts; 2000gal petrol; 500nm at 22kts
Complement:	10

HM/MTB 31-40, General arrangement (as fitted). Vosper, Portsmouth, c1940. In common with other drawings from Vosper this 'as fitted' covers a group of boats rather than an individual vessel. MTB31-40 were among the earliest of their 70ft (actually 71ft in this case) type and provide the basis for the company's later 72ft and 73ft designs. Of the original ten, four were destroyed by bombs while under construction – MTB33

in September 1940 and 37, 39 and 40 in January 1941. Although the drawing covers ten MTBs, only 31 to 34 had the three Isotta Fraschini engines indicated, the remaining six being fitted with Hall Scott engines due to the intended machinery supply being cut off by Italy's entry into the war. Note also the two Vosper V8 engines (each side of the main centre engine) geared to the outer shafts for economic cruising. The armament of two single 21in torpedo tubes and a twin

0.5in mounting aft was standard in all the early Vosper boats. The two tanks abaft the torpedo tubes are auxiliary fuel tanks (350 gallons each), fitted to extend the range and, being dangerous in action, arranged to be jettisoned. The three main fuel tanks are fitted forward of the engines and have a total capacity of 2004 gallons.
(Plan No 9238, Neg No 9238)

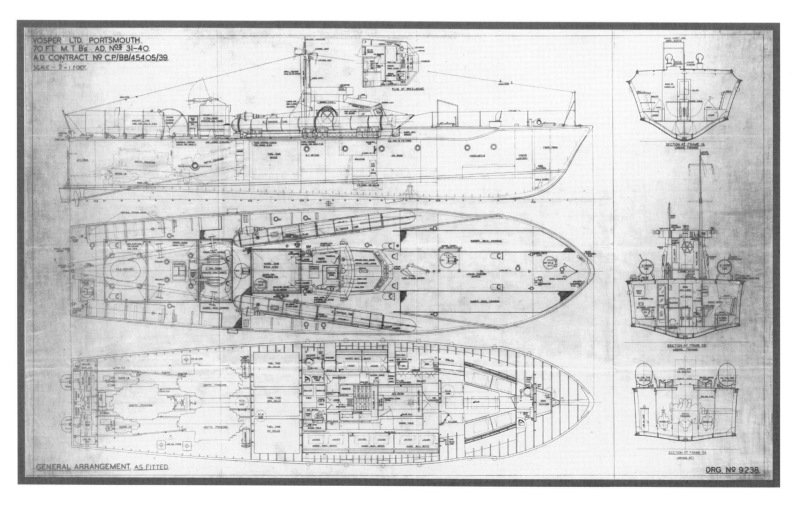

short-life vessels in time of peace would have been difficult to justify. Nevertheless, some experimental construction would have been worthwhile in order to pre-evaluate and develop the types of craft likely to be required. In the event it was not until 1935 that moves were made in this direction and then progress was slow so that most of the subsequent design evaluation and improvement had to be carried out under war conditions.

In 1935 the British Power Boat Company successfully gained Admiralty interest in the design of a 60ft wooden hulled, hard-chine motor torpedo boat. This vessel had a top speed of 38kts and carried two 18in torpedoes which, as in the First World War CMBs, were launched over the stern. As in the majority of later coastal forces craft, petrol engines provided the motive power, these being the only readily available lightweight high-power units capable of generating the required speed. However, these also represented a considerable weakness in an unprotected, wooden hull which had to accommodate a highly inflammable and possibly explosive fuel. The Admiralty eventually ordered eighteen, which became *MTB 1-12* and *14-19*, all of which entered service before the outbreak of war. British Power Boats followed these with a 70ft MTB but this was not taken up by the Admiralty who favoured a contemporary design from Vospers.[38] However, they continued to supply the Admiralty with vessels intended for service as coastal/harbour defence anti-submarine vessels. These MA/SBs (motor anti/submarine boats) proved less than successful in their intended role, being of too shallow a draught to adequately operate ASDIC, but found alternative employment as air-sea rescue launches or motor gun boats (MGB). British Power Boats subsequently produced a specific MGB design, based on their earlier MTB prototype, which occupied most of their construction capacity until 1942 when the roles of MGB and MTB were combined in their 72ft MTB which continued in production until the end of the war.

Vosper had originally approached the Admiralty at about the same time as British Power Boats and later produced a 70ft hard-chine boat, which was used for evaluation and comparative trials and was eventually accepted for service as *MTB 102*. She was originally fitted with an 18in torpedo tube forward firing through the stem and an 18in torpedo aft, which could be dropped over the stern. This complex arrangement was not successful and was altered at Admiralty instigation to two 18in tubes mounted one on each side of the upper deck abreast the wheelhouse. As modified, *MTB 102*, which had made nearly 44kts on trial, provided the prototype for the majority of war construction MTBs. Six similar vessels (four from Vosper, two from Thornycroft) were ordered under the 1938 Programme but no more were added until after the outbreak of war when orders were placed with Vosper, Thornycroft and White for *MTB 102* derivatives. Several problems manifested themselves in these early boats, primarily weaknesses in hull structure and inadequate propeller design/production which were respectively improved and corrected in later boats. A more serious problem occurred in 1940 when Italian entry into the war cut off the

supply of Isotta-Franschini petrol engines upon which the Vosper MTB relied for its high speed. The initial alternative was both less powerful and heavier and speed dropped from a maximum of 38kts to about 30kts but this was soon corrected with the introduction of the US Packard engine.[39] There is some irony in this particular provision of a suitable power plant for the Vosper craft in that British Power Boats was Packard's British distributor. They had, moreover, been directly involved in the improvement of the Packard engine for adoption in coastal force vessels as a result of their work in America which, in turn, had been largely prompted by the Admiralty rejection of their design in favour of Vosper. Other developments of the Vosper type followed the standard wartime pattern with increase in size and armament, improvement in endurance and the provision of radar and improved communications equipment. In the early boats the standard armament had been two 21in torpedo tubes and two pairs of 0.5in machine guns. Considerable variation on this was to be found in later boats and the ultimate standard was either two 21in/18in or four 18in and a gun armament of one 2pdr or 6pdr, two or three 20mm and two twin 0.5in machine guns. Towards the end of the war the search for increased firepower led to the introduction of a short barrel 4.5in which stood a good chance of stopping an E-boat with a single hit.

The third principal supplier of coastal force craft was Fairmile who approached the Admiralty in 1939 with a scheme for the mass production of motor launches. This initially resulted in the production of twelve 110ft Fairmile 'A' type in 1940 which, although of disappointing performance, served as a prototype for the highly successful 112ft Fairmile 'B'. The latter were an adaptation of 'A' with an improved hull form generated by the DNC's department and greater fuel stowage for improved endurance – over 650 were built in UK and Dominion yards. The Type 'A' also provided the basis for the Fairmile 'C', an MGB design with increased engine power which raised the speed of the 'A' type from 25 to 27kts. As with the contemporary conversion of MA/SBs and MTBs into MGBs these were primarily an expedient to counter the increasing threat of German E-boats to Channel and East Coast convoys but this soon led to specifically-designed MGB types. In the case of Fairmile this produced the 115ft 'D' which were originally designed as MGBs but, with few exceptions, completed as MTBs when it was decided to combine the two functions. These were very successful craft of which 288 were constructed during 1942-4 but unlike the smaller craft of Vosper and British Power Boats they had a fairly moderate maximum speed of 29kts. The only other British supplier of coastal forces craft was Camper and Nicholson which produced a small number of craft based on an outline design from the DNC's department. These were similar to the Fairmile 'D' but were of round bilge construction with steel frames and some were fitted with diesel engines. They were arranged so they could be fitted as either MTB, MGB or MA/SB but the majority of the thirty-nine constructed served as MGBs while seven of the initial group were employed as high speed transports for lightweight high-value cargoes from Sweden.

AUXILIARY AA SHIPS

Large numbers of merchant vessels were taken up for naval service during the war. The larger of these were generally employed in fairly passive roles but a few were modified to serve as true auxiliary warships. The best known of these ships were the armed merchant cruisers (AMCs) – generally fast merchantmen armed on the cruiser scale which served as convoy escorts and as patrol vessels. Others included armed boarding vessels, convoy escorts, patrol vessels, Q-ships and auxiliary AA vessels. The latter were subject to extensive modification as, to be effective in their new role, they required the addition of much more elaborate fire control and radar equipment than would normally be provided for a mercantile auxiliary. The superstructure changes involved a more navalised

bridge structure and other alterations, which gave them a much more naval look than was usual for conversions. Seven ships were rebuilt as ocean-going auxiliary AA vessels during 1940-1 and were fitted with three or four twin 4in HA/LA mountings and two quad pom-pom mountings controlled by a single HA director. They were primarily employed as convoy escorts and one, the *Springbank*, was fitted with an aircraft catapult and fighter. The last and largest ship of this type to be converted was the AMC *Prince Robert* of the RCN which was modified for her new role in Canada in 1943 and mounted five twin 4in. She and her two sisters, *Prince Henry* and *Prince David*, had been fitted out as AMCs in 1940 and were originally armed with four 6in and two 12pdr AA guns (the two sisters

INBOARD PROFILE.

were converted to LSI(M) in 1943 – see under Amphibious Warfare Vessels). *Prince Robert* was employed in the North Atlantic until 1945 when she transferred to the Far East; she was returned to merchant service in 1948.

Prince Robert

Gross tonnage:	6890
Dimensions:	366ft 3in (pp), 385ft (oa) x 57ft x 18ft 6in (mean)
Armament:	Ten 4in MkXVI (5 x 2); eight 2pdr (2 x 4); fifteen 20mm (6 x 2, 3 x 1)
Machinery:	Two shaft, geared turbines, 19,500shp = 21kts; six boilers; 1470 tons oil fuel
Complement:	241

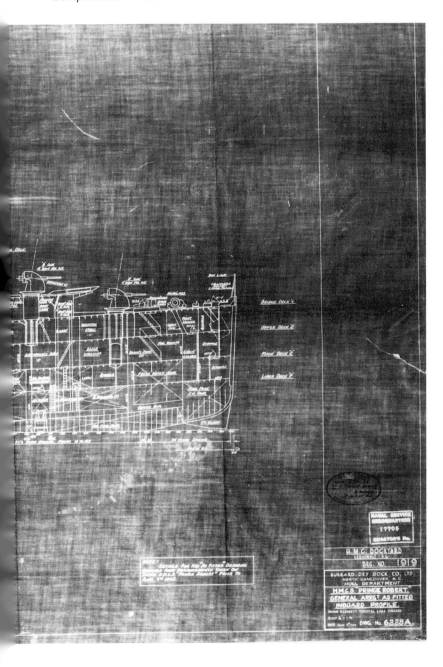

HMCS Prince Robert, *Inboard profile (as fitted) Esquimalt Dockyard, 7 June 1945. Another blueprint copy showing the arrangement of the sister-ship to* Prince David *and* Prince Henry *which, in this case, shows her appearance at the end of the war. The* Prince Robert *was converted from an AMC to an Auxiliary AA ship during 1943 and, apart from the heavier main armament and lack of landing craft, differed little in appearance, rig and radar fit from her sisters. Subsequent alterations involved the fitting of vertical tripod masts in place of the raked pole masts and additional/ improved radar and fire control gear. The main armament consists of five twin 4in MkXIX mountings, two forward and three aft, with control provided by a rangefinder director on the bridge. A later addition to this outfit is the barrage director with Type 283 radar on the raised platform abaft the mainmast. The original close range AA armament of two quad pom-pom mountings fitted abreast the main mast and six single 20mm Oerlikons has been enhanced by the addition of six twin 20mm Oerlikon mountings in place of the singles. The latter are located one per side, on the bridge structure and on the superstructure between the funnels and below the barrage director. Three of the original single 20mm guns were relocated – one forward of the bridge and one on each side of the fore funnel. The radar outfit includes Type 285 for the main armament, Type 277 combined*

BIBLIOGRAPHY

Brassey's Naval and Shipping Annual (Naval Annual 1936-39), various editions 1920-39 (London 1920-39)

Selected Papers on British Warship Design in World War II (London 1983)

Brown, D K, RCNC, *A Century of Naval Construction* (London 1983)

------------------------(ed), *The Design and Construction of British Warships 1939-1945*, Vols 1-3 (London 1995-6)

Buxton, Ian, *Big Gun Monitors* (World Ship Society 1978)

Friedman, Norman, *British Carrier Aviation* (London 1988)

Gardiner, Robert, (ed), *Conway's All the World's Fighting Ships 1922-1946* (London, 1980)

Hodges, Peter, and Friedman, Norman, *Destroyer Weapons of World War 2* (London 1979)

Lenton, H T, *British Battleships and Aircraft Carriers* (London 1972)

---------------, *British Fleet and Escort Destroyers*, Vols 1 and 2 (London 1970)

---------------, *British Submarines* (London 1972)

March, Edgar, *British Destroyers* (London 1966)

Preston, A, and Raven, Alan, *Flower Class Corvettes* (London 1973)

Raven, Alan, and Roberts, John, *British Battleships of World War Two* (London 1976)

--------------------------------------, *British Cruisers of World War Two* (London 1980)

----------------------------------- , *V and W Class Destroyers* (London 1979)

----------------------------------- , *Hunt Class Escort Destroyers* (London 1980)

----------------------------------- , *War Built O to Z Class Destroyers* (London 1976)

Roskill, Stephen, *Naval Policy Between the Wars*, Vol 1 (London 1968)

--------------------, *Naval Policy Between the Wars*, Vol 2 London 1976)

NOTES

1. Although the Admiralty collection contains few drawings of landing ships and craft, reasonably detailed general arrangements of these vessels appeared in the *Transactions of the Institution of Naval Architects* for 1947 (Vol. 89). The articles concerned ('Ships of the Invasion Fleet' and 'Notes on the Development of Landing Craft' both by R Baker, RCNC) were reprinted in *Selected Papers on British Warship Design in World War II* published by Conway Maritime Press in 1983.

2. In 1921 the Divisions of the Naval Staff were: Training and Staff Duties, Operations, Plans, Naval Intelligence, Trade, Gunnery and Torpedo. In the late 1920s several of the Divisions were combined, Trade being absorbed into Plans and Gunnery into Training and Staff Duties while the Torpedo Division was combined with the Tactical Section to become the Tactical Division. At the same time the Naval Air Section was raised to full 'Division' status. The 'Training and Staff Duties Division' was responsible for collating the Staff Requirements. Shortly before the outbreak of the Second World War, 'Trade' and 'Local Defence' divisions were added to the Naval Staff. During the war the Staff greatly expanded – the 'Tactical' and 'Training and Staff Duties' Divisions were combined to become 'Tactical and Staff Duties'; 'Naval Air' was split into two – 'Naval Air Warfare' and 'Naval Air Organisation and Training'; the Departments of 'Torpedoes and Mining' and 'Signals' were changed to divisions of the Naval Staff – the former split into two as 'Torpedo, Anti-submarine and Mine Warfare' and 'Minesweeping'; and three new divisions were added – 'Gunnery and Anti-Aircraft Warfare', 'Navigation and Direction' and 'Combined Operations'.

3. The senior Naval Staff members were the Chief of Naval Staff (CNS – First Sea Lord), Deputy Chief of Naval Staff (DCNS– title changed to Vice Chief of Naval Staff in 1940) and the Assistant Chief of Naval Staff (ACNS). The latter was the primary Staff Officer concerned with warship design. The official procedure required a meeting of the CNS, ACNS and Controller but this could vary with circumstances. Note that during the war the number of officers serving as an ACNS increased from one to seven but of these only two were Board members.

4. The number of sets of 'as fitted' drawings produced is not known to the author, however, David K Brown RCNC, believes it was normally three. (The National Maritime Museum hold two copies of the 'as fitted' drawings for the battleship *King George V* – there may be others but generally the Admiralty collection is strictly singular).

5. The twenty-one ships referred to are:

13.5in gun ships. Battleships of the *King George V* class (*King George V*, *Ajax* and *Centurion*) and *Iron Duke* class (*Iron Duke*, *Emperor of India*, *Marlborough* and *Benbow*) and the battlecruiser *Tiger*.

15in gun ships. Battleships of the *Queen Elizabeth* class (*Queen Elizabeth*, *Barham*, *Malaya*, *Valiant* and *Warspite*) and *Royal Sovereign* class (*Royal Sovereign*, *Royal Oak*, *Ramillies*, *Resolution* and *Revenge*) and the battlecruisers *Renown*, *Repulse* and *Hood*.

Of the remaining 13.5in gun ships, the *Orion* class battleships (*Orion*, *Monarch*, *Conqueror* and *Thunderer*) and the battlecruisers *Lion* and *Princess Royal*, all were either in reserve or serving in subsidiary roles; they were all disposed of between 1922 and 1926.

6. In 1921 the United States had eleven 14in gun battleships in service (all completed between 1914 and 1921) and four 16in gun battleships of the 33,000-ton *Maryland* class, of which one had just completed and the remainder were fitting out. The new construction programme consisted of six battleships (*South Dakota* class) and six battlecruisers (*Lexington* class) all of over 43,000 tons and armed with twelve and eight 16in guns respectively – construction of all twelve began in 1920-1. Japan had four battleships and four battlecruisers in service armed with 14in guns and two 16in gun battleships (*Mutsu* and *Nagato*) recently completed. Two fast battleships (*Kaga* and *Tosa*) and four battlecruisers (*Akagi* class) of c40,000 tons and armed with 16in guns were laid down in 1920-1 and construction was about to begin on a further eight fast battleships (four armed with 16in guns and four with 18in guns).

7. The overall limitation was based on total tonnage but Britain, the United States and Japan also agreed to a future limit on numbers of capital ships (15, 15 and 9 respectively by the mid-1930s). France and Italy, while accepting the total tonnage and qualitative limits, refused to accept a limit on numbers which gave them the option of building larger numbers of smaller replacement ships.

8. The United States was required to scrap two of their older ships on completion of these new vessels, thus maintaining their number of capital ships at eighteen. The total of ten for Japan includes the two new ships.

9. The 'Standard' displacement defined by the Washington Treaty was with a ship fully equipped for war and ready for sea but without fuel or reserve feed water.

10. Both France and Italy were allowed to increase the gun calibre and armour thicknesses of their older ships provided the overall increase in displacement did not exceed the 3000-ton limit.

11. The total tonnage allowed at 31 December 1936 was as follows:

	Britain	*USA*	*Japan*
Cruisers (guns over 6.1in)	146,800	180,000	108,400
Cruisers (guns under 6.1in)	192,200	143,500	100,450
Total for cruisers	339,000	323,500	208,850
Destroyers	150,000	150,000	105,000
Submarines	52,700	52,700	52,700

12. To allow for existing submarines over the 2000-ton limit, each of the signatories was allowed three submarines not exceeding 2800 tons.

13. The 1936 Treaty did not refer directly to cruiser or destroyer categories but to 'Light surface vessels', these being divided into three groups – (a) vessels with guns over 6.1in calibre, (b) vessels with guns less than 6.1in calibre but over 3000 tons in displacement and (c) vessels with guns less than 6.1in calibre and under 3000 tons displacement. The (c) group were included to accommodate the 2500-ton French *Le Fantasque* class super destroyers constructed in the early 1930s.

14. The four battleships of the *Yamato* class, one laid down in 1937, one in 1938 and two in 1940, had a standard displacement of 62,000 tons and carried a main armament of nine 18in guns. Only two, *Yamato* and *Musashi* were completed to their original design; the third vessel – *Shinano* – was

converted to an aircraft carrier during construction and the fourth – *Kii* – was never completed.

15. The 23kt speed of *Nelson* and *Rodney* was a reflection of the standard battleship speed of the period. The US and Japanese ships they were intended to answer were no faster and the requirements of the design in respect of armour and armament made a higher speed impossible to achieve with the machinery available at the time.

16. *Scharnhorst* and *Gneisenau* have been designated as both battlecruisers and as battleships. The distinction is far from clear-cut for the period between the wars. The Admiralty initially adopted speed as the prime differential (the heavily protected but fast G3 design was a battlecruiser) and in the early 1930s it was common for the designs of the fast battleships which ultimately led to the *King George V* class to be referred to as battle-cruisers. The fast battleship designs would by this criteria have all been battlecruisers but these types became generally accepted as the new form of the battleship. The *Scharnhorst* and *Gneisenau* were comparatively light in size, protection and armament in relation to later ships and their classi-fication as battlecruisers reflects this difference.

17. There was only one 16in gun sketch design drawn up to meet the Staff Requirements. In contrast there were eleven 12in gun designs with various arrangements of twin and triple mountings which followed the general principles of the staff requirements for the 16in gun ship but on a smaller scale. Similar remarks apply to the 14in, 11in and 10in gun designs of which there were two, one and two respectively.

18. An interesting side-light on the design adopted for the *King George V* is how closely it compared with the American design of the same period. The initial pair of the US rearmament programme – *North Carolina* and *Washington* – although they differed in detail from the British ships were also initially designed with three quad 14in gun mountings and were of generally similar dimensions and speed. However, the USA was not as desperate to begin their ships and when the armament escalator clause was invoked they redesigned them to mount three triple 16in mountings.

19. These four 15in twin mountings were removed from the light battle-cruisers *Courageous* and *Glorious* when those ships were converted to aircraft carriers in the 1920s.

20. Catapults were tried on the quarterdecks of *Resolution*, *Valiant* and *Hood*. The arrangement was not liked as the catapult aircraft were vulnerable to weather damage and blast from the after turrets. In addition they interfered with the arc of fire of 'Y' turret.

21. The *Hawkins* class consisted of *Hawkins*, *Raleigh*, *Frobisher*, *Effingham* and *Vindictive* (ex-*Cavendish*). The last named actually completed as an aircraft carrier but was reconverted to a cruiser (she retained a hangar and flying-off deck forward) in 1923. The *Raleigh* was wrecked in August 1922 and became a total loss.

22. Twelve 'Town' class cruisers remained in service – eight with the Royal Navy and four with the Royal Australian Navy – all but one (HMAS *Adelaide* which survived until 1949) were sold during the late 1920s and early 1930s.

23. The 1939 Programme originally included four cruisers, two of which were cancelled just before the outbreak of war, while the Emergency War Programme was for six cruisers of the *Dido* class, five of which were sub-sequently altered to become the Modified *Dido* class.

24. In addition to those mentioned in the table, Japan had built five light cruisers in the early 1920s with 5.5in guns mounted in single open shields

and four of their early Treaty cruisers were relatively small 7100-ton vessels armed with six 8in (mounted in single turrets in the first pair and twin turrets in the second pair).

25. Similar unfavourable, but for the most part ill-informed, comparisons were made with French and Italian cruisers which were generally designed for high speed.

26. The Washington and First London Naval Treaties terminated on 31 December 1936. The Second London Naval Treaty, although agreed in March 1936 to start on 1 January 1937 was not actually ratified by the British Parliament until 30 July 1937 being held up by the parallel treaties with Germany and Russia.

27. This number does not include the seven 'H' class and two 'I' class destroyers building for Brazil and Turkey respectively and taken over by the Admiralty on the outbreak of war.

28. The TSDS was designed to operate at 25kts but the towing wires were prone to break at this speed.

29. The well was covered with removable plates for normal low-angle fire.

30. These Japanese ships were lightly built and lacking in stability and were extensively reconstructed shortly after completion in order to restore stability and strengthen the hull. These alterations increased the standard displacement to 2090 tons (about 100 tons less in the *Akatsuki* class which were slightly lighter as built – 1680 tons) and reduced their maximum speed to 34kts.

31. The shell weight for earlier 4.7in guns was 50lbs.

32. One vessel of the 'M' class did not complete until 1943. This was *Mahratta*, laid down in July 1939 as the *Marksman*. A bomb knocked her off the slipway during an air raid in May 1941 and the hull had to be dismantled and rebuilt on another slip.

33. The conversion to AA destroyers originally included some 'O' class and some 'P' class ships but the names were reallocated while under construc-tion to give a uniform class of AA destroyers.

34. These five ships – the *Armada*, *Barfleur*, *Camperdown*, *Trafalgar* and *Hogue* – were the only vessels to be fitted with the intended 4in starshell gun.

35. This number does not include two sloops – *Hindustan* and *Indus* – built for the Indian Navy.

36. The distinction between landing craft and landing ships, apart from relative size, was that 'ships' were capable of deep sea voyages and had endurance to match while 'craft' were short-range types with limited seagoing potential.

37. Depot ships were also provided for coastal forces craft, patrol vessels, minesweepers and several other minor groups but these were all converted types some from merchant vessels and some from old warships. One mer-chant ship, the 10,000-ton *Bonaventure*, was specifically converted to an 'X' craft (midget submarine) depot ship during 1942-3.

38. Although BPB lost out to Vosper in supplying the Royal Navy they took their 70ft MTB to North America and succeeded in selling their design to both the US and Canadian Navies.

39. BPB had successfully employed the Rolls Royce Merlin engine in their 70ft MTB but by 1940 Merlin production was entirely concentrated on aircraft.

INDEX

Vessels named are Royal Navy unless stated otherwise. Page numbers in *italics* indicate draughts and their captions; page numbers in **bold** indicate specifications.

'A' class destroyers 7, 93-4, 96, 101, 123
'A' class submarines 126, 133
'A' type MTBs 151
Abdiel class minelayers 134
Abdiel (minelayer) 134
Abercrombie (monitor) *141*, 142
Acasta class destroyers *see* 'A' class destroyers
Acheron (destroyer) 96
Achilles (cruiser) 75
Activity (escort carrier) 125
Adamant (submarine depot ship) **148**, *148-9*, 149
Admiralty draughts 7-12
aircraft carriers 16-19, 21, 50-65
    armoured carriers 57-61
    catapults 10, *33*, 57, *67-8*, 74, 78, 87-8, 124
    deck parks 50
    see also Auxiliary AA ships, escort carriers, hangars, MAC, naval aviation, and flight decks *under* decks
Ajax (cruiser) *73-5*, 75
Akutsuki class Japanese destroyers 97
Alarm (minesweeper) *136-7*
Algerine class minesweepers 137
Amazon (destroyer) 90
Ambuscade (destroyer) 90
AMCs (Armed Merchant Cruisers) 151
amphibious warfare vessels 19, 143-5
Amphion (cruiser) 75
    class *69*, 75-6, 80
Anglo-German Naval Agreement (1935) 19
Anson (battleship) 39
anti-aircraft armament 12-13, 17, 19, 21, 25, *26*, *29*, *33*, *35*, *38*, 39-41, 45, 50, 57-8, *59*, 61, *68*, 80, 82, 87-8, *89*, 94, *98*, 98-101, *102*, *105*, 106-7, *108*, 111, *114*, *119*, 121, 124, 134, *141*, 142, 148-9, *149*
anti-submarine warfare and defence 12, 17, 25, 37, 39-40, 72, *98*, 99-100, *104*, 106-7, *108*, *110*, 111, *114*, 114-15, *116-17*, 118, 121, 125, 136-7, *140*, 146, *146*, 147, 149, *153*

Apollo (cruiser) 75
Apollo (minelayer) 134
Arethusa (cruiser) 76, 82
    class *69*, 76, 80
Argonaut (cruiser) 86
Argus (aircraft carrier) 51
Ariadne (minelayer) 134
Ark Royal (1937) (aircraft carrier) *50-1*, 51-2, **52**, *53-6*, 57-8, *59*, 61, 86
Ark Royal (1955) (aircraft carrier) 61
armour 9-10, *14*, 21, *23*, 25, 37, **43**, *48*, **52**, **66**, *67*, 70, **76**, 80, 86, **96**, 100-1, *102*, 127, 132, *138-9*, 140, 147, **148**
ASDIC *91*, 107, *135*, 147, 151
Atherstone (escort destroyer) 113
Attacker (escort carrier) *122-3*, **124**
Auckland (escort sloop) 107
Audacity (escort carrier) 125
Australia 19, 66, 70, 75, 99, 127, 137
Australia (Australian cruiser) 70
Auxiliary AA ships 151-2
Avenger class escort carriers 125

'B' class destroyers 7, 93, 96, 101, 123
'B' type MTBs 151
Bachaquero (LST) 145
Bangor class minesweepers 136-7
Barham (battleship) 41
Basset (trawler) 147
Bathurst class Australian minesweepers 137
'Battle' class destroyers 88, 101, 106
battleships 12-19, *13*, *16*, 21-49, 61, 75, 106
Béarn (French aircraft carrier) 50
Belfast (cruiser) 80
Bellona (cruiser) 86
Belvoir (escort destroyer) *112-13*, **113**
Berwick (cruiser) 70
'Bird' class trawlers 147
Birmingham (cruiser) 80
Bismarck (German battleship) 27, 30, 39-40, 61
Bittern (1) (escort sloop) *see Enchantress*
Bittern (2) (escort sloop) 107
Black Prince (cruiser) 86
Black Swan (escort sloop) 107, 111
    class 107, 111, 140
Bonaventure (cruiser) 86
Boxer (LST) 145
    class 145
Brecon (escort destroyer) 113
Brissenden (escort destroyer) 113

British Power Boat Company 151
Broke (frigate) 123
Brooklyn class US cruisers 80
Bruiser (LST) *142-3*, **143**, 145
Bryony (escort frigate) **116**, *116*

'C' class cruisers 82, 87
'C' class destroyers 7, 93-4, 96, 101, 106, 123
'C' type MTBs 151
'Ca' class destroyers 101
Caio Duilio (Italian battleship) 65
Cairo (cruiser) 87, *88-9*
Calcutta (cruiser) 87
Caledon (cruiser) 87
CAM (Catapult Merchant) ships 124
Camper & Nicholson (shipbuilders) 151
Canada 19, 99, 137, 145, 147, 151
Canberra (Australian cruiser) 70
Carlisle (cruiser) 87
'Castle' class corvettes 115
Ceylon (cruiser) 86-7
'Ch' class destroyers 101
Chacal class French destroyers 96
Charybdis (cruiser) 86
Churchill, Winston 40
Cleopatra (cruiser) 86
'Co' class destroyers 101
Codrington (destroyer) 94
Colombo (cruiser) 87
Colorado (US battleship) 17
Colossus class aircraft carriers 10, 61
Condottieri class Italian cruisers 97
Conti di Cavour (battleship) 65
Cornwall (cruiser) 70
corvettes 19, 114-15
'County' class cruisers 70-5, *70-5*, 80, 87
Courageous (aircraft carrier) 51, 57
Coventry (cruiser) 87
'Cr' class destroyers 101
cruisers 18-19, 66-89, **73**, **83**, 97, 106
    light cruisers *75*, 75-6, 97
Cumberland (cruiser) 70, 87-8
Curaçao (cruiser) 87
Curlew (cruiser) 87

'D' class cruisers 82
'D' class destroyers 7, 94, 96, 101, 123
'D' type MTBs 151
'Dance' class trawlers 147
Daring class destroyers *102*, 106
decks 9, *92*
    armoured 17, 21, *22-3*, 30, *31*, 41